S0-BEG-996

MASS MURDER MAILMAN

Shortly before 7:00 A.M. on a muggy August day in 1986, more than 50 postal workers toiled at sorting mail. They scarcely noticed as Patrick Sherrill entered the Edmond, Oklahoma post office carrying his mail delivery satchel over his left shoulder . . . and a pistol in his right hand.

Without warning, he began methodically shooting his fellow workers at random. The popping noises sounded like firecrackers. Two men were already dead before someone yelled, "He's got a gun!" Workers crawled under their stations or fled through nearby doorways.

By the time Sherrill had finished his bloody stalk through the post office, 14 people were dead—and six people were seriously wounded.

As helicopters circled above and police SWAT team officers prepared to invade the post office, Patrick Sherrill shot himself to death.

It was the third largest mass murder in U.S. history.

REAL HORROR STORIES!
PINNACLE TRUE CRIME

SAVAGE VENGEANCE   (0-7860-0251-4, $5.99)
By Gary C. King and Don Lasseter
On a sunny day in December, 1974, Charles Campbell attacked Renae Ahlers Wicklund, brutally raping her in her own home in front of her 16-month-old daughter. After Campbell was released from prison after only 8 years, he sought revenge. When Campbell was through, he left behind the most gruesome crime scene local investigators had ever encountered.

NO REMORSE   (0-7860-0231-X, $5.99)
By Bob Stewart
Kenneth Allen McDuff was a career criminal by the time he was a teenager. Then, in Fort Worth, Texas in 1966, he upped the ante. Arrested for three brutal murders, McDuff was sentenced to death. In 1972, his sentence was commuted to life imprisonment. He was paroled after only 23 years behind bars. In 1991 McDuff struck again, carving a bloody rampage of torture and murder across Texas.

BROKEN SILENCE   (0-7860-0343-X, $5.99)
The Truth About Lee Harvey Oswald, LBJ,
and the Assassination of JFK
By Ray "Tex" Brown with Don Lasseter
In 1963, two men approached Texas bounty hunter Ray "Tex" Brown. They needed someone to teach them how to shoot at a moving target—and they needed it fast. One of the men was Jack Ruby. The other was Lee Harvey Oswald. . . . Weeks later, after the assassination of JFK, Ray Brown was offered $5,000 to leave Ft. Worth and keep silent the rest of his life. The deal was arranged by none other than America's new president: Lyndon Baines Johnson.

Available wherever paperbacks are sold, or order direct from the Publisher. Send cover price plus 50¢ per copy for mailing and handling to Penguin USA, P.O. Box 999, c/o Dept. 17109, Bergenfield, NJ 07621. Residents of New York and Tennessee must include sales tax. DO NOT SEND CASH.

GOING POSTAL

Don Lasseter

Pinnacle Books
Kensington Publishing Corp.

http://www.pinnaclebooks.com

Some names have been changed to protect the privacy of individuals connected to this story.

PINNACLE BOOKS are published by

Kensington Publishing Corp.
850 Third Avenue
New York, NY 10022

Copyright © 1997 by Don Lasseter

Excerpts from *Shadow of a Massacre* © 1987 by Eugene B. Black.

All rights reserved. No part of this book may be reproduced in any form or by any means without the prior written consent of the Publisher, excepting brief quotes used in reviews.

If you purchased this book without a cover, you should be aware that this book is stolen property. It was reported as "unsold and destroyed" to the Publisher and neither the Author nor the Publisher has received any payment for this "stripped book."

Pinnacle and the P logo Reg. U.S. Pat. & TM Off.

First Printing: October, 1997
10 9 8 7 6 5 4 3 2 1

Printed in the United States of America

Foreword

He calmly walked into his place of employment, a U.S. post office, unsheathed a semi-automatic weapon, leveled it at his horrified supervisor, and pulled the trigger. As the victim fell, the killer opened an explosive barrage of fire against other coworkers, murdering. . . . .

Sound familiar? It should. Shocking accounts of assault, murder, and suicide have made headlines across this country *twenty* times since August 1983. Literally dozens of victims have lost their lives in United States post offices, leaving a gory trail from New York to Southern California, across Georgia, Alabama, up to New Jersey, and westward to Michigan.

The unsavory image of "disgruntled postal workers" has branded itself on the national psyche. What prompts the crazed assaults? Why is this happening? Are working conditions in the United States Postal Service (USPS) so arduous and stressful that employees have been driven to suicide and murder? Do other industries experience such tragedies? Is it likely to continue? With each new death-dealing outburst, stunned Americans search for answers. Has the USPS investigated the causes? What are their executives doing about it?

Newspapers, magazines, and television commentators chronicle highlights of the stories, but fall short of answering key questions.

If USPS officials are embarrassed by the long string of shocking homicides, in which their own employees murdered coworkers, they seem reluctant to acknowledge it, or even to discuss it. Their reaction, when I invited them to present the USPS side of the story in this book, suggested a defensive evasiveness. Maybe they wished the problems would quietly go away. Bureaucrats in the Washington, D.C. headquarters decided it would be better to slam the door in the face of requests for information. Rather than contribute a positive slant to the negative images that have proliferated in the press and entertainment media, officials chose not to respond. They didn't bother to disguise their hostility about being queried on the subject.

When reminded of the announcement by another government agency that murder was the second ranking cause of violent death among postal employees, disgruntled USPS damage control officers expressed anger about the "unfair" allegations. After all, the spin doctors argued, a higher rate of taxi drivers and liquor store clerks were murdered on the job.

They didn't bother to mention that cabbies and clerks weren't being slaughtered by *fellow cabbies and clerks.* Could these reactions by postal spokesmen be diversionary tactics or efforts to deflect the hard questions? Or did the executive representatives prefer to muddy the waters by quibbling about details? When I spoke to one officer and presented a long list of incidents which resulted in the bloody deaths of 40 USPS workers in post offices across the nation, he hurriedly protested that my tally included an incident that shouldn't be counted. In that specific case, the killer marched into the Montclair, New Jersey post office where he'd been previously employed, cold-bloodedly executed two supervisors and two customers, then sprinted away with a bundle of cash. Headquarters officials indignantly rationalized that it shouldn't be included in their statistical base of in-house homicides because the perpetrator was "only an ex-maintenance employee conducting a robbery."

Technically correct, perhaps. But it seemed to me that excluding the catastrophe wouldn't significantly change the appalling tally, cast any light on the growing enigma or help understand what drove postal workers to massacre people with whom they'd worked.

The long list had already caused a coast-to-coast rumble of questions by the American public. Shocked citizens wondered just what was going on behind those USPS walls that caused men to go berserk and unleash a savage hail of bullets against their colleagues and supervisors. "Disgruntled" became a word jocularly associated with postal workers. "Going Postal" found its way into the lexicon as a synonym for a berserk outburst of violence or murder. Comedians indulged in dark humor about the grim tragedies, while talk show hosts made cynical comments suggesting that it's a good idea to avoid any behavior that might anger a postal worker.

Such a rap is, indeed, grossly unfair to all but a very few of the over 850,000 USPS employees. Certainly, no one believes that violence and murder are endemic to the postal service. The vast majority of their people are responsible, hardworking, law-abiding citizens who detest the snide comments they hear, and stand up to defend their peers and their workplace. Steadfast USPS personnel provide admirable service, delivering billions of parcels and envelopes with remarkable speed and accuracy. It's an exceptional bargain they offer. For small change, we can still send a first class letter 3,000 miles and expect delivery in a couple of days. Mail carriers and behind-the-counter workers at post offices, for the most part, are reliable, friendly people whom we pleasantly encounter every day.

But the trend of violence and the long list of murdered and wounded employees, along with civilian victims who happened to get in the way, are not phantoms or figments of the imagination. Something went wrong with the men who opened fire inside the walls of 15 USPS offices across the nation. Something ignited their festering anger or frustration and sent them into an explosion of murderous destruction.

And like many other Americans, I wondered what was behind the horrible tragedies.

It is not widely known that the United States House of Representatives also questioned what was wrong and conducted a full investigation in 1992 of a particularly grievous slaughter in a Michigan post office.

When I launched my research for this book, I realized that the easiest course of action would be to write a sensational, tabloid-type exposé of the murders. But I decided that wouldn't be fair. I was certain that the USPS, with its extensive investigative branch, had intensively probed these deadly outbursts, identified the problems, helped administrators establish corrective action programs, and implemented plans to avoid future repetition. They would, no doubt, be proud of their accomplished efforts and welcome a chance to correct mistaken public perceptions.

With that in mind, I telephoned the media relation organization at 475 L'Enfant Plaza in Washington, D.C. to announce my intentions of writing a book about the tragedies and to offer the USPS folks the opportunity to tell their side of the story. Surely, they had nothing to hide, and would readily accept the challenge to inform the American public about their diligent efforts to curb violence in their workplaces.

I didn't expect to become privy to confidential matters. I expected the media relations folks to provide me with a stack of previously distributed press releases, perhaps give me some preprinted pamphlets and brochures, and possibly answer a few questions I might pose.

The representative with whom I first spoke, a friendly, courteous chap, did send a limited assortment of general information. He also gave me the names of some executives and suggested I write letters to them explaining my needs. I thanked him, and wrote the letters he suggested, along with a notification to the Postmaster General, Mr. Marvin Runyon, telling him of my project.

Most of us have experienced the frustration of dealing with the hopelessly slow labyrinth of government bureaucracies. It didn't surprise me that I received no answers. So I telephoned two of the staff executives to whom I had written. The one in the investigative branch referred me to the media relations boss.

I called his number, and his assistant referred me to the original media relations representative. Two weeks of inquiries landed me precisely back where I had started.

The friendly chap apologized and said he'd talk to his supervisor about my inquiries and my invitation for USPS participation. A couple of days later, the same man called me to say his boss needed some detailed written information about my personal background and my plans for the book. I had nothing to hide so I readily complied by sending a multi-page response to their requests.

After waiting several days and hearing nothing from the USPS, I called again. After all, I was dealing with an extension of the government, and knew I had to be patient. At last, I spoke with the man in charge. He opened his little speech with, "Let me be candid. . . ."

When those are the first words out of a bureaucrat's mouth, brace yourself. You know the rest of the message is not good news. He informed me that I wasn't a Ph.D. I already knew that. It seems that my failure to earn a doctorate somehow consigned me to the great unknown, therefore I held no status with the USPS media relations folks. How could an ordinary citizen dare to ask the imperial staff for information? And, he said, their investigative branch had opted not to provide any information for my project. Furthermore, I was told, they could find only one of my previous three books.

I wasn't very impressed with their investigative skills.

He was especially "offended" that I had singled out the USPS as a focus of murder in the workplace. Why wasn't I writing about violence and homicide across the entire scope of industry? I don't think he wanted to hear my explanation that national interest had already put the spotlight on the USPS. No one had been making jokes about disgruntled taxi drivers or killer convenience store clerks. I was right. He didn't want to hear that.

Finally, the official, whose attitude and words might be interpreted by some as arrogant, informed me that if I were a Ph.D. who planned to do an academic thesis on the subject of violence in the general workplace, they might be interested in cooperating. But they did not wish to be involved in a mass media book.

It seemed to me that the mass media might be exactly where a media relations executive would want to express the USPS story. His condescension made me wonder if the same kind of executive attitude percolated down through the rank and file of the whole USPS organization. If it did, that might explain some of the frustration and anger.

I couldn't help but wonder what they had to hide. Why wouldn't the USPS wish to make public their aggressive efforts to prevent violence in the workplace, if such efforts truly existed? Why not seize the opportunity to invalidate the public perception of "disgruntled postal workers" and boost the reputation of the hundreds of thousands of employees who efficiently collect, sort, and deliver tons of mail every day? The official's circular logic didn't make a whole lot of sense. He seemed to be concerned that I was going to write unpleasant things about the USPS. Wouldn't it be intelligent, then, to provide me with overwhelming evidence that would neutralize such an attack?

The executive chose, instead, to provide nothing. The media relations department decided to stonewall the media.

This attitude didn't come as a great surprise. The USPS reluctance to respond to an inquiry for complete information wasn't unprecedented, even when the request came from high places. When the United States House of Representatives Committee (on Post Office and Civil Service) conducted an investigation of a shooting at the post office in Royal Oak, Michigan, they encountered a certain degree of the same resistance. After the committee chairman had requested records in the possession of the chief postal inspector, he found the response incomplete. The subsequent Congressional report included the alarming comment: "The Chairman renewed his request for certain documents and requested additional documents and records by letter. . . . There was not a complete response to the Chairman's request."

When I saw that report, I realized that if a Congressional committee chairman faced such difficulty, a book author would probably have more luck swimming the Potomac in mid-winter than he would prying information from USPS headquarters.

Fortunately, there was a solid alternative. Employees of the USPS are represented by powerful and effective unions. The majority of the personnel are members of the National Association of Letter Carriers and the American Postal Workers Union. My requests to officers of these organizations were met with courtesy, professionalism, and dignity. Their answers, I found, would allow me to express the viewpoint of employees and to understand some of the problems inherent in certain management policies and conduct. The unions' point of view was probably far more candid and complete than anything the USPS would have provided.

Sometimes, it seems that officials in high government circles prefer that the public be left in the dark. So, if you readers, especially those of you who are employees of the postal service, would like to know more about the USPS investigations and executive plans to head off violence in the workplace, you might find the information in an academic doctorate thesis or in a university library somewhere. Maybe.

This book will tell you about the horrendous tragedies, the victims, the killers, the people involved, the shockwaves felt by survivors, analysis of the killers' behavior, what Congress found, the efforts of unions to improve working conditions for postal employees, and how justice was meted out.

When the USPS official in Washington, D.C. informed me that his organization, with its huge investigative branch, could find a record of only one of my three previous books, I had to admit some surprise. He said that I had apparently written only one book.

I will now refer him to a quote once used by the father of nineteenth-century politician Benjamin Disraeli: *"Cave ab hominie unius libre."*

It means, "Beware the man of one book."

Chapter 1

"Don't Move or I'll Kill All of You"

Johnston, South Carolina
August 19, 1983

In the "Peach Capitol of the World," as Johnston, South Carolina bills itself, it's easy to imagine being in the idyllic Mayberry of the old Andy Griffith show. A small town of 2,600 good people, in the rolling hills of the state's western edge, it retains the folksy charm of the Victorian era, which is also represented by the stately homes lining many of the streets. The police force is considerably larger than the Andy-Barney duo, but operates on the same first name basis with the folks they serve and protect. The citizens speak with southern color and mellifluous drawls, hunt deer and turkey in nearby woods, golf at Persimmon Hill eight miles north of town, and gather for Sunday picnics at Strom Thurmond Lake, named for the U.S. Senator who has represented them for most of the half-century since WWII. Main Street in Johnston is intersected by Lee Street at the city center, not far away from the post office where everyone in town eventually makes a stop.

Charles O. McGee, the postmaster for the last four years, also knew many of the townspeople by their first names. That's why they hated to see him leave. McGee, having accepted a transfer to the Hartsfield, Georgia post office, would complete his last-day duties on August 19, 1983. If necessary though, he told his boss, he'd stay in Johnston for another week to cover for his successor, who hadn't yet arrived.

Just a few months short of his 50th birthday, McGee looked much younger. A high, unlined forehead, narrow conservative face, neatly trimmed brown hair, and impeccable clothing gave him the look of a politician or a banker. His stay at Johnston had been, for the most part, a pleasant one, marred by only a few conflicts with some of the postal workers. The mail carrier who'd been the biggest problem had recently resigned, after a 25-year career.

Perry Bush Smith had started with the postal service in June, 1958. He delivered letters to Johnston residents for most of his quarter-century career. By 1983, he'd grown a three-inch salt-and-pepper beard, matching his hair color, and wore black-rimmed glasses. A slender, wiry man of average height, Smith was still strong and energetic at 55 even though he'd suffered a debilitating loss the previous November. Smith's only son, also a postal worker, had committed suicide. Perry's wife and grown daughter also suffered terribly with the tragic loss, but somehow, it seemed to take a heavier toll on the grieving father. His behavior changed. Already thin, he lost more weight, let his hair and beard become shaggier, started wearing dark glasses most of the time, and stopped bathing. Fellow employees couldn't help but notice. One man, who'd been a friend since childhood, said, "P.B. was a hard person to get to know. He wanted to do things his own way."

Smith's traumatic loss acted as a catalyst to inflame already sore relations between him and Postmaster Charles McGee. The quality of Smith's job performance slipped, his bosses noticed, and they reprimanded him for subpar production. To Smith, they seemed insensitive to the pain he suffered over the death of his son. How could they nag him about trivial mistakes? Didn't they understand how it hurt to lose someone so close?

A supervisor discovered that Smith left his letter satchel unattended for a few minutes while on his route, and warned him of possible disciplinary action. When Smith repeated the error a couple of times, the boss suspended him.

A proud and independent man, Smith had trouble accepting the discipline as constructive. A supervisor overheard him cursing the postmaster, and watched as Smith repeatedly exceeded the time limit for his breaks. Not serious violations of the rules, but violations just the same. So when Smith delivered a few letters to the wrong address, management came down hard on him with another suspension.

The postmaster was behind it all, Smith reasoned. These problems hadn't existed, at least in his mind, until the arrival of Charles McGee. Anger boiled in Smith's guts like corrosive acid. Other employees had trouble sympathizing with him, though, because of his rude attitude toward them. Maybe management could have shown more sympathy, but Smith's behavior did nothing to alleviate the problems. One coworker noted that Smith had gradually become more aggressive with his peers, undiplomatic in his criticism, and seemed ready to fight over the least misunderstanding. Yet, a few of his colleagues rushed to defend Smith, empathetic with his grievous loss.

The atmosphere of tension and the treatment by management, which Smith regarded as unfair, escalated in his mind. He approached Postmaster McGee, made some serious threats, and stalked out.

Worried that Smith might resort to violence, McGee had a chat with Police Chief Robert Waldrop. The chief asked McGee to swear out peace warrants against Smith. But after giving the matter some serious thought, McGee decided he didn't want to have Smith arrested, so he declined Waldrop's suggestion.

Unaware that the postmaster had given him a break, Smith continued to chafe about the negative twists his life had taken, and he still blamed McGee for making his job miserable. Smith's inner turmoil boiled over in the spring of 1983. "They're killing me," he muttered to his daughter. On May 27th, without giving any reason, he resigned from the USPS.

If he thought separation from the job would give him peace and serenity, he was wrong. Smith's world continued to disintegrate as the summer passed.

In a small town, such as Johnston, the grapevine is a powerful carrier of news. Over back fences, in parks, and along Main Street, current events are passed from person to person. The news that August 19th would be Charles McGee's last day on the job funneled through a number of people and reached the ears of Perry Smith.

On Thursday, August 18th, Smith walked casually into the post office, exchanged some brief conversation with ex-coworkers, then asked if it was true that McGee would be leaving after tomorrow. Yes, he was told. Well, Smith wanted to know, would McGee be in the office tomorrow? Yes, he would.

A few minutes before eight o'clock on Friday morning, Perry Smith left his Bland Street home and drove the short distance to the post office. Carrying a 12-gauge shotgun, he exited his dark four-door sedan, walked through the facility's rear entrance at 8:15, and locked it behind him. The first person he encountered inside was employee Josephine Gibson. Smith looked into her eyes and growled, "Jo, don't move." Other people he'd known for years looked up from their morning tasks, their eyes growing big at the sight of the weapon. "Don't move or I'll kill all of you," Smith shouted. Most of the workers complied.

From several yards away, Charles McGee overheard the commotion, caught sight of Smith wielding the shotgun, and dodged around a corner. Yelling, "He's got a gun. Everyone get out and run for your lives," McGee opened a side exit and bolted through it.

Standing near an interior door, 54-year-old Monroe Kneece watched in horror as Smith swung the gun's barrel in his direction and pulled the trigger, filling the room with an ear-splitting explosion and releasing a spray of buckshot. Some of the pellets and ragged fragments of the shattered door struck Kneece in the head.

After scrambling through the side exit, Postmaster McGee

sprinted across the street toward The Pantry, a convenience store.

Still inside the post office, Allen Thomas, 35, who had worked with Smith for ten years, saw his chance in the pandemonium and rushed out behind McGee, but a little late. Smith followed in close pursuit. Running with all the speed he could muster, Thomas crossed the street and dashed through a parking lot, heading for the nearby convenience store. He didn't make it. Perry Smith cut loose with another blast from the shotgun which dropped Thomas to the pavement.

Apparently realizing that his main target, Postmaster McGee had also sought refuge in The Pantry, Smith trotted toward the doorway.

Two clerks inside the store, Sandra Burkett and Ida Mae Heath, scrambled in fear when McGee ran in and told them to take cover. He slipped into a storage room and locked the door while they hid in the women's restroom. Seconds later, Smith charged in.

After glancing around for a moment, and reloading his weapon, Smith headed directly for the storage room, broke through the door, and confronted McGee. "I told you I'd get you," Smith shouted, and pulled the trigger. The first blast caught McGee in the stomach. Once more the gun discharged, slamming McGee in the chest. Through the cloud of smoke Smith yelled again. "I told you I'd get even with you, you sonofabitch!"

Retreating, Smith raced outside again, toward the rear of the post office.

Josephine Gibson, the first employee Smith had faced when he entered the post office, had made her way out the front door, and dashed up the street. She spotted Officer Robert Carroll, who had just finished his patrol shift, flagged him down, and breathlessly explained what was happening. He told her to call the police department for help, and moved toward the back of the post office. There, he spotted Smith carrying the shotgun. The officer dodged toward an air conditioner projecting from the wall.

Smith simultaneously saw Officer Carroll closing the few

yards between them, raised the weapon again, and fired. Part of the buckshot load caught Carroll in the left arm but most of it splattered against the air conditioner. Bleeding, but still able to function, Carroll raised his service pistol, aimed at Smith, and yelled for him to drop the shotgun.

Now an overwhelming silence replaced the explosions. Perry Smith, drained of venom, let his gun slip to the ground, raised his hands, and trudged toward the officer. He moved with weary, slow steps. As he approached the wounded cop, Smith said he wanted to surrender. After Carroll snapped cuffs on the shooter's wrists, Smith looked up into his eyes and showed recognition for the first time. "Oh," he said, "I didn't know it was you . . . I didn't mean to shoot you."

Help arrived. Uniformed cops took the now-acquiescent Perry Smith into custody. Paramedics loaded the three wounded postal employees into ambulances.

While other officers booked Smith into jail, Officer Carroll and postal employee Monroe Kneece received treatment for their wounds at Edgefield County Hospital. Doctors pronounced both men in good condition, but kept them overnight for observation.

Allen Thomas, who'd been shot while still inside the post office, needed more intensive care at Humana Hospital. He would eventually need spinal fusion operations, plastic surgery to his face, neck and shoulder, and reattachment of an ear. His hearing would never be the same and he wouldn't fully recover the feeling and full use of his right shoulder.

No amount of emergency medical help could save the life of Charles McGee. He died from the massive wounds to his chest and stomach.

Later on that sad Friday, the statement made by a postal spokesman didn't quite capture the magnitude of the tragedy. He said, "Mister McGee was well liked by all of us. He was an easygoing, likeable person. We feel terribly bad about this." He'd preceded those comments with, "This has put a damper on our day."

* * *

Perry Smith sat behind bars waiting for the legal process to begin. Circuit Court Judge George Bell Timmerman denied bail, and ordered Smith to undergo two weeks of intense psychiatric examination at South Carolina State Hospital in Columbia. Smith's bizarre behavior prior to and during the deadly outburst suggested the possibility of mental illness. The judge wanted to know if Smith understood his acts and if he was fit to stand trial.

If the case did go to trial, the prosecutor announced, he would not seek the death penalty. He really didn't have much choice, since capital punishment in South Carolina is applied only in murders of law enforcement officers and killings committed in the commission of rape or armed robbery.

By mid-October, Perry Smith appeared before the Edgefield County Grand Jury. Cleanly shaved, wearing a blue work shirt and denim pants, Smith heard them pronounce him mentally fit to stand trial.

The trial started on the first day of November with jury selection, however the judge had a shock in store for the next morning. He held a hearing requested by the defense at which psychiatric experts spoke. At its conclusion, Judge Timmerman announced to the gathered assembly his ruling that Perry Smith was mentally incompetent to stand trial!

The judge based his decision on testimony that Smith regarded himself as Moses, and was determined to smite evil in the world. Dr. Harold Morgan stated that Smith believed Charles McGee, the dead victim, had represented a mortal threat to him. Morgan said, "It was [Smith's] mission, like it was the mission of Moses, to rise up against these forces of evil." Smith's mental stability, the expert said, had been declining during the past two years. This partially accounted for his troubles on the job and led him to resign. The loss of his son had led to "rapid deterioration" of Smith's mind.

Prosecutor Donald V. Myers harshly criticized Morgan and two hospital-appointed psychologists who presented opinions that Smith was not capable of aiding in his own defense. The defense tactic, Myers charged, was nothing but an effort to preempt the trial. Myers asked Timmerman to assign new medical personnel to monitor Smith's case for future hearings. The judge agreed.

Perry Smith walked meekly out of the courtroom between armed officers. He would be confined and tested at the state hospital to determine the need for future court involvement.

Thus began one of the most contested legal battles in the state's history. Psychiatrists eventually agreed that Smith could face murder charges and he came to trial in Edgefield County. It lasted over one month, but the jury required only three hours of deliberation to find him guilty. In mid-1985, Judge Hubert Long sentenced Smith to life in prison. Eighteen months later, the South Carolina Supreme Court overturned the conviction citing that "improper questions" had been asked by one of the trial lawyers. When the retrial came, a change of venue was granted due to the publicity given the case. A McCormick County jury would hear the evidence against Smith, but the long, slow hand of American justice delayed the new hearings to the final months of 1987. The new jury, ten women and two men, decided after prolonged deliberations that they couldn't reach a decision. The judge reluctantly declared a mistrial, commenting to the hung jurors that "it's sad, because it means twelve other citizens will have to do the job you couldn't, or wouldn't, do."

A third trial, in a third county, began one month later. The jury, with the same make-up of ten women and two men, at last found Smith guilty of murder. Ninth Circuit Judge William Traxler sentenced Smith to life in prison. The state Supreme Court rejected a new appeal to overturn the verdict. After four years of court battles, state prison bars slammed on Perry Smith.

* * *

But the interval between the day he committed the murders and the next grisly outburst in a post office was only four months. Another postal worker, about 200 miles west of Johnston, South Carolina, couldn't suppress a seething rage building up inside him.

Chapter 2

"We Never Know What to Expect"

Anniston, Alabama
December 2, 1983

Oscar Gerald Johnson shook off the morning chill and slipped out of his overcoat after he entered the Anniston, Alabama post office on a frigid Friday, December 2, 1983. At age 49, Johnson had been postmaster there for five years, and felt comfortable with his reputation among the employees. At one time, soon after joining the postal service in 1957, Johnson had been the only mail carrier in nearby Oxford. As the area and the number of employees grew, Johnson became an officer of the National Association of Letter Carriers (NALC) union. During this time he developed a strong sympathy for the workers' side of labor disputes. Management executives spotted Johnson's potential and convinced him to accept supervisorial duties. Over the next few years he moved gradually upward and finally earned a promotion to postmaster in 1978. Johnson remembered his roots, trying to see both sides of every issue, and administering his duties with even-handed common sense. His colleagues, non-management employees, and the townspeople, for the most part, held him in high regard. The African-American community, nearly 6,000 strong, took pride in Johnson's achievements and status, and the Lions Club welcomed him as a member. One acquaintance called him a fine fellow who never asked anything of his subordinates that he wouldn't do himself. "He always had time for everybody." Another commented, "I've never seen him mad. He's quiet, very unassertive. We've been in some rough situations together and I never saw him change his expression."

Within minutes after entering his office on that December morning, one of the roughest situations Johnson had ever faced occurred. He figured he could handle it, though. Two days earlier, on Wednesday evening at the Grace Baptist Church, Johnson had heard the Reverend Don Gentry deliver an inspiring sermon to the congregation. To a chorus of Amens, Hallelujahs, and "Yes, brother," the church leader had spoken of the fleeting nature of life. The complexity of life, he said, ". . . is such that we never know what to expect." Johnson had often been buoyed by Gentry's delivery of sensible religion.

Religion plays a major role in the daily lives of people who live in Calhoun County, Alabama, which boasts of more than 350 churches. Many of the more picturesque and historic places of worship are in the town of Anniston.

Nestled in the foothills of the Appalachian range 25 miles west of the Georgia border, Anniston is the seat of Calhoun County where "time honored traditions still hold true and a shake of the hand is still as good as a man's word." Local business owners express those sentiments and point proudly to a variety of attractions in their county, including Talladega Superspeedway where the shrill whine of race cars fills the air each spring during the "Winston 500," a museum celebrating the history of the Women's Army Corp, a charming covered bridge over Coldwater Creek, and a park where a 90-foot waterfall is named for Noccalula, a young Cherokee maiden who plunged to her untimely death rather than forsake her true love.

Laid out as a model city by "eastern architects and European artisans," Anniston was built by industrialists and incorporated in 1873. They'd established textile mills and iron manufacturing soon after the Civil War to take advantage of the region's abundant natural resources. Originally called Woodstock, it was changed after one of the moneyed founders, who had a wife named Annie, exerted considerable influence to change it to something like Annie's Town. The thriving municipality, now boasting a population of more than 31,000, owes some of its economic stability to government establishments. Fort McClellan Military Reservation occupies land on the northeast sector while Morrisville Maneuver Area and the Anniston Army Depot form the western border.

Picturesque and historic brick buildings are scattered throughout Anniston, contrasting with modern steel and glass multistory towers in the commercial center. The various religions are represented by magnificent nineteenth century churches, including Parker Memorial Baptist, a double-steepled stone structure, German Gothic style, dating from 1888. Just two blocks from Parker Baptist, down Quintard Avenue, which has a center divider landscaped with rows of trees, at the corner intersected by 11th Street, sits a contemporary concrete and brick post office.

Before the sun came up that December morning, at 4:30 A.M., James H. Brooks had started his predawn duties of cleaning the interior of the post office. Brooks, like Oscar Johnson, had also been deeply involved with his union, climbing to the post of Local president. But he became disillusioned with it, and felt alienated. Other similarities existed between Postmaster Johnson and maintenance worker Brooks. Both men were well liked in the community, and both men attended Baptist churches. A bank guard said of Brooks, "He's always jolly. I've never heard him say a mean word." Brooks had spent 20 of his 53 years in the U.S. Navy before joining the postal service. He'd settled in Anniston to live near a retired police officer brother and a daughter who worked for a local bank. People who knew him described Brooks as friendly, good-natured, and always willing to lend a helping hand. Physically, Brooks seemed healthy enough except for a tendency toward high blood pressure. But close acquaintances worried about his inconsistent demeanor. He's a very "quiet fellow," said Wayne Jackson, post office foreman of deliveries and collections. But not everyone agreed with that assessment. Postal clerk Dewitt Morgan called Brooks a "pretty vocal" guy and said he was easily agitated. Some called him a restless "loner."

The troubles started for James Brooks early in 1983. His supervisors, he complained, treated him unfairly. Much of his discontent centered on overtime issues and was aimed at his immediate boss, J.H. "Butch" Taylor. The 38-year-old supervisor, in addition to his regular job, was also a deacon at Parker Memorial Baptist Church down the street. But neither Taylor's church training nor his management skills helped. The disagreement couldn't be resolved at that level.

When Brooks sought assistance from the union, he felt doubly frustrated at the results, which he perceived as ineffective. Angrily, he withdrew his membership and filed a complaint with the National Labor Relations Board (NLRB). The union, he said, unfairly and arbitrarily refused to file his grievances and sought to prevent him from selecting his own representative to negotiate with management. Ultimately, Brooks and the NLRB reached a mutual agreement to drop the complaint.

James "Bucky" Walters, national vice president of the American Postal Workers Union, tried to negotiate a peaceful solution. On more than one occasion, he traveled from Washington, D.C. to Anniston. He commented, "The last time I saw [Brooks] I came over and stayed a complete day trying to iron out the problems. . . . He could be reasonable, and he could be unreasonable." There is no record available of upper level management attempting to seek resolution.

Still acting like a person caught in an inescapable trap, James Brooks wasn't finished. He decided to handle the matter himself by embarking on a campaign to bypass his supervisor and personally express his dissatisfaction directly to the postmaster, Oscar Johnson. Starting in mid-November, Brooks confronted Johnson at least once each week, and argued his case.

The Thanksgiving holiday passed, but the celebration for

Brooks was an empty one. He cornered Johnson again, this time complaining about mistreatment in regards to overtime hours and pay.

By the time Johnson parked near Brooks's car in the lot on Friday, December 2nd, and entered the building, Brooks had already put in three hours of work cleaning the offices. He had been interrupted at 6:00 A.M. by the arrival of clerk Dewitt Morgan, for whom he had to unlock the entry door. Morgan thought Brooks seemed to be acting in a normal manner.

Two hours later, Morgan caught a glimpse of Brooks stepping into the postmaster's office. Morgan overheard only part of the conversation. He recognized Brooks's voice saying, "I want results." There was no shouting, just the firm demand. Then silence.

Shortly afterwards, Brooks stalked out of the building and headed for his car in the adjacent lot. He leaned inside, retrieved a .38-caliber revolver, and rushed back into the post office. Once more, he entered Oscar Johnson's office.

Johnson, as was his custom when he received visitors, took off his glasses, laid them on the desk, and looked up.

During day-to-day activities in the work areas of most post offices, there can be a din of racket at times, especially when someone drops a large tray loaded with mail. Dewitt Morgan hadn't noticed Brooks return, and when he heard the first loud crack, he thought someone had dropped a tray. A second burst of noise caused Morgan more than ordinary concern. Within seconds, he heard someone shout, "Johnson's been wounded!" A customer collecting mail from his P.O. box in the public area heard a pair of pops, then what seemed to be some commotion on the other side of the wall separating him from Johnson's office.

Up on the second floor, Brooks's supervisor, "Butch" Taylor had stepped away from his desk for a few moments to examine some nearby files. He stopped to chat with clerk Don Dulaney.

When Brooks appeared wild-eyed at the top of the stairs, wielding a weapon that looked like a cannon, Dulaney ducked down and scrambled for cover. A mail carrier standing around the corner couldn't see what was happening, but could hear some of the ensuing exchange. Neither he nor Dulaney heard a word from Brooks. Only the pitiful voice of Butch Taylor was crystal clear as he pled, "Please, man! No! No!" Dulaney crawled away to seek help and made his way downstairs. Two more shots exploded, echoing through the room. A moment of silence, then one more loud blast.

As he reached the lower floor, Dulaney shouted to his fellow workers, "Get out ... Jim's got a gun." A mad scramble ensued with frightened employees seeking shelter and racing for the exits. Dulaney escaped through a rear door, sprinted across a parking lot, crossed Leighton Avenue, and burst into an office building. Grabbing the first phone he saw, he dialed for emergency help, breathlessly describing the terror he'd witnessed.

Sirens screamed and tires squealed as emergency vehicles braked to a halt on Quintard and 11th, as well as the surrounding parking lots. Risking the possibility that the gunman would open fire again and ignoring their own safety, paramedics dashed inside directly to Oscar Johnson's office, pointed out by horrified employees. They found him slumped on the floor leaning against a wall, his head a bloody mess. Kneeling beside the victim to check for vital signs, they found a faint pulse. Moving as rapidly as possible, the technicians strapped the victim to a gurney and hurried him outside to a waiting ambulance.

Simultaneously, a second paramedic team, taking the stairs two at a time, rushed to the aid of Butch Taylor. Finding him alive and conscious, they rapidly transported him to the Northeast Alabama Regional Medical Center (RMC), where he arrived 16 minutes after Johnson. A triage nurse sent the bleeding Taylor to a second ER room.

Back at the post office, Anniston Police Department Officers Ken Murphy and Paul Rowell had cleared the building of all remaining nervous employees who'd been hiding. As the two cops moved cautiously into the large work area called the mail room, they spotted a figure standing at the far end. He held a big revolver pointed toward the floor. "Drop the gun," Rowell shouted, his voice making it clear that he meant business. James Brooks hesitated only a moment, turned to face the two uniformed armed cops, and let his weapon drop to the floor. Still holding their own handguns at the ready, both officers advanced toward him, and hurriedly slapped the cuffs on Brooks's wrists behind his back. Brooks hung his head in acquiescent silence. Rowell and Murphy hustled him to a waiting patrol car outside, and transported him to the jail, only four blocks away.

Meanwhile, at RMC, emergency surgeons worked feverishly on Oscar Johnson from the moment he arrived, at 8:03 A.M. But within a few minutes, they realized it was hopeless. They pronounced him dead at 8:24 that morning. His friend, the Reverend Don Gentry, would be left to ponder the sermon he'd delivered on Wednesday night, the last one ever heard by Johnson, in which he'd said, "Life is just a vapor . . . we never know what to expect." Gentry had never spoken truer words.

In the other emergency room, three hours of intense surgery to remove bullets from the stomach and arm of Butch Taylor worked a minor miracle. He survived.

U.S. Postal Inspectors, accompanied by the F.B.I., swarmed over the crime scene. As soon as they finished, a cleanup crew scoured away any signs of the earlier carnage. Management ordered the reopening for business at noon, the same day. The only sign of the tragedy was the flag out front, lowered to half staff.

Federal officers whisked James Brooks from the local jail to a lockup in Birmingham. Charged with premeditated murder of a federal official, a judge set bail at $250,000. Brooks would face trial in a U.S. District Court.

* * *

On Sunday, three weeks before Christmas, Oscar Johnson's friends and family gathered in Grace Baptist Church in Oxford, where he'd once been the only postman delivering mail. Johnson's wife wept softly, seated beside his three sons. After the tearful eulogy and the church hymns, at Forestlawn Gardens Cemetery, Dewitt Morgan, who'd been close to the shootings, helped five other pallbearers carry Johnson's casket to the grave site.

In Birmingham's Homewood City Jail, Brooks sat silently, beginning the long wait for trial.

Sad coworkers wondered if Brooks considered the horrible pain and trauma he'd inflicted justified, or if he now realized that his grievances seemed petty by comparison.

When James Brooks faced trial, he drew a jury very similar to the one in Perry Smith's second trial. In the United States District Court, Northern District of Alabama, a jury announced their "inability to reach a unanimous decision" on April 5, 1984. Four months later, a second jury found him guilty of first degree murder. Judge Sam C. Pointer sentenced Brooks to prison for the rest of his natural life. In Federal law, there is no parole for a life sentence.

If post office officials were concerned about the second outburst of murder within 15 weeks, they made no announcement of it. Surely these were two anomalies, nothing to get excited about. It probably wouldn't happen again for decades.

Fifteen months after Brooks shot Oscar Johnson to death, the hope of USPS officials went up in the smoke of a gun once again.

Chapter 3

The United States Postal Service, Then and Now

Postal service in the United States has been the provenance of the government since shortly after the Revolutionary War. Prior to this country breaking away from England, mail service in the Colonies was overseen by Postmaster General Benjamin Franklin. Two more men took the office before 1789, when Congress granted the federal government sole power to provide postal service. The top man in the new structure, the Postmaster General, would be a member of the U.S. President's cabinet.

Early letter carriers received no salary. Instead, they were authorized by Congress to collect two pennies for every letter delivered. Most customers opted to go to the post office to pick up their mail. There, they would often find the contents of incoming mailbags dumped onto a table for anyone to rummage through.

The first postage stamps were printed in 1847, but were not required on letters until seven years later.

During the Civil War, in 1863, the U.S. Post Office Department upgraded the operations by establishing three classes of mail and free rural delivery. Money orders, postcards, and registered mail soon followed.

Perhaps the most colorful and storied episode in the service took place from 1860 to 1861, with dashing young men riding fast horses in relays from St. Joseph, Missouri to Sacramento, California. The Pony Express took only 10 days to transport letters 1,400 miles. They faded rapidly, though, when railroad tracks spanned the country. Behind a coal-burning locomotive, postal clerks sorted the mail en route, while specially designed catcher arms picked up bundles of mail without requiring the train to stop.

Labor-management problems developed early. Poor working conditions for postal employees go back to the end of the 19th century, when letter carriers were often forced to stay on the job 10 or more hours daily. An 1890 national survey showed that 90 percent of post office clerks worked an average of 14 hours a day. Along with long workdays, workrooms were filthy and their air was polluted. Tuberculosis was such a common occupational disease among postal employees that it became known as the "clerk's sickness."

Conditions were ripe for the growth of labor unions. City letter carriers organized in 1889 and postal clerks became a national organization by 1908. It became common for postal labor unions to heavily lobby Congress, who held the purse strings.

Post offices proliferated in every state, from about 75 in 1789 to 77,000 in 1901. Today, there are about 42,000 offices and over 850,000 employees.

The most important change in the history of the postal service took place during the presidency of Richard Nixon. He first asked Congress in 1969 to pass the Postal Service Act, calling for the removal of the Postmaster General from the Cabinet and the creation of a self-supporting postal corporation wholly owned by the federal government. The following year, after extensive hearings, the House Post Office Committee watered down the proposal with a compromise measure containing many of the President's suggestions, and adding a moderate pay increase for all postal workers. At that time, Congress controlled postal service wages. To the employees, the tiny boost in money was insulting. In mid-March, a huge postal strike took place.

On the condition that employees would return to work, Postmaster General William Blount agreed to bargain with the seven recognized unions involved. Within a few weeks, an agreement was reached to recommend to Congress that the postal service be reorganized and that employees be awarded adequate wage increases.

After the bill, HR 17070, finally was passed by the Senate and the House of Representatives, the new United States Postal Service replaced the old Department of the Post Office on July 1, 1971. Its mission, as described in Title 39 of the U.S. Code: "The Postal Service shall have as its basic function the obligation to provide postal services to bind the Nations together through the personal, educational, literary, and business correspondence of the people. It shall provide prompt, reliable, and efficient service to patrons in all areas and shall render postal services to all communities."

The USPS would be directed by an 11-member board of governors, nine of them appointed by the President, with Senate confirmation, for nine year terms. Those nine members would, in turn, appoint a Postmaster General (PMG). The new head officer would join the nine to appoint a deputy PMG.

A Postal Rate Commission would consist of five members appointed by the President. The USPS operations would be financed through its revenues and securities, with authorization to borrow up to $10 billion from the general public until profits made it self-supporting. The USPS reached that goal for the first time in 1983.

To the employees, one of the most important new elements was the establishment of collective bargaining to establish wages and working conditions, plus the provision of binding arbitration on issues unsettled after an impasse of 180 days. Strikes by postal employees were prohibited. Contracts between labor and management would spell out the working conditions, and would contain provisions for disciplinary measures, also subject to binding arbitration.

By becoming a separate agency, the USPS severed its connection to Congress. The House of Representatives would still maintain a committee to oversee the service, and would be able to make recommendations, but would have no firm authority to intervene in operations.

The House Committee would see a powerful need to conduct an investigation and make recommendations following a 1991 tragedy in Royal Oak, Michigan. They suggested some changes in the role played by the Postal Inspection Service.

Internal investigations had long been conducted by the Postal Inspection Service, originally installed by Benjamin Franklin to protect and defend post offices, and the mail, nationwide. They also probe crimes committed on postal property. Consisting of more than 2,000 employees, including inspectors and uniformed police officers, they investigate scores of mail-related crimes including robberies, theft, fraud, assaults, and murder. A question came up, after Royal Oak, regarding their responsibilities to provide security and respond to threats.

The current Postmaster General, number 72 in the long line, is Marvin T. Runyon who took office on July 6, 1992. He and his USPS executives have often expressed anger about news and entertainment media using the "disgruntled postal worker image" as an object of humor. They don't appreciate the jokes. In a recent *Newsbreak* flyer distributed for bulletin board posting by the USPS, Pacific Area, titled "Study Reveals Postal Work Place Not Dangerous," the corporate relations folks objected to the jesting thusly:

> In the recent adventure movie, *Jumanji*, starring Robin Williams, the villain goes wild and shoots up a store, prompting another character to ask him, "You're not a postal employee, are you?"
>
> The image of the Postal Service as a violent place to work is largely a creation of the media, which has often exaggerated and sensationalized postal violence. Violence in the workplace and the safety of all employees are issues that the Postal Service takes very seriously and has taken steps to prevent.
>
> In a recent report by the National Institute for Occupa-

tional Safety and Health of the most dangerous jobs in America, the Postal Service doesn't even make the list. The 15 jobs that do make the list as the most dangerous in America include (in order of the number of homicides per 100,000 workers): cab drivers; sheriff/bailiff; police; gas station/garage worker; security guard; stock handler; supervisor/owner, sales; salesclerk; bartender; logger; hotel clerk; vehicle salesperson; other salespeople; butcher; firefighter.

The study also reveals that 73 percent of work place homicides stem from robberies and are committed, not by co-workers, but by strangers to the victims. The authors of the study hope their efforts will get people thinking about violence in the work place and help make all jobs safer for employees.

The bulletin almost came to grips with the real issue; not that post offices have a high rate of homicide, but that they have an exceptionally high rate of employees who kill coworkers.

Most people are well aware that statistics can be manipulated to support almost any point of view. USPS officials continued to cite homicide *rates* and workplace violence *rates* to whitewash the problems. The rank and file work force, and the public in general, want to hear less about rates and more about what the executives intend to do to protect workers from those few employees who have been pushed over the edge by real or imagined demons.

Damage control officials in the USPS evidently didn't realize that Americans have always had a sense of humor, and historically use laughter to cope with tough times. Young cartoonist Bill Mauldin created "Willie and Joe," the two grizzled G.I.s in World War II, to satirize the horrors of combat and the drudgery of life in the trenches. Police officers are known for dark humor that helps them mentally survive the grisly crimes in which they are immersed every day. *The Los Angeles Times* prints a daily "Laugh Lines" column in which humorists find

the light side of news events. Laughter is good medicine, and
humorists can often pinpoint crucial issues with a few barbed
quips.

The image of the disgruntled postal worker was a natural
for whimsical parody, and most USPS employees laughed right
along with America. They could see the humor in a newspaper
cartoon asking, ''Do you want to spice up your life?'' The
drawing depicts three rifle-toting men on a hunting trip, with
one saying, ''What, me disgruntled?'' The punch line is ''Try
hunting with a postal worker.'' On television, the sitcom *Sein-
feld* includes a wacky postal worker, as did *Cheers*. *Saturday
Night Live* introduced an androgynous character named Pat
who became the subject for a spinoff movie. In an early scene,
Pat, wearing a postal worker uniform, is told by the supervisor
that he/she is being fired. While saying it, the boss hurriedly
slips into a bulletproof vest.

Audiences laugh, while USPS executives issue angry denials.

Even the Internet has a Website titled http://www.disgrun-
tled.com/fed.html. Some of the contributors tell dramatic stories
of their own mistreatment while working for the post office,
while others submit humorous anecdotes.

While a little defensiveness on the part of USPS executives
is understandable, perhaps they should temper it by dealing
head on with the issue of in-house murder and be more forthright
about why it's happening and what can be done about it.

Chapter 4

"Somebody Must Pay For Bettye's Dying"

Atlanta, Georgia
March 6, 1985

The main post office in Atlanta, Georgia, is not in Atlanta. It can be found in Hapeville, a community at the southern tip of the capital city near the international airport. A giant central mail processing location, the sprawling facility buzzes with hundreds of employees busily crisscrossing inside the complex work area, handling and sorting tons of mail around the clock. With so many people, it might be extremely difficult to spot a potential killer among them—unless administrative policy allowed special handling of an employee who'd been receiving treatment at a mental hospital. Whether or not it was necessary or practicable to single out such an employee for individual treatment is arguable. After all, it had been over a year since the tragic murders in Anniston, Alabama.

Steven Brownlee, it was said, feared for his personal safety and sometimes heard voices when no one was around. The postal clerk had worked 12 years for the USPS, most recently operating one of the 12 positions along the 60 feet of a letter-sorting machine during the night shift. Sometimes, he could be heard talking to himself. If anyone had listened closely, they might have heard the 30-year-old man muttering about being the target of white evildoers who were out to get him because he was black. Even though it was recognized that Brownlee didn't mix well with coworkers, he did manage to avoid any serious disciplinary measures from management.

At the condominium complex where Brownlee lived, in building number 27, neighbors didn't know him very well, despite his having been there four years. Some of them thought of him as a quiet man who kept to himself, as described by one woman who lived just a few paces away. She said, "He always kept very much to himself. I never saw anyone come to his place. I didn't even know his name. If he came to my door, I wouldn't even recognize his face." Brownlee never associated with anyone, she added.

Right next door to Brownlee's unit, the neighboring resident could hear each afternoon the constant beating of drums coming from the reclusive loner's apartment. But the rhythmic beat was not unpleasant. "The only thing I could hear were those drums," she said. "He played them beautifully, and he never played them at night." She wondered why she never saw any-one but Brownlee go in or out of his place. Possibly, she didn't realize that his abstinence from drum beating at night was because he worked the late shift at the post office.

Coincidentally, the occupant on the other side also worked for the postal service. He knew Brownlee much better than the other residents. The two men sometimes exchanged greetings and had short conversations about the Atlanta Falcons's football fortunes, or the Hawks's performance in basketball. Of course, the job would come up, too, but since they worked different shifts, they never met during duty hours. Brownlee was an okay neighbor, the coworker said, because he was usually quiet and caused no trouble. The only activity he'd ever noticed was Brownlee's frequent workout with a punching bag, outside on his patio, which he did with noticeable vigor and determination.

* * *

Positioned at his mail sorting station, Steven Brownlee performed his duties alongside coworkers Phillip T. Sciarrone and Douglas Adams. All three men reported to supervisor Warren M. Bailey, who had spent 26 years with the USPS. For a portion of that time, Bailey had served as president of the Atlanta chapter of the National Association of Postal Supervisors. At age 45, he had no thoughts of retirement despite his long seniority. If there is a record of friction between Brownlee and Bailey, postal inspection executives aren't talking about it. Neither are they revealing anything about Brownlee's relationship with Sciarrone and Adams.

From a large family that included six siblings, Warren Bailey and his wife continued the tradition by having four children of their own. One of their daughters admired her father so much, she chose his profession, and joined the postal service in nearby Smyrna. Bailey's younger brother also looked up to him, proudly saying that his older sibling "set a good example for me when we were growing up." He called Warren "a good Christian." The concern Bailey held for his fellow man could be seen in a card he carried in his wallet, willing his organs for transplant in the case of his death.

Phillip Sciarrone held the esteem of most of his coworkers, one of whom said that he "got along well with all the guys at work." With his wife and children, Sciarrone lived in Riverdale, a community of 7,000 a few miles southwest on I-85. Some days, the 32-year-old Sciarrone, who'd been with the USPS for eight years, joined other employees at a park to play in the postal service softball league.

Douglas Adams's family chose an even smaller town several miles north of Atlanta to call home. Woodstock, which had a population of fewer than 3,000, and was situated off the main highway, offered solitude and safety. Perhaps that suited Adams's special needs. Mute, age 42, and classified as a handicapped employee, Adams had started with the postal service in 1970. Regarded as a gentle and congenial person, he was treated with great respect and affection by most of his coworkers. One of them said that Adams was "the nicest guy you'd ever meet." It was unimaginable that anyone would want to harm him.

While Steven Brownlee didn't appear to maintain close relations with most of his coworkers, it later became apparent that he felt a kinship for Bettye T. Eberhart, a 35-year-old clerk who sorted mail at a station fairly close to Brownlee.

The troubles about which Steven Brownlee fumed, whether real or imaginary, turned into rage in early March 1985, when he heard that Eberhart had been brutally murdered in her Decatur home. The man suspected of strangling her to death turned out to be Eberhart's estranged husband. The killing seemed to have a profound effect on Brownlee who couldn't stop talking about it. It fueled his seething anger. After he'd changed to the afternoon shift, several coworkers overheard him say, "Somebody must pay for Bettye's dying!"

On Wednesday, March 6, 1985, a gentle breeze brushed away the afternoon clouds over Atlanta, making a beautiful day for visitors who walked along Peachtree Street, trying to imagine the days when Margaret Mitchell's Scarlet and Rhett drove along the avenue in a handsome carriage. The temperature leveled off in the low 70's, perfect for people paying homage at Martin Luther King's memorial tomb, or for picnickers and hikers in the huge park around Stone Mountain.

In the busy main post office, Steven Brownlee wore an impassive mask, giving no clue to his mental turmoil. Many of the employees had been asked to come in two hours early to cope with a mountain of mail, unusually large for that period. The heavy volume of work and pressure to hurry would naturally increase tension. Hundreds of employees coped with it. One did not.

Shortly after two o'clock that afternoon, Steven Brownlee stood at his work station, about six feet away from Phillip Sciarrone. With no warning, other than a nearly unintelligible comment about Bettye Eberhart's death, Brownlee produced a .22-caliber handgun, quickly closed the distance between himself and Sciarrone, and pulled the trigger at point-blank range. The bullet slammed into the middle of Sciarrone's chest.

Many of the workers may not have heard the light pop of the small-caliber weapon due to the noise in the room. Even if they had heard it, Brownlee moved quickly before they could react. He hurried along the floor, the full length of the sorting machine, circled to the other side, and found supervisor Warren Bailey standing near a desk. Once more aiming only inches away from Bailey, Brownlee opened fire. The wounded man crumpled to the floor. Blood from a head wound soon formed a crimson pool on the polished tiles.

Approximately eight feet away, Douglas Adams stood mutely watching the horror, his mouth agape. He lunged forward in what witnesses would later speculate was an effort to stop the slaughter. But Brownlee spun around, spotted the silent man, and squeezed off another round. A gusher of blood poured from Adams's head as he, too, crashed to the floor.

At last, the workers realized that the noise wasn't just the dropping of heavy, mail-filled trays or the clatter of metal-wheeled carts on the hard floor. Terror broke loose all over the room. Some of the startled crowd ducked behind any barriers they could find, seeking safety, while others ran aimlessly. One witness recalled the scene. "People were running. People were hysterical. And the ladies were crying ... After that, I don't know what happened. I'm not exactly sure where [Brownlee] went. People were running and I was trying to keep out of the firing line."

Someone yelled, "Stop that man!" Several courageous individuals surrounded Brownlee. One of them lunged forward, grabbing the gunman and wrestling him to the floor. Several of the men then pinned Brownlee down to hold him until police arrived. He offered no resistance. All the anger and fire in Brownlee had apparently been quenched.

Emergency medical technicians arrived to whisk the three

wounded men to nearby hospitals. Uniformed officers shackled Steven Brownlee and transported him to the Atlanta City Jail.

The employee who had observed the confused flight of coworkers told investigators that the shooter seemed to have carefully picked his targets, but had no idea why the three men were selected for Brownlee's vendetta. "I don't think it was random," the witness said. "If he was shooting people at random, I think he would have shot me and the people around me."

The chances of dying from a bullet wound are unpredictable. Sometimes, a single small-caliber gunshot will cause instant death, while at other times victims have sustained several injuries from larger weapons and still survived.

The slug that struck Phillip Sciarrone in the chest drained his life away in just a few minutes. He died on the post office floor, although he wasn't officially declared dead until his arrival at South Fulton Hospital.

Warren Bailey fought valiantly for his life while Mrs. Bailey and her family waited outside the Emergency Room hoping and praying late into the night. The wounded man lost his battle and succumbed a few minutes before midnight. As Warren Bailey had wished, and with the consent of his family, surgeons removed his vital organs to be used for transplants that might save other lives.

At Grady Hospital, Douglas Adams lay on the operating table for hours while surgeons probed with meticulous skill to remove bullet fragments from his fractured skull. He evidently had been grazed by a disintegrating slug. When the doctors finished the job, they pronounced him in stable condition. He would survive.

That same night, officers removed Brownlee from the Atlanta jail to the psychiatric detention ward at the same hospital where surgeons worked to save Adams's life. Brownlee had shown enough symptoms of insanity to require the change of location for his confinement. Officials filed charges against him for murder and aggravated assault.

* * *

Following the usual procedure, USPS officials opened the main post office for business on Thursday morning. The mail had to be processed and delivered. Employees who'd heard about the tragedy reported to work wearing black arm bands or black clothing.

Three months after the shooting, Steven Brownlee sat in an Atlanta courtroom charged with two counts of murder and one count of aggravated assault. If convicted, he would face a sentence of life in prison.

Defense attorney Tony Axam took on the formidable task of defending a client about whom there was no doubt of guilt. Axam watched in amazement as the judicial system struggled to decide if Brownlee would be tried in federal court or the county superior court. It seemed to him that the feds backed away because they hadn't been able to get a conviction against John Hinckley Jr. in June 1982, for shooting President Ronald Reagan. The jury had found Hinckley not guilty by reason of insanity, a verdict which would send him to a mental institution instead of prison. Prosecutors might stand a better chance of imprisoning Brownlee for life by trying the case in the state's superior court system.

Assistant District Attorney Wendy Shoob had drawn the duty of presenting the state's case, and she realized it would be an uphill battle. The defense had pled not guilty by reasons of insanity, and produced evidence that Brownlee had shown symptoms of mental illness. Shoob told the jury that mental illness may be present in any number of people, but most of them can discern right from wrong. Brownlee, she argued, knew what he was doing when he shot two men to death.

Not so, countered Axam. An eloquently soft-spoken lawyer, known for his compassionate ability to drill right to the core of a problem, Axam had arranged for Brownlee to undergo a series of tests. In addition, the attorney personally scrutinized the working conditions to which his client had been subjected, and came away appalled. Brownlee had been laboring 70 to 80 hours each week to keep up with the supervisor's need to process exceptionally heavy volumes of mail. The noise of the sorting machine, the long hours, the stress, and a predisposition toward anxiety disorder had jeopardized Brownlee's mental health.

A contributing factor to Brownlee's ultimate collapse, Axam contended, was the failure of managers at his workplace to recognize the red flag being waved in their faces. It appeared that no concern existed for the mental health of postal employees. No one responded to the snide jokes being circulated. Management ignored hints that Brownlee might be on the edge of a breakdown. If he'd been sent to a professional counselor, tragedy might have been prevented.

In his client's mind, Axam learned, the repetitive groaning noise Brownlee heard at the sorting machine became a voice telling him that he would soon be killed. He must protect himself. His mind became a twisting whirlpool of exhausted confusion. The machine spoke to him, and imitated the sounds of sliding steel doors slamming around him. A mental prison. Escape! Kill! Break the bonds of pressure and danger!

During the trial, two psychiatrists took the witness stand to inform the court about tests they had conducted on the defendant which, in their opinions, proved that he was legally insane. Brownlee had told his attorney that the sorting machine at work spoke to him. Axam wanted the jury to understand how the grinding, repetitive noise affected his client, so he took a big risk. Seated at the defense table while questioning the experts, Axam placed his hands over his mouth and dramatically imitated the demonic voices his client had heard.

In his summation, Axam appealed to jurors to avoid basing their verdict on fear, and asked them to give serious thought to his client's mental state. "There is no doubt that Steven Brownlee shot and killed two people," he said. "What's true is that [he is] not guilty by reason of insanity and he did not know the difference between right and wrong."

The 12 jurors filed out on Friday, June 21st, to begin deliberations, a process many people thought might take several days.

They were astonished when the 12 people filed back only 45 minutes later. The old rule of thumb is that a quick decision is usually indicative of a guilty verdict. There are always exceptions.

Steven Brownlee, they found, was *not guilty* by reason of insanity. That meant he would be placed in the custody of the state to be treated for his mental illness. It also meant that when psychiatrists decided that Brownlee was no longer mentally ill, he could be released back into the public and face no prison time. Superior Court Judge Frank Eldridge, who had presided over the trial, would be responsible for periodic hearings to evaluate the patient's progress.

Defense Attorney Tony Axam, in an attempt to cushion the shock to the victims' outraged families and the public, stressed that Brownlee was not a free man. But the appeasement was short-lived.

In August, less than two months after the jury's decision, Judge Eldridge heard evidence of Brownlee's treatment and progress at the Georgia Regional Hospital. Dr. Cassandra F. Newkirk, who had joined the hospital staff only a few days after Brownlee's arrival, testified in his behalf. At the end of the hearing, based on what he had heard, the judge ordered the patient to be freed!

A quick request by the district attorney's office for a new hearing was granted. Pending the outcome, authorities put Brownlee's release on hold. On August 29th, the district attorney brought in Dr. Martin Youngelson, a clinical psychologist, who had been transferred out of his job at the hospital in July. There had been discussions and misunderstandings, he said, aggravated by an extremely heavy work load and a shortage of bed space in the mental wards. In his testimony, Dr. Youngelson reported having tested Brownlee, and finding that the patient "continues to have thoughts of hurting others, both physically and sexually." The psychologist also pointed out that the patient was inconsistent about taking prescribed psychotropic medication given for the purpose of controlling his symptoms.

Absolutely furious that Youngelson's testimony hadn't been offered at the earlier hearing, Judge Eldridge reversed his previ-

ous ruling, and ordered that Steven Brownlee continue his
residency and treatment at the Georgia Mental Health Institute.
The court would still have the responsibility of monitoring
Brownlee's progress and holding periodic hearings to determine
his future.

Chapter 5

"He Shaded The Truth"

New York, New York
May 31, 1985

Ten weeks after Steven Brownlee heard machines talking to him, and opened fire in Atlanta's main post office, a New York City letter carrier simmered in rage over his pending dismissal. David Perez had spent too many years with the postal service to give up easily. In his mind, he'd been treated unfairly. At age 45, and with his seniority, he figured they couldn't push him around so easily.

At 1:50 p.m., on the last day of May 1985, Perez stepped into an elevator of the multistory post office building at 90 Church Street in Manhattan. Slipping his mailbag off his right shoulder, Perez punched the button for the sixth floor.

From the elevator, he marched to supervisor George Grady's office, and asked a clerk where Grady was. She pointed to a conference room. Perez nodded his thanks, gripped his bag, and headed in the direction indicated. Moments later, he stepped into the conference room where he confronted his boss.

George Grady felt justified in having made the decision to fire David Perez. In the last couple of months, he had suspended the mail carrier twice for violating rules of the workplace. Perez had failed to respond to warnings about his tardiness, and had shaded the truth during an interview regarding his disregard of proper procedures.

As soon as Perez opened his mouth, Grady responded. Their voices rose as they argued, each man absolutely convinced the other was wrong.

Postal Clerk Carlos Siratt, age 50, grimaced as he watched the growing conflict. Better break it up, he thought, before it gets out of hand. He stepped forward and suggested they calm down.

Perez, his tanned square face darkened with anger, his black curly hair bristling, turned to face Siratt. Without a word, he reached into the mailbag still slung over his shoulder, pulled out a .30-.30 rifle, and pointed it toward Siratt's chest. No warning. No waiting. Perez pulled the trigger. The slug tore into Siratt's chest, dropping him in stunned agony to the floor. Then Perez turned toward an astonished George Grady, and motioned with the rifle for him to move. Both men entered an empty office adjacent to the conference room.

Horrified, clerks at their desks throughout the office scrambled for cover. One of them telephoned for emergency help. An ambulance arrived along with uniformed members of New York's finest. Medical techs hoisted Carlos Siratt onto a gurney and rushed him to the elevator. At New York Infirmary-Beekman Downtown Hospital, surgeons worked over two hours to remove the bullet from Siratt's chest. They pronounced him in serious but stable condition. He would survive.

Back on the post office sixth floor, David Perez didn't know what to do, so he waited. The police, he knew, wouldn't rush in and try to subdue him as long as he kept the rifle pointed at George Grady.

A flurry of activity outside choked off the traffic lanes, backing up honking taxis and tangling pedestrian traffic along Church Street. Police finally sealed off the entire block, hoping to avoid any more casualties.

A hostage negotiator spoke in soothing tones to Perez, pleading with him not to make the situation any worse. He'd only wounded his first victim, but more shots could end lives. The skilled officer told Perez that he would be given help to work through his problems.

After nearly two hours, Perez at last saw the futility of his actions. Like a scolded child, he handed the rifle to his relieved boss, and submitted to arrest. Surrounded by uniformed and plainclothes officers, and with his hands cuffed behind his back, Perez exited the building. From a distance, curious onlookers gawked. Perez forced a tight grin, deepening the crow's feet at the corners of his eyes.

Charged with attempted murder and assault under federal laws, David Perez would face trial in a U.S. district court.

On January 30, 1986, a judge in the U.S. district court, southern district of New York, dismissed charges of attempted murder, attempted manslaughter, and possession of a firearm against David Perez. Finding the defendant guilty only on the charge of assault, the judge sentenced him to five years of imprisonment, but suspended the term. Instead, Perez would be on probation for five years and would be required to perform 750 hours of community service. A second condition demanded that Perez seek and maintain "gainful employment."

Chapter 6

Prelude to a Massacre

Edmond, Oklahoma
August 20, 1986

Oppressive, muggy heat smothered early risers and commuters in central Oklahoma just one hour after sunrise on August 20, 1986. Distant clouds hovered on the horizon, threatening to bring lightning-streaked thunderstorms later that day when the temperature would climb past 90, typical summer weather for the region. Those residents lucky enough to stay home near air conditioners watched morning television shows.

Light traffic rolled along Broadway in the town center of Edmond a few minutes before 7:00 A.M., many of the drivers heading south to pick up a main route for the quarter-hour drive to Oklahoma City. If any of them had chosen to spend that evening in the city to catch a movie, they could have gone to the South Park theater complex to see a thriller titled, *Armed and Dangerous.*

In Edmond, one of the early motorists pulled into the quiet parking lot behind the modern, five-year-old red brick post office on Broadway between Campbell and Edwards Streets. The driver stepped out and strode resolutely toward a back entrance he'd used hundreds of times during his previous 18 months of employment. He wore the standard summer uniform; blue-gray walking shorts cut above the knees, black over-the-calf socks, soft-soled shoes and a short-sleeved light blue shirt bearing the eagle logo patch on the left shoulder. Despite the early hour, perspiration had already soaked through the back of his shirt. In his left hand, he toted a mailbag laden with something heavy he had brought from home, and his right hand gripped a metal object. As he stepped through the door, he could see a myriad of fellow employees sorting and processing mail to be delivered that day. Many of the workers had been there since 1:30 A.M., the starting time for the early shift. Past the entry, he moved quickly toward the center of the work area. Moments later, without warning, a burst of gunfire erupted inside the post office. The ensuing bloody massacre brought the proud and stunned community to its knees.

Guns have been an integral part of Oklahoma's old west heritage. The boom of a cannon had started it all at noon on April 22, 1889, setting in frantic motion the first of five massive land runs which allowed homesteaders to scramble across the rolling hills in horse-drawn wagons, bouncing carriages, astride fast mounts, or precariously balanced on bicycles, to stake out claims on precious 160-acre parcels of land. It didn't matter that the U.S. Government had reneged on promises to allow relocated Native Americans to occupy the Indian Territory "as long as the grass grows and the water runs." Fevered speculators, farmers, and businessmen reveled in the news that Congress had declared the land open to white settlers.

As Oklahoma City and Guthrie had, Edmond literally grew into a town overnight. Two years earlier, the Santa Fe railroad had laid tracks up and down Oklahoma, from Texas to Kansas. An abundance of good well water at mile 103 led railroad builders to establish a coal and watering station atop the highest point between two major rivers. They named the site Summit. The "boomers" in the 1889 land rush (preceded by the "sooners'' who found ways to arrive at choice sites early) charged toward Summit to grab the valuable sections adjacent to the railroad.

Tents and rough-hewn buildings instantly mushroomed among the blooming redbud trees, blackjack oaks, cottonwoods, and along grassy hills where bison had once roamed by the millions. Summit became Edmond. The village grew and boasted several Oklahoma Territory firsts: public schoolhouse, church, and library.

In the 20 years from 1966 to 1986, Edmond flourished from a quiet town of 8,000 residents to a thriving, bustling community of nearly 45,000. A place of community pride and loyalty, Edmond was a magnet to Oklahomans searching for the best place to live. Commuters from bustling Oklahoma City found escape in the quiet residential sections. Arcadia Lake on the eastern city limits underwent construction of campgrounds and boat launches to offer fishing and water sports. Shoppers strolled sidewalks downtown where shops maintained original mid-American charm, and a revolving candy-striped pole still marked the barbershop's location. The stores along both sides of the street bore small brass plaques engraved with the history of each building.

However, strife and tragedy were not completely unknown in Edmond. In July, the previous year, three supermarket workers had been slaughtered during a robbery. Within hours after the shocking crime, local businessmen had raised a reward of $11,000 for information leading to the killers. It worked. Two young men from Oklahoma City were subsequently arrested and convicted for the savage murders.

Ten months after the supermarket homicides, in May 1986, a tornado ripped through the western section of the town and destroyed 39 homes.

But Edmond residents were resilient, possessing the will and the courage to put tragic events behind them. On that quiet Wednesday morning in August, though, they would be confronted by a disaster unlike anything they could ever imagine.

* * *

Among those postal service employees who toiled with the day's mail on that hot, stifling morning was Paul Michael "Mike" Rockne. Mike's grandfather was the legendary Knute Rockne who had played football at the University of Notre Dame from 1910 to 1913. Following graduation, Knute Rockne had taught chemistry there, then coached the gridiron team from 1918 to 1930 compiling an incredible record of 120 wins, only 12 losses, and 5 ties. He pioneered game techniques and strategies that would later be used by most coaches across the country.

In the early part of 1931, a Hollywood mogul offered Knute Rockne a small role as a football coach in a forthcoming production, which appealed to him both financially and creatively. He took a train from South Bend, Indiana to Kansas City where he boarded a Los Angeles bound Fokker Tri-motor plane belonging to Transcontinental and Western Airway. On the last day of March, southwest of Bazaar, Kansas, an orange ball of flame lit up the clear blue sky. Knute Rockne died in the aerial disaster.

His name would forever be associated with Notre Dame football lore. But Knute Rockne had held a job prior to his university years. It wasn't widely known that the immortal coach, just after dropping out of high school, worked five years as a postal clerk to earn the $1,000 necessary to enroll in college.

Mike Rockne was born within shouting distance of Notre Dame on March 15, 1953, just two weeks before the 22nd anniversary of his grandfather's death. One of seven brothers, all of whom worshiped their one sister, Mike Rockne revered his grandfather's alma mater, but chose to earn his degree at Oklahoma State University. He took time out from his future plans to serve in the Vietnam War. One year after marrying his wife, Lynda, Rockne made the decision to buy a home on a quiet Edmond cul-de-sac called Rick's Court in 1978. He, too, joined the postal service in 1981 as a city mail carrier.

Well-muscled and stout, Mike Rockne wore a constant grin

under his bushy Groucho Marx-style mustache, the same dark color as his heavy arched eyebrows and the shock of thick hair tumbling down over the left side of his forehead. Acquaintances knew they could always depend on him for an uplifting laugh with his repertoire of jokes and quick-witted quips. His serious side could be seen on Sundays, when Rockne took his wife and seven-year-old son to St. John's Catholic Church. Never a passive man, he participated actively on several parish committees and in the local chapter of the Veteran's of Foreign Wars. And he had not forsaken his grandfather's roots in football, continuing the tradition by coaching a Little League team.

The work environment can sometimes create strain between fellow employees, but just as often it bonds close friendships. One of Mike Rockne's best pals, Richard "Rick" Esser had recently been promoted to supervisor after six years of service which coworkers described as "dedicated and loyal." Originally from Sedalia, Missouri, Esser still spoke with a soft Midwestern drawl, but with clear articulation that came from earning a degree at Oklahoma's Central State University. The camaraderie between Esser and Rockne was partially founded on and strengthened by another factor—both men had survived the rigorous hell of combat experience in Vietnam. While they often shared war stories between themselves, neither man spoke much about it to others. Another Edmond postal worker hinted to them that he'd been "in country" during the controversial jungle conflict, but Esser and Rockne doubted the veracity of the man's claims.

Rick Esser and his wife, Janet, met Mike and Lynda Rockne occasionally at social activities and post office functions, but while they were also Catholic, they lived 15 miles away in Bethany, so they attended a different church. With their two sons and a daughter, the Essers worshiped at St. Charles Borromeo Catholic Church. In the evenings and on days off, Esser could be seen turning soil and pulling weeds in the garden at his home. His brother, Ron, sometimes tried to persuade him to join the U.S. Army reserves, where Ron held a commission as a lieutenant. But Rick good-naturedly refused, rationalizing that the military might require him to shave off his short, neatly-trimmed dark brown beard and mustache. Esser's earlier tour of military duty had been a reluctant one. His smiling brother teased him about it, saying, "Rick was drafted. He went kicking and screaming into the Army. . . ."

Standing side by side and chatting quietly, Rick Esser and Mike Rockne paid little attention when the man carrying his heavy mailbag and holding something in his right hand entered through the back door.

The first person to notice the grim-faced employee's entrance was Jerry Ralph Pyle. At age 51, Pyle proudly accepted his niche as one of the older mail carriers on duty that August morning. He had completed sorting his daily delivery load, and stood near the back door preparing to leave when the man charging through the entry nearly collided with him. Glancing up, Pyle shook his head, but thought little about it. In his years of service, he'd seen the entire spectrum of behavior by employees, and had learned to ignore most of it.

A slender wiry man, who looked taller than he really was, Pyle was born in Edmond during the Great Depression, on July 14, 1935, the same day headlines announced that 100,000 New York welfare recipients would get jobs under the new Project Works Administration, later known as the WPA. Just nine days before Pyle's birth, President Franklin Roosevelt had signed into law the National Labor Relations Act, which insured that management would recognize and bargain collectively with unions. It also authorized government investigation of unfair employment practices. The events of August 20, 1986, combined with other similar incidents, would raise serious questions about USPS management practices and cause union officials to invoke some of the rights guaranteed by that act.

Nothing could have been further from Jerry Pyle's mind that humid morning, though. His loyalty to the job was unquestioned and supervisors had grown accustomed to his efficiency. Off the job, Pyle loyally followed the football fortunes of Oklahoma

University's Sooners. He frequently drove his old Volkswagen south to Norman, walked across campus through carpets of autumn leaves to sit in Owen Stadium and root for the team on Saturday afternoons. Pyle had been working at the Edmond post office since March 1961, the last 12 years delivering mail on Rural Route 3. Each of his customers knew him well, and looked forward to the time of day when Pyle would stop by. They knew the friendly face, topped by a pile of dark hair combed to a high pompadour, the wide forehead, black-rimmed glasses, prominent ears, and the thin-lipped smile that deepened facial creases etched by years of exposure to the Oklahoma sun. His friends, customers, members of the Baptist Church, and relatives characterized Pyle as "a real quiet and lovable guy," extremely well organized in his work, and a man who "was a hardworker and dedicated." One kinsman said, "He wanted to do everything to high perfection."

While the taciturn Pyle prepared to leave, a junior member of the force, Patti Lou Welch, age 27, who was also known as a "perfectionist," had started her morning duties as a full-time clerk. One of five employees (four women and a man) sharing the name Pat or Patty, Welch still wore the rosy bloom of a newlywed. She and her husband, Randy, had exchanged vows just four months earlier, on April 12th. Soft spoken with a dazzling smile, a dimple in her chin, and dark curly hair reaching to her shoulders, Welch traveled each day from her home on Windswest Court in Oklahoma City. A native Oklahoman from Lawton in the southwestern part of the state, she'd graduated high school in her hometown and later attended college at Cameron University. Shortly after moving to the capital city, Welch joined the USPS in 1981, following the path of one of her parents, Pat Ford, director of customer service at the Lawton post office. She and Rick had met through a mutual friend and she fell for his calm dignity, wavy dark hair, and trim mustache. Coworkers shared the joy reflected in Patti's face, and the happiness marriage brought her. And they sympathized with her problem of working different shifts from her husband, which limited the amount of time they could spend together. The couple made up for it, she told associates, by leaving love notes for each other.

One of Welch's newest friends had joined the work group just four days before. Judy Denney still spoke with a charming southern drawl. At age 39, Denney seemed much younger, probably due to the frequent flash of her quick smile and wit, large luminous eyes, and platinum blond hair. She had worked the front counter of the post office at Kennesaw, Georgia for 11 years before moving to Edmond, where she accepted the duties of part-time clerk. Her husband, Ron, also a career employee of the USPS, had spent most of his time in the Atlanta main post office. In June, their move to Oklahoma was prompted by a promotion which elevated him to director of marketing and communications for the large metropolitan area.

In a sad twist of irony, Ron Denney had been in Atlanta's main post office, located in Hapeville, on March 6, 1985, when wild-eyed employee Steven Brownlee blasted away with a .22-caliber handgun, killing a supervisor and a coworker, plus wounding a third employee.

Now, in their new rural surroundings, Judy and Ron Denney would be far removed from the urban strife and danger of big city life. They both thought this new environment would be much safer. They couldn't possibly be exposed to the brutal type of terror meted out by killers such as Steven Brownlee.

Marriages between postal employees seemed to be the norm. Betty Jarred had met her husband in the Edmond post office. She left her native Colorado in 1981, where she had worked nine years at the Rocky Ford postal facility. Soon after beginning her duties in Edmond as a full-time clerk, the exceptionally attractive Betty met supervisor Melvin Jarred, the man who had accepted her transfer, and promptly fell in love. He couldn't resist her sparkling dark eyes, full lips, soft wide smile, and multifaceted personality which mixed serious intelligence, curiosity, and mischievous wit. Married in 1983, the couple didn't work together very long because he transferred to Oklahoma City.

Melvin and Betty Jarred saw no dark spots in their future. They had found their life's dreams in Edmond, and their union produced two beautiful daughters. Nothing but serenity and happiness, they felt, lay before them. They eagerly anticipated celebrating their third wedding anniversary on Monday, August 24th.

The USPS, in some instances, pioneered efforts to poke holes in the "glass ceiling," the metaphorical barrier preventing women from ascending the management ladder. As a result, an Edmond employee received the opportunity she sought. Patty J. Husband had worked for an Oklahoma City firm, Aero Commander, for several years. At age 43, she decided to change careers, so she took a job delivering mail in Edmond. Husband, a single woman, had a clear-cut goal in mind and worked hard to achieve it. After five years of dedicated service, she proudly accepted her appointment as a supervisor on July 18, 1986.

If any of her coworkers felt envious about the promotion, none of them showed it. They offered congratulations to the soft-spoken woman, whose blue eyes reflected her gentle demeanor. A "people"-oriented individual, Patty Husband would fit smoothly into her new duties as a sensitive boss who could understand the job pressures of the postal workers. She had been there.

Patricia Gabbard had also been there, having worked a variety of jobs all over Oklahoma. Hailing from the tiny crossroads town of Crescent, a few miles north of Edmond, Gabbard had labored at everything from waitress to nuclear fuels plant technician. Because of her good looks, intelligence, and upbeat personality, Gabbard had no trouble landing a job, but often found the work boring or tedious. She had applied for a position with the USPS in 1984, and had been finally accepted just five months before as a full-time clerk. At age 47, she felt that she had at last found something solid upon which she could depend. Like her previous jobs, her marriage had failed some years earlier. But she took a great deal of pride in her two grown daughters who had found reliable husbands. One had moved up north, to Wichita, Kansas, while the other lived in Oklahoma City. Having settled into her new employment, Gabbard launched a search for suitable housing.

A close friend called Patricia Gabbard a "free spirit," and observed that she dabbled at writing rather good poetry. He enjoyed her company, and commented that everyone she met seemed to love her.

At age 41, Patricia Ann Chambers had found peace and serenity in marriage, family, and her church. She commuted 25 miles from Wellston, east of Edmond, to her job as a part-time clerk, but regarded the long drive as well worth the trouble, considering the site of her home. She and her husband Gary, with their young daughter and son, lived what many would consider an ideal existence in their country house, equipped with a large-screened porch and situated on 15 acres of gently rolling hills and forest.

Leroy Phillips, like Patricia Gabbard, also found a new career late in life. The difference was in their backgrounds. Phillips had spent 23 years on his previous job, serving with the United States Air Force. After retiring, Phillips spent a few months of leisure before taking on the task of delivering mail in Edmond at age 42. At home in Choctaw, east of Oklahoma City, his wife, Carla, and two young boys expressed pride in dad's new job. And they celebrated the change. There'd be no more moving around the world from post to post, as required by military assignments.

Originally from Portland, Maine, Lee Phillips adapted well to the constant winds and weather extremes of central Oklahoma, as well as the long distance from any ocean. Portland, of course, has its share of snow. But Oklahoma has more freeze-thaw cycles than anywhere else in the United States. Phillips' reputation for adaptability and determination served him well in coping with weather conditions, and in struggling through his first three months with the postal service. Delivering mail looks much easier than it really is. Extensive rules and regulations must be learned along with complex procedures. Phillips studied doggedly, and shaved a few seconds each day from the hours it took him to efficiently deposit all the mail on his rural route. He refused to take any breaks, saying he would join his coworkers for coffee and short rests only after he mastered the job well enough to spare those precious minutes.

Finally, at the end of his first three months, Phillips laughed out loud with his announcement that he had conquered the routine. He could now take his place as an accomplished mail delivery expert. Phillips had retired his Air Force wings, and earned his USPS eagle. On the morning of August 20, 1986, Phillips said, "I feel that I can really start to enjoy myself."

The delivery of mail on rural routes also filled the work time of Kenneth Morey, who looked forward to his 50th birthday in September. His wife, Judith, loved the positive attitude he held for his job, as reflected in his daily comment about distributing mail to farms and woodland homes. With a wave and a grin, Morey would say, "It's a nice day for a ride in the country." During his entire five years with the USPS, Morey displayed that same upbeat outlook. His personal image was more consistent with that of a banker or executive, clean-cut, hair neatly trimmed and combed, slim and tastefully dressed. At home in Guthrie, north of Edmond, Morey spent as much time as possible with his Arabian horses and his family. Whenever his wife found an opportunity, she would point with pride to their wedding rings, to explain that her wonderful husband had designed both of them.

* * *

Horses occupied a special place in the heart of another Edmond postal worker, Jonna Gragert Hamilton. Known for her wide, sparkling smile, honest clear eyes, and the almost childlike radiance of her round face, Hamilton frequently visited the commercial stable where she kept her horse, Cinnamon. Observers noted that when Hamilton gave the animal food, she would invariably share some of it with the horses in adjacent stalls. Someday, she said, her dream of owning her own horse farm would come true. Previously Hamilton had worked as a licensed practical nurse. She still dropped in to pay her respects to the elderly folks whom she'd attended in a local nursing home. Competent in nearly everything she tried, Hamilton even used her skills as an amateur auto mechanic to keep her own car maintained. Having started with the postal service in 1982, she worked the early shift in predawn hours sorting mail. She told her parents, who lived in a small community two hours north of Edmond, that she hoped and prayed for a reassignment soon to a day shift. She never complained, though. Her mother said, "She was a devout Christian . . . born with a smile. When the doctor handed her to me the day she was born, she looked at me and smiled."

Hamilton dutifully reported to work at the usual time long before the sun rose on August 20th.

Several of the male employees at Edmond wore beards and mustaches, but perhaps only one man sported more facial hair than part-time clerk Thomas Wade Shader. His full, wavy locks, parted in the middle, extended down both sides of his face into bushy sideburns and flourished into a four-inch beard, complete with wide mustache, all of which formed a circular frame for his thin face. On the shift that began at 1:30 A.M., Shader could be counted on to wake up drowsy coworkers with his hilarious wit and good cheer. He knew how to make his colleagues feel good. Flashing a toothy grin, he'd greet arrivals with, "Hey, that's a sharp outfit." Or he might ask, "How'd the ballgame go last night?'' Each comment would usually be followed by something to make them laugh.

At age 31, Shader maintained a youthful exuberance. Fellow employees knew they could always rely on him to offer a helping hand or lighten a tense moment with an offhand remark. Every work group needs a Tom Shader to shoo away problems through the use of humor.

Born in Arlington, Virginia, Shader attended the U.S. Air Force Academy in Colorado for one year. Later, he tried several jobs and a marriage in Minnesota, but realizing none of it was working, he divorced all of it. After settling in Bethany, not far from Rick and Janet Esser, he joined the postal service in the latter part of 1985. Off duty, he pedaled the countryside on his 10-speed as a member of the Oklahoma Bicycle Society. To his closest friends, Shader expressed an unusual wish. When the time came for his departure from this earth, he said, he would like to be cremated and have half of his ashes spread on a beautiful camping meadow in the Rocky Mountains and the other half scattered at Arlington National Cemetery across the Potomac from Washington, D.C. His pals assured him that his death would be a long distance into the future.

The beard that gave stiff competition to Tom Shader's belonged to William ''Billy'' Miller. His full, dark crop of whiskers cascaded all the way down to the top button of his shirt. He balanced it with an equally dark thatch of hair parted high on the left side and swooping down to his right eyebrow. His oversized glasses gave him a professorial look, consistent with his thin frame. Like Jerry Pyle, Leroy Phillips, and Ken Morey, Miller delivered mail to the rural areas surrounding Edmond. Born in Oklahoma City, and raised in the tiny town of Piedmont, Miller started with the USPS at age 28 on the last day of February 1985. During his one-and-a-half years at the Edmond post office, he earned a reputation of unselfishness. Proficient with auto mechanics, he compiled debts of gratitude from several of his coworkers by helping them repair stalled cars in the parking lot.

Completely dedicated to his wife, Cathy, and his little daughter, Nikki, Miller often spoke about them to his fellow employees, affectionately boasting of Cathy's cooking skills, her church involvement, or her singing skills. And his baby girl, he laughed, had helped him repair his jeep.

When Billy Miller entered the red brick building on August 20th, he generously handed out some of his wife's homemade chocolate chip cookies.

He didn't have time to give one to the man who walked in carrying a heavy mailbag in his left hand, and the white-knuckled fingers of his right hand tightly folded around the grip of a .45-caliber pistol. The grim-faced man probably wouldn't have accepted it anyway.

He had other, more serious matters on his mind.

Chapter 7

"Do You Know Who I Am?"

Edmond, Oklahoma
August 20, 1986

For the most part, post office employees in Edmond maintained a convivial relationship among the workplace family, with one major exception. Patrick Henry Sherrill set himself apart like a hermit uncle, generally refusing to socialize or even linger a few moments for friendly conversation. Aloof and sometimes rude, he ignored attempts to include him in coffee break chatter or the exchange of cordial greetings. With few exceptions, his personal life at home wasn't much different, characterized mostly by odd and reclusive behavior. At age 44, the ex-Marine had few friends and a strange reputation.

No one could reliably say when Sherrill's problems first started. Life began for him in the tiny hamlet of Watonga, 60 miles northwest of Oklahoma City, on November 13, 1941, three weeks and three days before the U.S. entered World War II. Sherrill had an older brother and sister. The family owned a marginally profitable farm and operated a small café in town. They sold everything and moved to Oklahoma City in the mid-1950s.

It can be traumatic for a teenager to make the transition from farm life to an urban existence, and Sherrill may have begun his inward withdrawal at that point. When he enrolled at Harding High School in Oklahoma City, his grades were barely passable. A yearbook photo portrays a young man who still had a country-boy appearance, with a long oval face, protruding ears and a shy grin. It didn't help that he was already balding. Sherrill was already slightly taller than his peers, and as farm work had given him muscular strength, he turned to athletics. Even though he earned a letter in football, team sports didn't appeal to Sherrill, a trait which would stay with him permanently. He preferred track and field where he could perform as an individual. The teenager tried out throwing a discus and apparently felt a strong desire to succeed with it. He borrowed one of the circular, metal-rimmed wooden plates from school, took it home, and practiced at night. The efforts earned him another school letter, as did his skill in wrestling. For the first time in his life, Sherrill could feel equal to his peers. He may not have been able to impress authority figures in the classroom or socially, but in the sports arena, Sherrill could hold his own, and coaches gave him the approval he needed. One of them later recalled that the young man seemed to be "a normal teenager" who didn't cause any trouble.

Sherrill's parents, the coach had heard, were "older people" when he was born and that "the father passed away while Patrick was in his teens." One of the youth's few friends would remember that Sherrill was troubled by what he regarded as a family secret. Finally, he confided the problem to his pal. His father, Sherrill whispered, was mentally ill. With a pained expression, the teenager continued. "I'm never going to get married, cause I don't want to pass on those bad genes to any kids."

In his junior year, Sherrill noticed a pretty young coed but couldn't seem to attract her attention. Years later, he succeeded in making his presence known to her in a most unwelcome way.

He graduated from Harding High School in June 1959, the same month conservative U.S. Postmaster General Arthur E.

Summerfield declared *Lady Chatterly's Lover,* by English novelist D.H. Lawrence, too racy to be sent through the United States mail.

That fall, Sherrill enrolled at Oklahoma University on a wrestling scholarship and posed in a group photograph printed in the 1960 yearbook. It pictured several young men who resided in the Lincoln House dormitory on the campus periphery. All of them wore expressions of relaxed confidence except Sherrill, who seemed out of place. He dropped out of school that same year.

On January 15, 1964, while the nation still mourned the assassination of President John F. Kennedy, Patrick Sherrill enlisted in the U.S. Marine Corps. In boot camp, where young "gyrenes" learn the skills of warfare, Sherrill qualified as an "expert" with an M-14 rifle. He seemed to adapt fairly well to military life despite a tendency to resent those who exercised authority over him.

In later years, it would be rumored that Sherrill had served in Vietnam, a reputation he did nothing to dispel, but actually, he spent most of his Marine Corps tour in Camp Lejeune, North Carolina. When it came time for him to requalify on the rifle range, he dropped down two steps from the top classification of "expert" to "marksman." It didn't seem to bother him, though, because he earned an "expert" medal with a pistol.

Other than the badges for firearms qualifications, Sherrill earned no medals, ribbons, or awards. His general behavior record was clean, showing no disciplinary actions against him. Four days after Christmas 1966, after serving almost three years, he received a general discharge under honorable conditions, one step down from an honorable discharge.

Perhaps Sherrill had forgotten the difficulties he'd encountered in civilian life. Once again, he couldn't seem to settle into a career or hold any long-term jobs. Instead, he enrolled at Edmond's Central State University in mid1967 taking general education classes. Directionless, he couldn't seem to make up his mind about a major. If a course didn't excite him, Sherrill would simply drop out and enter a new one. He received grades on the low end of the scale, winding up with a string of "Ds" and "Fs." Without ever earning a degree, he dropped out for the final time in the spring of 1970.

In those unsettled student years, he lived with his mother in a modest white frame house on Northwest 27th Street, a working class sector of Oklahoma City. An old school chum who dropped in periodically thought Sherrill had a "short fuse," and hated to see him yell at his mother. But relatives later insisted that he gave her attentive care.

The same fragmented pattern of indecision and unrest marking his academic record also influenced Sherrill's employment history. For long periods of time, he simply ignored the responsibility of working, choosing instead to live on his mother's limited income. One of the few jobs he held in the mid70s came as the result of a government program making federal dollars available for municipalities to hire needed technicians. Sherrill served a short stint, October 1974 to July 1975, as an electronics technician repairing traffic lights in Oklahoma City. His supervisor thought "he was kind of an eccentric person . . . kind of strange."

After he resigned, Sherrill again spent time lounging around home and operating his ham radio set. On the airwaves, he met another ham who was a member of the Oklahoma Air National Guard at Will Rogers Air Base (now Will Rogers World Airport). The man convinced Sherrill to take a trip to the recruiting office. Sherrill bicycled the 10 miles out to the air base several times before the military unit accepted him in 1976. A female civilian employee of the 219th E-I Squadron encountered Sherrill several times while he was attempting to enlist, and periodically afterwards. She formed some distinct ideas about him, later saying, "I just got the impression, you know, he's a weird guy. . . . He always struck me as one of those men that, you know, peeped in windows and molested little kids." Asked what gave her that impression, she replied, "Just his mannerisms. The way he would look. He's the first man ever in my life—and I have dealt with men all my life and worked with them—that I felt like I was nude standing there talking to him.

Or sitting there." She commented that she had told her male associates, "Don't leave me in the building by myself with him."

She thought he was "Guard bumming" which meant an unemployed person just hanging around the military unit because he had nothing else to do. She was right about the unemployment. But through military reserve contacts, Sherrill managed to land a job as a civilian maintenance employee at Tinker Air Force Base in the southeast quadrant of Oklahoma City.

Visitors to the tidy home Sherrill shared with his mother always remarked about the neatness of the house's interior. But that ceased in 1977 when Sherrill's mother retreated from the real world, her abilities ravaged by Alzheimer's disease. By the end of the year, she needed full-time care at a nursing home. The few remaining callers at the house were appalled at how it became increasingly cluttered. Sherrill's longstanding interest in ham radio grew to major proportions during that period. He spent everything he could spare on related electronics gear and appliances. Using his skill and equipment, he volunteered his free services to the emergency operations center of the American Red Cross. As he acquired a vast array of gadgets, the house, garage, and yard filled with boxes of tubes, wires, microphones, and receivers. Five unsightly radio antennas towered over the roof like aluminum skeletons. Soon, the yard sprouted with empty cable reels and discarded, rusting junk. Piles of magazines, including *Penthouse, Playboy,* and paramilitary publications, took up space inside the house. Neighbors labeled Sherrill a "pack rat."

When his mother died in 1978, Sherrill continued to occupy the home, and let it fall into even worse disrepair.

Even though he had a small income from her insurance, Sherrill found it necessary to seek work again after being dismissed at Tinker Air Force base. He landed a job at a radio store as an installer and technician. Eight months into his tenure, a senior coworker made an innocent mistake that infuriated Sherrill. When a customer asked for assistance, the older employee nodded toward Sherrill and suggested that the "young man over there" would help. Glaring in anger, Sherrill snapped out loud, "I have a given name and it's Patrick Sherrill." With that, he stalked out of the store and never returned.

Years later, the store manager would say, "I turned around and the customer was gone. So was Pat." Asked about Sherrill's personality, he recalled, "I had no real problems with him except when he quit for such a ridiculous reason. [I think] he was just a lonely man. . . ."

That same year, Sherrill found another job with the Federal Aviation Administration (FAA) as a file clerk. One coworker who knew nothing about his previous background figured that Sherrill must have been in the military because he always stood ramrod straight, walked as if he was marching, and wore shiny army-style shoes. The colleague commented that Sherrill never seemed violent, angry, or even upset. The only troubling thing about him was a whispered rumor that he had "exposed himself" to a young female temporary employee.

The rumor was heard by Herb Cardwell, an FAA manager who was also an avid ham radio operator. Cardwell gave little credence to the rumor, but still considered Sherrill an "odd duck," who was "hard to talk to." If anyone attempted conversation, Sherrill would either respond with some arrogant remark, or "act like he was out in space somewhere." Something that later stood out in Cardwell's mind was Sherrill's out-of-style clothing with "pants people wore back in the 'fifties." A common interest in ham radio was the only bond between the two men. Cardwell said that he did respect Sherrill, whose operator code was N5PS, for consistently observing the rules of ham radio while on the air, refraining from cursing or injecting commercial messages into the traffic. But in face-to-face conversations, Sherrill often seemed "arrogant and bull-headed." One afternoon, while exchanging some thoughts about their mutual hobby, Sherrill asked several technical questions. Each time Cardwell tried to answer, Sherrill would interrupt with, "I know that." After three repetitions of the rude conduct, Cardwell gave up and kept his distance thereafter.

Sherrill made it difficult when he showed up at Cardwell's home one evening, just before dinner time. Cardwell stepped outside, making it clear that he had no intentions of inviting the impromptu visitor to stay for the evening meal. They discussed ham radio, on the porch, for 30 minutes. Finally, Sherrill left.

In Cardwell's duties as an investigator of airplane accidents, he had another strange experience with Sherrill. When a small plane crashed in northern Oklahoma City on a weekend, Sherrill immediately radioed and asked Cardwell if he planned to visit the site and investigate the accident. Cardwell said no, someone else had drawn the duty. Sherrill announced that he was going to go and have a look. Cardwell all but ordered Sherrill to stay away. He later heard that Sherrill had ignored his advice and showed up at the scene, where officials had to shoo him away.

Another FAA employee remembered Sherrill for allegedly sexually harassing women in the office. He said Sherrill never showed any violent behavior and was "real quiet." But he recalled that women complained about Sherrill because he was always "staring" at them and "rubbed up against them" near the file drawers. Sherrill was fired because he had cornered a woman in the elevator and "wouldn't let her out."

Something about military life must have appealed to Sherrill. After serving six years with the Oklahoma Air National Guard, he dropped out then immediately joined the U.S. Air Force Reserve in August 1982, where he became part of the 507th Tactical Fighter Group. The regular meetings, drills, and periods of active duty gave him not only a sense of identity, but filled in the large gaps of idle time in his life.

Most of his days had been spent with his newest activity, bicycling, or spending endless hours at the console of his ham radio. The bike became his major mode of transportation and his primary physical recreation. He informally joined group tours, usually uninvited, such as the annual "Freewill" tour in which members pedal across the entire state of Oklahoma. Sherrill showed up without the necessary provisions or the required sleeping bag. One of the club officers provided him with a blanket. At the overnight camp sites, Sherrill crawled under a trailer to use as shelter while he slept.

It is quite probable that, in his bicycling activities, Sherrill ran across another enthusiast during that period. Edmond USPS employee Thomas Shader belonged to the Oklahoma Bicycle Society, and spent a great deal of his spare time touring the country astride his state-of-the-art bike. If they ever did ride in the same group, no one could recall either man ever mentioning it.

Sherrill's first real attempt to tackle long term employment, other than his Air Force Reserve activities, came in 1982 when he applied at the USPS. The postal service put him on the payroll, but it lasted only 89 days. Hired in Oklahoma City as a "multiple position" letter sorter, Sherrill was accepted on the condition that he qualify for the job by demonstrating competent performance and by passing certain tests within 90 days. He fell short on both levels, threw up his hands in disgust and resigned a day before the three-month deadline. A coworker later recalled that Sherrill hadn't created any serious problems in the workplace, but was "strange, kind of eccentric."

When he found himself again needing a source of income, he turned to the Oklahoma City Chapter of the American Cancer Society in March 1984, and filled a position in the stockroom. It probably helped that his sister, who lived in Edmond, was the organization's director of professional services. Even with her sponsorship, the job lasted only five months. Sherrill complained that he needed to earn more than the minimum wages they paid, so he left in September.

With the 507th Air Reserves, Sherrill attended an extensive training course at Lackland Air Force Base near San Antonio, Texas, to become a firearms instructor. According to an officer stationed there, the school is one of the finest available for instructor development courses in small arms training. Shaking his head in disbelief, the officer said he had observed Sherrill in the classroom and on the firing range and could not understand how he could have successfully completed it. Sherrill, he said, was nonproductive in the classroom and would make a poor firearms instructor, seeming smart enough but often acting "slow." His demeanor, the officer said, was such that people did not want to associate with him or help him. The rumor circulated that Sherrill was homosexual, but the officer saw nothing to substantiate it. In any case, he said, he wouldn't want Sherrill to babysit any kids.

Other personality characteristics in Sherrill bothered the officer as well, prompting his comment that Sherrill was the type of individual one wouldn't want to humiliate or push too far "as he might knock your head off."

Despite the officer's personal opinions, he acknowledged watching Sherrill shoot a .45 pistol at the air range on a drill weekend, and said the man was "an excellent shot."

A classmate at the firearms training saw a different Patrick Sherrill in several respects. Vincent Stubbs was assigned to quarters in the same barracks with Sherrill and 40 other class members during the nine-week course. He became one of the few people to befriend Sherrill. The two men ate their meals together and toured San Antonio during off duty hours. They would later keep in touch by mail. Stubbs described his 42-year-old buddy as an "overweight bachelor who always expressed concern that he was going nowhere," and whose main interests in life were guns, ham radio, and bicycling. Sherrill, he said, was very intelligent, understood electronics, and "was the most precise person" he'd ever known.

During the rigorous training, Stubbs said, they were taught how to handle and shoot almost every kind of weapon. Sherrill, he thought, was an excellent shot whose favorite handgun was the .45 automatic. For some reason, Stubbs recalled, Sherrill disliked one of the female instructors and took every opportunity to give her a hard time.

Described by most people as uncommunicative and reticent, Sherrill opened up to Stubbs. He spoke of his college years, his experiences on the wrestling team, and his time in the Marine Corps. He even mentioned a girlfriend who sang with him in a church choir. Sherrill read a lot, Stubbs said, usually picking "good books." Stubbs was particularly impressed with

Sherrill's choice of reading material each night before going to sleep: the Holy Bible.

Sherrill's home life on Northwest 27th Street sometimes seemed relatively normal, but periodically took on some bizarre twists. One of his neighbors stated that as far as she could tell, no one could get along with Sherrill. Louise Eastman, who lived on the same block for years, said that in her opinion, "He was a nosy kind of guy, always wanting to know what everyone else was doing."

In one instance, she recalled, some kids were trying to sell candy door-to-door. They stood at her entry making their childish pitch, when Sherrill walked up the street and asked what they were saying. "None of your business," Eastman told him.

"Do you know who I am?" Sherrill demanded.

"Yes, I know who you are. Now get off my property and get away from my house," Eastman ordered. Sherrill stared intently at her, but backed away into the street when Eastman stepped off her porch in his direction.

Eastman remembered that Sherrill would take late-night strolls in the neighborhood, pacing furtively up and down the sidewalks in the darkness and making frequent stops to stare into unshaded windows. Sometimes, he would turn up the paths leading to front porches and edge toward the houses, to get a closer look. When Eastman's mother made overnight visits, she'd see Sherrill peeping in. She told her daughter that if he ever came close enough, she would throw cold water in his face. Several of the residents called the police over a period of time, but no one ever saw Sherrill arrested. Eastman heard some talk about Sherrill using a telescope after that to make his nocturnal observations. Asked if she thought Sherrill was a violent man, Eastman pondered the question for a few moments, and said she had actually seen nothing in his personality to suggest violence, but that he could give a very "hard stare" when angered.

The occupant of another house on Sherrill's street corroborated the accounts of his peering into his neighbors' homes.

"Pat would stand out on the street and look in windows." When the police were summoned, she said, they did nothing "because Sherrill was only looking and never tried to break in a house." Troubled by his persistent peeping, she bought an air conditioner so she could keep windows and drapes closed at night.

Except for a homely pit bulldog he acquired, Sherrill lived alone. He usually kept the fierce-looking pooch in the house, but one day it escaped outside and immediately attacked a smaller terrier next door. Sherrill heard the growling scuffle, and rushed out just in time to see his neighbor kicking at the pit bull in an attempt to separate them. A witness reported that Sherrill became furious and loudly berated the terrier owner. When the animals were finally pulled apart, the badly injured small dog required treatment from a veterinarian. The pet healed, but the relationship between its owner and Patrick Sherrill didn't.

The cute classmate Sherrill had watched at Harding High School showed up in his life again. Long after graduating and getting married, she moved into Sherrill's neighborhood. She was there only a short time when she began receiving obscene phone calls. The voice sounded familiar, and she soon connected it to the strange young man from her school days who "had an older-looking face because he was already starting to go bald." The next time she heard the caller spewing obscenities, she calmly said, "Pat, quit calling me." The unwelcome telephone intrusions came to a screeching halt.

The folks on 27th Street agreed that Sherrill was more of a nuisance than a danger. They said he never really did anything spectacular or violent. The children liked to taunt him and call him "Crazy Pat," which stemmed from his paranoid accusations that they were always laughing at him. He'd catch sight of a group of kids giggling, and charge over to the parents' house demanding they put a stop to it. But they just humored him, and the children found it great fun to laugh, run, and taunt him from a safe distance. No one wanted to make Sherrill too angry at close range. Standing six feet tall, and weighing nearly

200 pounds, Sherrill's appearance discouraged the thought of physical confrontation.

In October 1984, Sherrill ended his tour with the Air Force Reserve. Within days, he telephoned the woman who'd been so wary of him during his previous six years with the Oklahoma Air National Guard, the same one who felt naked when he looked at her. Sherrill asked her advice about his reenlisting. She didn't want to encourage him, but suggested he contact the appropriate officials. Shortly after that, an officer approached her to solicit her opinion about accepting Sherrill. She answered, "You can do what you want to, but, you know, I wouldn't accept him . . . Do what you think's best."

The officer took a chance, and Sherrill became a member of the 137th Squadron as a combat arms instructor, with the rank of sergeant.

Not long after rejoining the National Guard, Sherrill accepted an invitation to try out for the post's marksmanship team. Another member recalled meeting him at an indoor practice range. In a courteous manner, Sergeant Sherrill offered him some pointers about accurate shooting which the member thought was good advice. Sherrill asked him about weapons issuing procedures for the marksmanship team. The member passed on what he knew about obtaining permission, checking out the guns, how to get ammunition, and the importance of keeping the weapon secured at home.

The following spring, April 1985, Sherrill decided to give the USPS another try. He applied in Edmond, utilizing the extra points routinely awarded by the USPS to help veterans qualify, and passed the written and physical examinations. He was not given a psychological exam, despite the peculiar behavior seen during his former short stint in Oklahoma City. Sherrill joined the Edmond force as a part-time letter carrier in April. "Part-time" in the post office isn't what it sounds like. The classification means simply that the employee works for an hourly wage, not an annual salary and is not guaranteed certain working hours. Because of the high volume of mail funneling through the Edmond facility, which employed about 100 people, Sherrill was able to put in the normal 40 hours each week. With some overtime, he earned approximately $13,000 in his first year.

Initially, Sherrill's performance seemed adequate, but his social skills continued in the same negative mode. He just didn't seem to mix well with colleagues, other employees, or supervisors. As he struggled through the summer, the problem festered beneath the surface.

In August, Sherrill ran into his old military pal, Vincent Stubbs, during two weeks of active duty with the Air National Guard at McChord Air Force Base near Tacoma, Washington. Stubbs and his family invited Sherrill to tour the Seattle area with them and later join them for dinner at the home of some relatives. Sherrill seemed deeply grateful, saying, ''No one has done this for me before.''

Alone with Stubbs, Sherrill spoke proudly of his USPS job, but said that he was unhappy about the way he was being treated, and didn't like being forced to stay in one place sorting mail for long periods of time.

Upon parting, the two old buddies made promises to get together again. They never would. Vincent Stubbs would one day say about Sherrill, ''Pat was the loneliest man I have ever known.''

Back on the job in Edmond, more friction developed. In October, Bill Bland, Supervisor of Mails and Delivery, signed a letter which was handed to Sherrill, informing him that he was suspended for seven calender days. The reason stated was, ''Failure to discharge your assigned duties conscientiously and effectively.'' It stated:

On September 19, 1985, you did fail to protect mail entrusted to your care, as evidenced by the fact you left two trays of mail and three parcel post items unattended, overnight, at 601 Vista Lane. Your failure to discharge your assigned duties conscientiously and effectively resulted in a one day delay in delivery of approximately 500 pieces of mail which had been entrusted to your care.

Five months later, Bill Bland issued another letter, this time suspending Sherrill for 14 calender days:

> On March 31, 1986, you acted in a very unprofessional manner by telling a customer ... that you did not need her help in finding the apartment mail boxes and did not care if the tenants received mail or not. The customer reported this incident ... [and] stated that you were very rude to her, adding that she was only trying to help you find your way around the complex.
>
> ... you again acted in this manner ... The customer reported by phone and by customer complaint form ... that you sprayed his dog with dog spray. The dog was and is behind a 5 foot fence with a locked gate. When questioned about the incident you admitted that you have walked past him many times in the past and was [sic] fully aware of the dog's presence behind the fence. You also stated that you had just received a new can of dog spray and was [sic] not sure it would work but decided to use it on this dog anyway. You also asked the customer when questioned by him about the incedent [sic] if he wanted his mail delivered or not.
>
> This type of service seems consistent with you [sic] past performance evidenced by a suspension given you on October 2, 1985 and several discussions and a letter of warning. This type of behavior will not and cannot be tolerated.

Sherrill confided to a longtime friend that he'd been suspended for spraying a dog with Mace. Asked if the dog had attacked him, Sherrill admitted that it hadn't, but it had growled and barked at him the day before. At that time, Sherrill had tried to spray the intimidating animal, but the propellent hadn't worked. He obtained a new can and when he came to the dog's yard, he leaned over a fence, aimed the nozzle, and sent out a stinging mist to "test the can and see if it worked." Unfortunately for Sherrill, the resident witnessed the whole thing and reported it to postal management.

When confronted, Sherrill admitted what he'd done. But after management suspended him, he told his friend that the supervisors were "making book" on him. That meant, he explained, they were accumulating every infraction, no matter how minor, in an effort to get rid of him. To one of his few close friends, Sherrill complained that his supervisor was timing him on his route on the days when he had heavy loads of mail to deliver, and timing a female carrier on the same route when the load was light. "He didn't appear to be too upset, but Pat never did appear upset over anything."

Through it all, Sherrill maintained his middle-of-the-road demeanor, showing no extremes in behavior or emotion. One associate said, "You'd never know what was going on inside his head."

Some of the mail carriers, including Sherrill, liked to stop in at the Christian Nursing Home in Edmond for lunch or a glass of lemonade. An employee there described Sherrill as friendly, personable, and quite pleasant. He'd often speak to one of the nurses. "Not a great conversationalist," she would later say about him, but if she kidded him about the shorts he wore with the summer uniform, he'd "kid right back."

On April 5th, Sherrill checked out a Colt .45-caliber semi-automatic pistol from the Air National Guard marksmanship unit. The privilege of keeping such weapons at home was limited to members of the team

The Air National Guard took Sherrill to England for two weeks of active duty in late July 1986. He told an officer that he was "really getting hassled" by the postal service managers about his request for a military leave, and emphasized his need for the documents verifying that he was, indeed, serving with his Guard unit in England. The officer assured him there would be no problem.

When the group arrived in a town not far from London, Sherrill had expected to be lodged with another unit member in civilian quarters, but found himself billeted alone in an on-base single room. Disappointed, he requested a change to off-post facilities which required two people per room. An attempt

to accommodate him failed because no one could be found
who would double up with Sherrill.

One of the unit members would later discuss the trip and his
interaction with Sherrill: "I can recall a conversation very
vividly that we had in England. Several of us . . . were planning
a trip to London through American Express . . . I personally
asked if he would like to go with us, and he said no, he was
going to ride around the countryside and get a firsthand look
at the local culture. He said they were having difficulty staying
busy; there wasn't work for them to do. They had to go to a
[weapon firing] range away from our base . . . I said, 'Please
try to stay busy or at least be out of uniform so that you are
not conspicuous.' He did, thereafter."

Asked if Sherrill seemed angry or moody, the member said
no, and that he seemed to be a pleasant person who was usually
smiling.

Upon the unit's return to Oklahoma in early August, one of
Sherrill's relatives heard his views of the duty in England. "He
expressed disappointment in the trip, calling it unsuccessful
and placing blame on his commanding officer. He said the C.O.
had them doing menial, trivial tasks and that he restricted their
free time for sightseeing off base." Sherrill seemed at first to
enjoy his Guard involvement, the relative said, especially his
participation in the marksmanship team. In recent months,
though, his interest appeared to diminish and he stopped talking
about the team members and competition. More often, he spoke
of his problems at the post office, focusing often on two supervisors who he thought were trying to get rid of him. He'd been
criticized for misdelivering mail, but rationalized that it wasn't
his fault, that the mail hadn't been properly pre-sorted.
According to the relative, Sherrill said that only one of his
customers complained about his deliveries, a woman in a mobile
home park who was hostile toward him for an unknown reason.
His boss, he complained, was going overboard in meting out
disciplinary actions. Sherrill said he wanted to transfer to
another job with the Postal Service, perhaps to the maintenance
crew or something more technical than delivering mail.

Shortly after returning from England, Sherrill checked out

a second pistol, a Remington .45-caliber semiautomatic, from the chief of the Air National Guard marksmanship team. On the next weekend, before practicing with the group, he picked up his authorized 200 rounds of ammunition.

The humidity of August days in Central Oklahoma can be oppressive. It was that way on Tuesday afternoon, August 19th, in Edmond. The air conditioning inside the brick post office building labored to keep the atmosphere comfortable. One of the employees glanced up from her work and could see through the glass panel of the supervisor's office where another kind of heat shot up to danger levels. "I saw one of our uniformed mail carriers, Pat Sherrill . . . with supervisors Rick Esser and Bill Bland. Although I could not hear, it was obvious that Pat Sherrill was being reprimanded. I could see the look on his face which struck me as being very strange, eerie."

A mail carrier also watched the glass-enclosed conflict. "When I returned from my route about one o'clock P.M., . . . Pat Sherrill was in the supervisor's office. . . . Bland and Esser were talking to him with the door closed. It appeared he was being reprimanded."

A third coworker would recall a conversation she had with Sherrill a week earlier on August 12th. "I was alone with Patrick in the break room. He was angry at management over some annual leave he had to account for. He said Bland didn't think he [Sherrill] was much to worry about, but he'd be sorry. I said we all knew he [Pat] had been having trouble with management. He said they'll be sorry and everyone would know."

Chapter 8

"I Froze . . . I Knew I Was Next"

Edmond, Oklahoma
August 20, 1986

Patrick Sherrill entered the post office from the employee parking lot, on the east side of the building, a few minutes before seven o'clock on that muggy morning of August 20, 1986, carrying his mail delivery satchel over his left shoulder, and a pistol in his right hand.

He stepped inside where more than 50 employees toiled at sorting mail and various other tasks. One of them, Mike Bigler, spotted Sherrill as he approached a table where Mike Rockne stood chatting with his friend, supervisor Rick Esser. Bigler recalled it: "I was at my case [work station]. I heard some popping like firecrackers. I thought it was a practical joke to scare employees, so I kept working. My friend Mike was standing behind his own case." When the noise started, Bigler said, some of the people rushed outside. Neither Esser nor Rockne made it. "Mike [Rockne] fell to the floor and I could see he was lying in a pool of blood." Esser dropped next to him.

Horrified, Bigler headed toward an exit. "I was fifty or sixty

2130 Almaz

TRN 2889 NOV11'97 8:44AM

```
   032097005996
1 5.99 BOOK              5.99
   072440102392
1 ST SWIMSUIT SUPE       9.95

   Subtotal             15.94
   Tax                   1.04
   Amt Paid             16.98
   Cash                 17.00
   Change Due            0.02
```

feet from it and was shot in the back . . . felt a stinging sensation. I just played dead. Sherrill kept walking around several times . . . just went around shooting methodically, saying nothing. Some of the clerks were huddled in the post-office box area. He went up to them and shot seven rounds and they were all screaming.''

Darrell Fesler reeled as he saw what was happening. ''I heard a gunshot, and hid behind some big boxes. I looked up and saw a man shooting a gun. He shot Mike Bigler and then just turned in a circle shooting at random. He went towards the front lobby shooting and we ran out the back. He followed, still firing, and then returned inside.''

Bleeding profusely from the back wound, Bigler saw his opportunity to sprint out the door when Sherrill disappeared from view. As a precaution, he put his hands over his head in the surrender position just in case the police had arrived outside. He didn't want to be shot again, by friendly fire.

Inside, someone had yelled, ''He's got a gun!'' That alarm would be remembered by many of the employees who paid scant attention when the first popping noises began.

One of the mail carriers Gene Black remembered:

> *Crack—crack, and then crack again. I was jolted from my concentration. It sounded like plastic letter trays falling to the floor. I turned to look and heard the footsteps of people running across the hard tile floor.*
>
> *''Get out—get out of here—he's shooting a gun,'' I heard someone yell. I saw Steve Vick fall to the floor clutching his stomach. He was in the row of cases close to the supervisor's desk. Others run to help him. Crack— crack the gun sounded again. I heard more shouting and people running—and then more screams.*
>
> *''Run, get out, he's got a gun!'' someone yelled. My heart pounded loudly in my ears as confusion gripped me. I couldn't move. Someone grabbed my arm and pulled me down the aisle.*
>
> *''Run,'' he said. ''He's killing people over there.''*

The gunfire sounded to some like firecrackers, and to others, such as Larrie Parrish, "like someone slapping a tray against the floor repeatedly." Parrish, too, quickly realized it was not someone "just fooling around" and instinctively crouched low. A woman "crawled under my case. Then I thought maybe it was dry-run practice to see how we'd react to a holdup, like a drill. I got under the case and asked her what was going on. She didn't know."

Several employees scurried out the east door where Sherrill had entered. The gunman swiveled from his position near the fallen bodies of Rockne and Esser, and followed the panic stricken runners. As Sherrill stepped out, he sprayed the area with another fusillade of bullets.

Jerry Pyle, the senior carrier, had made it to the parking lot. As he tried to seek protection close to his old Volkswagen, a slug dropped him in his tracks. He became the third person to die that morning.

Sherrill reversed his direction again, reentered the post office work area, and walked past the bodies of Esser and Rockne.

Hubert Hammond, like many others, at first thought he was hearing some practical joker throwing firecrackers. But, ". . . all of a sudden, everyone panicked. At that time I was at station C-13. I took a step out to see what was the confusion. I saw Pat Sherrill walking towards C-9 (William Nimmo) and shoot him twice. Then he turned toward me and lifted his gun at me, but didn't shoot. By then I was running with my back to him, to the front office. As I got out, I heard a lot of shooting inside." Hammond saw Nimmo fall, critically wounded.

Gene Black remembered:

> . . . *running hard through the row of sorting cases. Fear gripping my mind and body. I ran to escape the flying bullets, from the fear of pain, from the fear of sudden death. He could be right behind me. I couldn't turn around and look.*
>
> *I ran to the superintendent's office, on the north wall, slipping and almost falling as I turned to run up the aisle to the front. The doorway to the front counter appeared*

*and I told myself to jump. The counter looked as tall as
the building itself.*

*I sailed over the counter and crashed down on the
other side, feeling other bodies moving with me. I got up
and ran through the open double doors into the lobby.
Frantically, I shoved open the first set of glass doors;
they crashed against the outer doors as they swung back
toward me. I ran outside, then down the front sidewalk
to the public parking lot, running until I felt free of the
building.*

*I turned and saw Phil Crabtree and Larry Wilson half-
carrying, half-dragging Bill Nimmo out the doors I had
just run through. Nimmo was holding his side with his
left hand, his legs doubled back underneath him. His blue
shirt was red with blood and his face showed the intense
pain from his wound. Crabtree opened the back door of
a car parked at the front of the building. Then they forced
Nimmo's nearly limp body into the backseat of the car.*

*"Go with him," Crabtree said, pushing Wilson into
the car. It drove through the empty parking lot and disappeared around the corner of the building.*

"A loud bang" startled Diane Mason, who had peered
through a glass partition the previous day and seen Sherrill
being reprimanded. "I thought someone had dropped a tray of
mail, as we often do, which makes the same sound. . . . Then
I heard screams so I hid behind my tub of mail. I got down on
the floor and curled up in the smallest ball I could. I heard
more shots and smelled gunpowder. I was praying to God that
when he got to me, he'd kill me quick and it wouldn't hurt.
But when I heard the shots getting farther away, I ran to the
front windows area, rolled over the counter, and out the front
lobby door which is always unlocked."

Stepping past his first two victims, Sherrill headed to the
southwest sector where employees in three rectangular bays
had been stuffing mail into the back side of post office boxes.

Clerks Nancy Limbecker and Becky Davis heard their supervisor, Patty Husband, who'd been promoted just one month

before, yell, ''Get down!'' Husband crouched in the far southwest bay along with Betty Jarred, who had been looking forward to her third wedding anniversary, and Thomas Shader, the bicycler.

Sherrill marched toward the bay and turned to face the trio. Employee Debbie Smith remembered: ''The supervisor yelled to get down. I was trying to hide in the second box section . . . Pat Sherrill was dressed in his postal uniform [and] went to the first box section. I heard Patty Husband say, 'No, Pat, No!' And then he shot the gun . . .''

Husband, Jarred, and Shader died in spreading pools of crimson, all three sprawled on the hard tile floor

Near section 2, Debbie Smith prayed that she wouldn't be next. ''I saw him walk on past with the gun and go to the next section. I heard him shoot . . . and a woman scream.''

Smith knew that several terrified employees were seeking shelter in the adjacent post office box bay. ''In that section,'' she said, ''were Pat Chambers, and a new lady named Judy, Patti Welch, Patricia, and I'm not sure who else. I crawled around the boxes and I heard him empty his gun, but I couldn't see him. I froze. I couldn't run. He came to shoot the clerks in the box section next to mine. I just knew I was next. I ran for the front door and got out of there.'' Smith's escape was miraculous. For some reason, after Sherrill slaughtered the three victims in the first bay, he strode right past the spot where Smith crouched in fear and stopped at the next section, closed on three sides like a small room trapping more terrified workers.

As Smith accurately recalled, Patty Chambers was in there, along with four others seeking safety. Chambers would never see her husband and two children again. Nor would ''the new lady named Judy,'' get out alive; Judy Denney, the platinum blonde from Georgia whose husband had brought her to the safety of Edmond after a postal worker named Steven Brownlee had killed two people in the Atlanta Main Post Office. In addition to Patty Chambers, two more women fearfully huddled in the cubicle. Patricia Gabbard, who had worked for the USPS only five months and newlywed Patti Welch. Jonna Gragert

Hamilton, cornered in terror, would never again visit her horse, Cinnamon.

Patrick Sherrill ended the dreams of all five women with a hail of deadly fire from the .45-caliber semiautomatic pistol he wielded. He slaughtered them with cold merciless cruelty before turning left and striding toward the north side of the big work area.

Employee Peggy Gibson also narrowly missed being killed. "I heard gunshots and stepped out from my case . . . Someone yelled to get down. I saw a man with a gun. There was one person [Gene Bray] between me and the man with the gun. He got shot and was lying on the floor. I hid under my case and behind the parcel tub. I ran to the back doors [found locked] . . . then ran to the side door and outside." The bullet that struck Bray in the back penetrated his right kidney.

Richard Tompkins recalled, "I ran around behind some rural carrier cases trying to hide. When it got quiet I headed for the back door and saw Gene Bray lying on the floor in a pool of blood . . . The shooting started again toward the front of the post office, so I went to the back and got a door open. I headed across the parking lot for an apartment building to try to raise someone." Unable to find help, Tompkins flagged down a passing motorist and asked for a ride to the police station.

As Sherrill approached the office at the north wall, he encountered Ken Morey, the upbeat rural mail carrier. Sherrill leveled the .45 and ended the life of Morey four weeks before his 50th birthday.

Tracy Sanchez watched in horror. "I was at my case near the break room [northeast corner of building] and I heard a series of bangs. I looked across the room and saw people yelling and falling on the floor. Then Sherrill walked by with a gun, shooting people . . . He walked right past me and I ran to the back door, but it was locked. Another man tried to get out with me. We ran back and there was a storage closet nearby. We hid in there, but we couldn't lock it so we turned the light off and stayed quiet. Sherrill stood by our door and kept emptying his shells and reloading his gun—about three times. Each time we could hear him walk around the room shooting, over and over. People begged him and he would yell at them and shoot them several times. Then, finally, it got quiet. But we stayed hidden until we heard the police.''

With Ken Morey lying dead on the hard tile floor, Sherrill turned east, toward the coffeebreak room in the corner. Halfway there, he found William Miller. Just that morning, Miller had passed around a plate of his wife's marvelous cookies to coworkers. Patrick Sherrill didn't care. He blasted Miller's life away with no more compassion than he'd shown in spraying Mace in the face of a fenced-in dog.

Postal workers sometimes refer to each other by their delivery routes, rather than names. Elizabeth Hilchey, when nervously reporting her experience that morning, used this technique. ''I heard gunshots. At first, I thought it was a joke, until I saw City 4 fall on the ground, bleeding. I could smell gunpowder. I heard several shots and people falling and moaning. When it became quiet for a few minutes, I decided to get out because I knew he would probably kill me, too. I ran for the back door with Route 5, Joe, Route 6, Vernon, and jumped in the car with Route 20. He drove us to the police station. Once there we were told the police already knew. I never saw Sherrill's face, just his legs as he walked around shooting people.''

Larry Wilson recalled making an effort to stop Sherrill's mad slaughter. He said, ''I kicked the gun out of Pat's hand but he recovered it and started shooting again.''

As the seconds ticked by like hours, Sherrill continued his destructive path, at last heading toward the break room in the northeast corner. He stepped in and found Leroy Phillips. Sherrill ended his life in a burst from his .45 semiautomatic, making a total of 14 dead victims, 13 scattered throughout the interior of the post office and one outside on the pavement near his Volkswagen.

Police cruisers and ambulances swarmed Broadway and the parking lots. Those workers who had escaped dragged the wounded to safety. Six employees, William Nimmo, Gene Bray, Michael Bigler, Steve Vick, Judy Walker, and Joyce Ingram were rushed to the hospital for emergency care. Though some were badly wounded, they would all survive.

Gene Black remembered:

I stood on the front sidewalk with a few other employees and watched as two policemen ran toward the post office. One positioned himself near the front door. The other ran to the southeast corner of the building near the loading docks, then dodged to the front of my mail truck. He crouched down and peered out.

"Help me, help me, I'm shot," someone shouted.

Gene Bray stumbled down the loading dock stairs, his uniform shirt covered in blood. He staggered about 30 feet from the steps, stumbled, and collapsed over a low brick wall on the south lawn.

I rushed toward him at a dead run, desperate, wanting to help him. Others followed behind me, but the closer we got to his motionless body, the stronger my fear became that my friend was dying.

The policeman crouched beside my mail truck waved his hands and shouted, "Get back! Get back!"

Four of my colleagues, friends, spurred by the need to help our wounded, possible dying buddy, paid no attention to the well-intentioned warning.

We snatched Gene Bray's limp body from the blood-soaked lawn as if he were a small child. Hoisting him up, Mark Lumin, Phil Crabtree, Ken Lobdell and I ran for safety. We were not being heroic; we were damned scared for Gene. We carried him face down, the way we found him, each of us taking an arm or a leg. As we ran, I could see on his shirt the mass of blood from the wound in his back that now splattered on our uniforms.

Finally reaching the front sidewalk again, we were met by two AmCare paramedics. We gently lowered our colleague to the concrete as the excited paramedics pushed us aside.

"Oh, God, don't let Gene die," I said. "Do something for him."

The Edmond Police Department had been swamped with reports by telephone calls, by people running into the station only two blocks from the post office, and with patrol cars flagged down by terrified employees who had escaped the carnage.

As they converged on the brick building, they saw bleeding victims being helped by coworkers on the lawn and in the parking lot. Several of the workers reported that a tall, bald man inside was shooting up the place and killing people. Many of them knew his name, Patrick Sherrill.

With weapons drawn, officers cautiously advanced toward the doors, mostly to assure the killer didn't escape or to help victims who fled. The police would wait for the arrival of the SWAT team to invade the interior.

One officer reported, "When I arrived at the post office, I saw one man drenched in blood lying on the grass with emergency fire department employees attempting to carry him to the southwest corner where the ambulance was parked. I also saw another postal employee standing by the emergency vehicles being treated and that his shirt was drenched in blood."

Joined by several other officers, he helped surround the building, taking a post near a brick wall at the south side. "We were there approximately thirty seconds when a blonde female came running out of one of the back doors with a white male [Mike Bigler]. Bigler showed us that he had been shot in the back and stated that the man doing the shooting was Patrick Sherrill.

"A couple of minutes later, we saw [through the windows] a subject inside the post office walk up and bar the back doors, look out the windows for an instant, then disappear from view. The man was bald-headed and there was blood on his forehead." With his attention riveted on the windows, the officer saw the bald man pacing back and forth for several minutes, then vanish again. "Approximately thirty seconds after he walked away [from view], at approximately 0715 to 0720, I heard the distinct sound of a muffled gunshot." Silence ensued and no more movement was observed. The SWAT team arrived, and rushed inside.

"We stayed in position guarding the south doors until we were told that the SWAT team had made entry and found the suspect dead, an apparent suicide."

Gene Black remembered:

> Someone called my name from close range and I saw Mike Bigler stumbling towards me. I ran to him and took his arm. He groaned as I tried to support him and help him to where the medics were working. As he lay on the sidewalk, I could see the blood seeping from a hole in his shirt.
>
> I glanced for another paramedic and saw Steve Vick standing nearby, looking dazed, pale, and about to fall. He, too, was covered with blood. I hurried to help him to the sidewalk. The paramedic ripped his shirt away to get at the large bleeding hole in the right side of Vick's abdomen. He'd turned white with shock and passed out.
>
> No one was attending Mike Bigler's wounds. In a panic, I asked "Where in hell are more medics? Is this all the damned help we're going to get?" I knew I was ranting and raving out of control, but my friends were dying here on the sidewalk.
>
> Someone grabbed me by the arm and said, "It'll be okay man. It'll be okay. They're coming."
>
> I pulled away and knelt beside Mike Bigler. I heard him sobbing and praying, ". . . By His stripes I am healed, by His stripes I am healed. . . ."
>
> Brakes screamed behind me as another AmCare unit of paramedics pulled up.

Black remembered he was left to stand across the street from the post office and watch helplessly.

He says:

> Uniformed and plain clothes officers walked around the building carrying shotguns and rifles. Cameramen

took pictures as news reporters pried details from anyone who would speak. Two AmCare units waited to receive more wounded. Helicopters circled above as officers spoke into walkie-talkies, trying to develop a strategy for invading the building to bring out the killer.

The survivors were asked to gather at the nearby City Council chambers. Many stood in small groups outside, some crying, others looking dazed. Family members of the employees had also been asked to assemble. An officer requested everyone to come inside to fill out a police report.

A crowd of dazed, confused people funneled through the doorway. Officials handed out forms and we did our best to fill them out. The crowd milled around in the hot, stuffy area, not knowing what to do. Some stepped out for some fresh air.

A city official and his associates arrived. He requested everyone go back inside for a roll call. "When I call out the names of the fatalities, I would like for their family members to please come to the front of the chambers. We have counselors available to talk with each one of you."

"Oh, God!" said someone next to me.

I was speechless. How could they say that with the friends and families listening?

One by one the victims' names were called. A wail of emotional pain sprang from someone in the crowd. The sound of crying in the chamber grew louder and louder, like shock waves rippling through the room, as each name of a fallen loved one was called. Many families cried out in horror, some collapsed and had to be helped to the front.

"Ah, man, how can they do this?" I said.

The room started to close in on me. I headed for the exit, pushing and shoving until I was finally outside. I leaned against the bed of a pickup, gasping for air. My head reeled from anguish and disbelief as tears ran down my face.

Seven men died.

Seven women died.

Six employees were seriously wounded.

Patrick Henry Sherrill made himself the 15th fatality in the Edmond post office on August 20, 1986.

If Sherrill's main target had been the supervisor who suspended him, fate had interceded in Bill Bland's behalf. He had slept late that morning and was not present during the massacre.

At that time, it was the third largest mass murder in U.S. history. James Oliver Huberty, on July 18, 1984, slaughtered 21 men, women, and children at a McDonald's restaurant in San Ysidro, California. And 20 years before the Edmond tragedy, Charles Whitman climbed the clock tower at the University of Texas in Austin, and gunned down 15 innocent people before being killed.

Chapter 9
Gene Black: Witness to Horror

Edmond, Oklahoma

How would it feel to have been one of the employees in the Edmond post office that ghastly morning? To have known Patrick Sherrill and many of the victims? What would it be like to suffer post traumatic stress over the incredible events? Most of us cannot even imagine the psychological impact or the subsequent torment.

Gene B. Black was there. He lived through it and through the aftershock. No one can tell his story better than Gene himself, in his own words.

Evening and the Day After
August 20, 1986.

I looked at my watch. It was 8:00 P.M. Hours have passed since I came home to my small apartment. I'm a postman in Edmond, Oklahoma. This morning, Patrick Henry Sherrill shot and killed 14 of my friends and coworkers at the post office.

Through the physical exhaustion and numbness in my mind,

I feel anger and disbelief. While staring at the walls, I've gone over the horror I experienced, bit by bit, in an attempt to make some sense of it.

This morning, I arrived at work as usual at 6:30, and by 7:30 I found myself standing across the street in a parking lot, watching helplessly as the local police and other law enforcement agencies played a waiting game. It seemed an eternity. I wanted them to do something, to find out what was happening in there. When were they going to do something? What were they waiting for?

Now, in my apartment, I turned out the lights and made my way to the bedroom. I lay down and waited for sleep to help me escape into blessed nothingness for at least a few short hours.

My clock radio is sounding its usual alarm—five-thirty A.M. It's still dark outside.

"I'm still alive," I say to myself. "My God, I'm still alive. Yesterday wasn't a nightmare." I survived, for what reason? So many are dead, so many families wrecked and destroyed. Lives changed forever. I could still see the bloody, mutilated bodies all over the post office workroom floor. Why? I could only ask why? How would I ever know why when Patrick Henry Sherrill, the killer, was dead too? How could he murder 14 people I saw and talked to each day? How could someone kill others the way he did? What kind of a sick son of a bitch does it take to pull the trigger of a .45-caliber pistol and see a human being die? Did it give him pleasure? Did he even realize what the hell he was doing?

Too many questions flashed through my mind all at once. They were the same questions I had asked myself last night as I sat in my living room. Pushing aside the unwanted thoughts of yesterday did little good. New ones rushed in to take their places.

Can I go back into that building again? Can I really open that door and go back to work today, as if nothing had ever happened? It was almost 24 hours since the deaths of my friends and coworkers. The pain and suffering hadn't ended with the close of yesterday. The fires of sorrow and grief still raged out of control.

Before I had become a postman, I had always felt kindly to the person who brought my mail. How could someone kill the nice guy that shows up in the rain, sleet and snow? How could someone kill the fellow who greets you warmly and hands you the mail each day?

The question of why wasn't going to be answered today. All I wanted to do now was to stay in bed and shut the world out. But I pulled myself up and off the bed, made my way into the bathroom, showered, and put on a clean, pressed uniform.

Opening the front door of my apartment took more willpower than I thought. I stood there a few seconds, hesitating, holding the knob. My muscles tensed as if to pull the door toward me, but stopped again. What I really wanted to do was call the office and tell them I felt ill. It wasn't a lie. The more I thought about the post office building, the more nauseated I became. Taking a deep breath, I finally shrugged off the fear, jerked the door open, and stepped out onto the porch. I felt vulnerable to the outside world, missing the safety of my apartment's walls.

"Well, I believe I can do it," I said under my breath. "I wonder who else will show up this morning? Maybe the police are still at the post office today." The thought of someone being there to protect us now encouraged me somehow.

I drove to Broadway and headed north. But as I narrowed the distance to the post office, the uneasy feeling took hold again. The closer I got, the less I wanted to reach my destination. I kept telling myself I could turn around and go home. I could try again tomorrow, but what about tomorrow? Would it be harder to make the trip then? How could I do it tomorrow if I couldn't do it today? Tomorrow would always have another tomorrow and what then?

As I crossed Main Street, the crowded roads around the post office came into view. The news media had haphazardly parked in the front lot and on every street surrounding the building. In the early dawn light, the brick structure stood as a reminder

of the horror I had experienced the morning before. A live
newscast was being held with three city carriers, Ron Blackwell,
Ray Walker, and Mike Bigler. I was surprised to see Mike, as
he had been wounded by Sherrill.

At the south entrance to the parking lot, postal inspectors
and a crowd of milling reporters stopped me. I could hear the
cameras clicking away as the flashbulb lights lit up the interior
of my pickup.

A reporter ran to my open window and asked if I had been
in the building during the shooting. A postal inspector shoved
him out of the way, then leaned over to peer into my window
for a better look at me in the light. "May I have your name
please?" he asked.

"Gene Black. I'm a carrier."

"Do you care to talk to reporters at this time, or would you
like to enter the lot?"

I shook my head. "No, I just want to go to work."

"Go ahead then, Mr. Black."

The inspector cleared a path through the reporters for me
and I eased forward into the lot. Once parked, I sat staring at
the back of the building. The long outside loading areas were
well lit by the night lights. Dark shadows loomed between the
mail delivery jeeps backed up to the building, giving the place
a haunted look. There were empty gaps in the lot with familiar
cars missing, and I didn't want to think about why. Most of
the vehicles I saw belonged to early-shift clerks. "How hard
was it for them to enter the building at one-thirty this morning?"
I whispered to myself.

Walking slowly toward the rear entrance, I inspected every
shadow. Closer to the two sets of steel double doors, my heart
started pounding and the uneasiness crept inside me again. My
legs cramped with each step. Cold sweat ran down my temples.
I rubbed my hand across my forehead. Just short of the first
set of doors, I stopped to look through one of the glass panels.

For a moment, I really wanted to run, to go somewhere else,
anywhere except here. I felt nausea, as if I had been kicked in
the stomach. My breath came in short, rapid bursts. With blind
trust, I lunged at the door, not even knowing if it had been

unlocked. My shoulder crashed hard against the cold metal and
I bolted into the foyer facing another set of double doors. I'd
made the first step, but I felt my heart rate increasing, pounding
harder and harder until I could actually hear it.

"It's a warning not to go in there again," I told myself.
"Go back home, damn you."

With a tentative step forward, I peered suspiciously inside.
The workroom looked empty.

"You okay, sir?"

I turned quickly, startled to see another person standing next
to me. I stood staring at a uniformed policeman, shaking and
unable to answer his question.

"Sir, you okay?" He took my arm.

"Yeah—okay—I'll go on in." I still felt shaky.

The policeman pushed the door open and held it for me.
Hesitatingly, I walked inside. I stopped and took a deep breath,
then continued out onto the workroom floor.

Tears came streaming down my face as if the floodgate to
my emotions had burst from the hidden pressure inside my
head. I turned and walked back toward the double doors, and
saw a face staring back at me. Chills ran up and down my
spine until I recognized the policeman I had just encountered
in the foyer and suddenly felt embarrassed for my emotional
display.

Once more, I turned toward the workroom. Looking around
the room, I could see that the large metal racks we used to
transport our letter trays to and from our jeeps outside had been
replaced with canvas hampers, neatly placed in the center of
the room. The sorting cases remained in their usual positions,
lining the outside area of the city carriers' workroom floor. The
canvas hampers overflowed with two days worth of parcels.
Of course, nothing had been delivered the day before.

The polished floor had been cleaned overnight and a new
heavy coat of wax applied. All this couldn't cover the stench
of spilled blood. The air still smelled pungent.

Dan Lipscomb appeared from the last row of cases at the
west side of the room. I walked toward him. We stopped in
the center of the workroom floor and just looked at each other.

I could see how red his eyes were and the pallid look on his face. It was probably much like my own.

"I'm glad you're here, Gene."

I responded without thinking. "I'm glad you're here too, Dan."

As the tears ran down my cheeks, I could see the moisture welling up in Dan's eyes. He stood, not knowing what to say or do next.

Finally, I managed to mumble, "I think I'll go check out my case."

"There's a lot of mail back there," Dan said, and walked away toward the break room.

It took a lot of effort to make my legs move. I made it to my case at the west side of the building. All I could do was stand at the tall stack of two-foot plastic trays filled with mail.

I wondered if we could really pull this off. Were we all going to go back to work today as if nothing had happened. How many coworkers would show up? Would they, too, have the terrible feelings of anguish I was having? Would we look for our fallen friends expecting to see them here just like we always had?

"Why did this happen?" Tears were flowing down my cheeks. I missed my friends, realizing now that they would not be here for me today. They'd never be here again.

Wiping my eyes, I moved closer to my case. The letters were still in the slots exactly as I had left them yesterday. I remembered that I had mail, letters, in my hand when I ran from the building yesterday morning.

"Oh, my God, what did I do with them?" I couldn't shake the worry. Then I remembered—I threw them on the ground outside.

I looked at my watch. Already six-thirty, time to clock in. By the time I had reached the time clock by the east double doors, many of the other carriers were arriving at their cases. I watched them as they surveyed the mountains of mail, just as I had done a few minutes before. Their faces were drawn up tight as if they were trying to hold back their emotions.

After clocking in, I started working the mail at my case,

wondering how I was going to get this huge mound efficiently sorted. I had always felt proud of myself for being one of the first carriers to leave for the street. This morning, I realized very quickly the pile of mail wasn't going to be my only problem. The noise—where was the noise? The post office is always a noisy place, music blaring from the overhead speakers, canvas carts squeaking as they're pushed from one place to another, and people always talking and joking. Today, it was so quiet, I could hear the ceiling fans squeaking 10 feet overhead.

As I tried to concentrate on my work, I realized I had to focus all of my attention just to place the letters into the proper spaces. Normally, sorting letters was like typing; you don't have to really think about each word you see. You know all the streets and house numbers. When you look at a letter you place it in its proper slot without thinking about it. And you instantly recognize when one is misplaced. On this morning, though, each letter required all the concentration I could muster.

About mid-morning a voice came over the loudspeaker with an announcement. "I want everyone to come to the center of the building for a meeting. City carriers, rural carriers and clerks—everybody."

Slowly I walked with the other city carriers to the center of the room and we were joined by the other crafts.

There were a lot of new faces present in the group. Apparently, we had been sent help from Oklahoma City stations. It was a grim sight, this group of people. Not at all like the lively bunch I was used to.

The speech from the gentleman in the center of the workroom floor was about pulling together, doing our best. I heard him say he was proud of the people who worked here. Only one person had failed to show up for work this morning. At the end of his speech, he asked us to bow our heads for a moment of silent prayer. I had never known the post office to be like this, the stillness almost stifling.

I walked back over to my case and thought about my friend and supervisor, Rick. I had talked to him only a minute or so before he was killed. At least I had gotten to say something nice to him that day. Rick was about my height, five-eight or so, with dark brown hair and neatly trimmed beard. He was friendly, outwardly happy and easy to get along with. When he was assigned as a 204B, a part-time supervisor, he always praised my work and assigned me to work his mail route. After Rick was picked for the full-time supervisor position, he assigned me to the new auxiliary route number C29. I was still on this route when Rick died.

After the meeting, the workroom turned quiet once more. A few minutes later, the loudspeaker shattered the silence again. "Take as much mail as you think you can carry. Make sure all first-class mail is worked first. If you need help, fill out a 3996 (auxiliary assistance request form)."

As quickly as the quiet was shattered, it returned and closed in around me again. Concentration still came hard. I couldn't get my mind off the eeriness of the building. Every small noise was like a sonic boom. Everything was a distraction, any sound coming from the far side of the building. I concentrated on remembering the lay of my case, but this extra effort gave me a massive headache. By the time my eight-thirty break rolled around, my headache desperately needed attention.

On the way to the break room, I stopped momentarily at the first-aid box to select a remedy, then went straight for the Coke machine. After swallowing the pills down with a big gulp of Coke, I sat down to wait for the relief I hoped was possible.

"You having trouble getting the letters to fit the case?" Larry asked as I sat down next to him.

"It's not going very fast today, is it?" I responded, holding my head between my cupped palms.

"I'm having trouble keeping my mind on my work, Gene."

"Yeah, I can't seem to keep my mind on anything but what's been happening around here for the last day or so."

About 10:00 A.M., the temporary supervisor, Rausse, went around to each of the cases and told the carriers what mail was to be left until the next day. I had just finished casing most of my first class when he arrived at my station. About 45 minutes later, I finished and tossed the rubber-banded bundles in the trays. I loaded my hamper and pushed it toward the east dock doors to clock out for the street. The squeaking hamper wheels broke the silence again, drawing attention to my advance across the hard tile floor. As I passed by the other carrier cases, each person turned and looked as if I was deliberately making the noise.

Before today, each carrier would look around to see who was leaving and say, "Have a good'n," or "Gene's leaving," or "Say goodbye to Gene." This morning was quite different. Each carrier looked around to see what or who was making the noise, then turned back to continue casing in silence.

Rausse stopped me as I was leaving and said, "Call us if you need any help and we'll send someone out."

"Okay," I said, and continued on my way toward the south doors and the loading dock.

The dock doors swung back heavily, then shut behind me. I saw a mass of reporters, onlookers, and cameramen standing at the south entrance to the parking lot. The local police and postal policemen were doing a good job of holding the crowd at bay.

After I had loaded my mail trays into the back of my truck, I drove slowly toward the crowd not knowing what to expect next. I stopped abruptly as a man jumped in front of my vehicle waving his hands over his head. Before he got all the way around my truck, I could see an identification badge pinned on his coat. "Post Office," it read in large red letters. Probably a postal inspector.

I opened the door as he started speaking. "Do you feel like being interviewed?"

"No," I said bluntly.

"Then I'll get them to move out of your way," he said, and trotted back to the exit gate. I drove out onto Campbell Street glad to be clear of the mass gathering.

It felt good to be outside in the fresh air again. Blue sky and the rising temperature told me it was going to be another hot summer day.

My first delivery was at a small shopping center at 15th and Boulevard. I'd emerged from my truck and taken just a few steps when I realized that people were staring at me. The massacre had apparently made me, as a postal employee, an object of curiosity. I felt conspicuous as if I were a freak on display. The stores were already crowded and many of the shoppers smiled and said, "Hello." Being accustomed to working unnoticed, it felt odd to be the center of attention.

Today, it felt different to take a quiet lunch alone. I usually went down on Broadway to meet Bruce Johnson, Mike Harris, and Roger Nelson. But today, I'd left the post office wanting to get out of the building in solitude. I couldn't possibly discuss the details of yesterday and doubted if anyone of the others could either.

The morning slipped by into a humid afternoon. When I arrived back at the post office, the street was clear except for a few lingering, die-hard reporters. For the most part, the media had given up, at least for now. After I backed the truck up to the south dock, I sat there looking out over the south lawn. Tears formed again, and started running down my cheeks as I thought of my friend, Gene Bray, lying bloodied on the lawn.

The sound of another truck backing to the dock jolted me from my thoughts. It activated me, though, into getting out and pushing my hamper toward the dock doors. I paused for another glance at the lawn. My nerves felt frazzled from thinking about the blood, and my friends Gene, Steve, and Mike suffering there. I hoped going back into the building wouldn't be as hard as it had been this morning.

The heavy doors swung shut with a groan, making me feel as if I'd entered a tomb. When I pushed the hamper through, and entered the building, the smell of blood returned. For a few seconds, I had an almost irresistible impulse to make a run for the outside. The feelings were as strong as they'd been this morning. The deeper I walked into the building, the more my uneasiness grew.

I checked on my accountables—registered, certified and postage due letters—and pushed my hamper to my case.

Most of the day, I'd felt better. But returning to the post

office rekindled my overwhelming desire to escape the building's interior. After unloading my trays, I stood in my small work space just staring at the case.

"What do I do now?" Confusion kept me from routinely doing what I knew had to be done. "Am I always going to feel this way?" I shouldn't have come back this morning. I should have stayed away.

Chapter 10

Gene Black: Days of Pain

Edmond, Oklahoma
August 22, 1986.

Day Two:

6:30 A.M. The drive to work the second morning was much easier. Reporters no longer blocked the parking lot entrance and no policemen or postal inspectors hung around. The brick building still looked haunting and lonely in the absence of 14 good people.

Again, I inspected all the dark shadows as I had the previous morning, but entering the post office was not as sickening. One Edmond PD officer remained on duty watching each person who approached the back entrance. His presence gave a feeling of some security to the workroom.

I walked over to the end of the line of carriers waiting to clock in. They were unusually quiet again today. Normally, there'd be good-natured chatter about families, sports, or playful teasing of each other. Today, the grim looks on their faces were different. No puffy eyes, no tears, just sadness. A stunned expression still showed on some, but mostly they were just quiet.

Before long, I was past the clock and tackling the mail left over from yesterday plus today's new mail. The anxiety I'd felt all day yesterday hadn't subsided until evening at my apartment.

I knew I was pushing myself physically, forcing back depression and avoiding memories of the graphic scenes in my mind. All this had torn my insides and left me exhausted. I'd slept as well as could be expected under the circumstances, but that wasn't saying much.

About an hour into our workday, we were again called to the center of the workroom for a group meeting to hear the schedules for funerals. Rick Esser, 2:00 P.M. Friday in Bethany; Bill Miller, 2:00 P.M. Friday in Yukon; Patty Welch, 10:00 A.M. Friday in Lawton: Jerry Pyle, 3:00 P.M. Saturday in Edmond; Pat Gabbard, 2:00 P.M. Sunday in Crescent; Lee Phillips, 2:00 P.M. Saturday in St. John; Betty Jarred, 10:30 A.M. Sunday, in Edmond; Ken Morey, 1:00 P.M. Saturday in Edmond; Patty Chambers, 2:00 P.M. Friday in Wellson; Mike Rockne, 11:00 A.M. Saturday in Edmond; Patty Husband, 10:00 A.M. Saturday in Oklahoma City; Judy Denney, 2:00 P.M. Saturday in Piedmont; Jonna Hamilton, 4:00 P.M. Friday in Edmond; and Tom Shader's funeral would be announced at a later time. Some of the funerals were out of town and I wouldn't be able to attend them. Many were scheduled at conflicting times, making a choice difficult. Rick Esser's funeral was today, and I had been asked to be a pallbearer. It wouldn't be until two in the afternoon. In order to attend, I'd have to turn over part of my route to another carrier.

Yellow ribbons tied on nearly every mailbox in the town fluttered in the hot summer breeze. The city of Edmond mourned the loss of friends and relatives. I was surprised as I retrieved cards and letters from many of the boxes expressing condolences, addressed only to "Our Post Office." It was heartwarming to see so many caring attitudes.

I returned from my route early enough to go home, change uniforms, and arrive at Rick's funeral on time.

Roger had asked if he could ride with me to the funeral. We

drove to the church in silence, neither of us caring much for small talk. We arrived a few minutes before the funeral, and stood outside with other carriers who were to be pallbearers. A funeral director came out and asked us to follow him into the church and be seated with rows of solemn mourners.

As I entered the church, I felt a clammy feeling under my clothes. My heart pounded in my ears and my temples became moist. I followed the funeral director down the aisle toward the casket in front of the pews. As soon as I fixed my eyes on the casket I felt dizzy and faint. I stumbled. Larry caught me by the arm and pulled me back toward him.

I kept my eyes away from the casket until I had taken my seat. As I looked at it again, knowing Rick was in there, I felt the queasiness return. Earlier in the day, I'd known it might be difficult, but I hadn't anticipated feeling this sick. Perspiration soaked my clothing and my hands felt clammy. I wanted to go outside for some fresh air. It was all I could do to sit quietly and try to recapture my composure.

Glancing around, I saw coworkers and other acquaintances entering. I wanted out of this place, but said to myself, "Hold on, hold on, not now. It would be disrespectful to Rick."

Now I could hear other carriers seated close to me sniffling and taking deep breaths. I wasn't the only one having trouble. Here we sat, the six of us, facing indescribable pain, all caused by Sherrill. "Damn him," I thought to myself. "That's my friend in the casket up there. My supervisor, one of the best I'd ever had. Why? Why did it have to be Rick?"

The funeral service started. At its end the priest and others with him in the ceremony started a procession up the aisle. The casket was pushed along behind them. A director assembled us at the front door in preparation for carrying it. As soon as I took hold of the front handle in my left hand, my knees felt weak, and my palms sweaty, making it hard to hold on. I was wringing wet as we walked down the church steps. I felt it slipping and reached over with my right hand to stabilize my grip. As I tried to regain my hold, I felt the other pallbearers behind me tugging frantically, trying not to let it slip from their grasps. Larry, opposite me at the front, struggled as well. At another row of steps, we did better. Cameras clicked from across the street where reporters stood. We reached the hearse and slid the casket in with no more difficulty. I saw Janet crying so hard that she had to be helped down the steps to a waiting car.

The slow, quiet procession to the cemetery seemed to take forever. I settled back against the seat and closed my eyes.

At the cemetery, we lifted the casket and walked across the lawn. I could hear the other pallbearers clearing their throats trying to control their emotions. It was a long last walk we took with Rick.

I missed him, knowing he'd be out here forever and never again join us at work.

As we pushed the casket onto the chrome rails over the grave, I could taste the salty wetness in the corners of my mouth. I stood at the end of the casket not knowing what to do next. Finally, I stepped back and stood next to Larry and the others in the warm sunshine. I stared at the casket that held my friend Rick, not hearing much of what the priest said. I looked at Janet and her kids sitting under the tent. I felt so sorry for her. She had lost so much.

Day Three:
August 23, 1986. 2:00 A.M.

I awoke in the dark, scared and seeing shadows moving around the interior of my apartment. Security lights outside my window usually illuminated my room, but tonight, for some reason, they remained dark. Headlights from cars passing on the street cast strange shapes on my bedroom walls.

When I realized what was happening, I settled down to sleep again. The clock radio woke me at 5:30 and I dragged myself out of bed, still tired.

At the post office parking lot, I couldn't find a vacant space and had to park on the street. Flowers had been placed around the flagpole on the lawn where I'd tried to help my wounded buddies. It looked like half the town had sent floral wreaths and bouquets.

Inside, I saw several carriers I didn't know and found that 20 to 30 employees had been borrowed from other stations. One of the on-loan men came over to my case and said he'd been assigned to help me. I kept waiting for him to start asking about the massacre and felt grateful that he refrained from it. Shortly after eight, the loudspeaker sounded again. ''I need all Edmond personnel to come to the center of the workroom floor for a meeting.''

A new supervisor greeted us there. He said, ''I'd like to introduce Mr. Orsi of the Edmond Support Center. Mr. Orsi and several other counselors have established a temporary center across the street in the ReMax building for Post Office personnel and their families. Anyone needing to talk to a counselor may go to the support center at any time during working hours or may make appointments for after hours.''

Jim Orsi stepped up to the center of the room to speak. ''This morning we're going to have a group session. We feel that it is necessary to have at least one group counseling session for all employees. After today, the support center will be available from seven-thirty each morning to six P.M. If you feel it necessary to come to the counseling office during working hours, you will only need to check out with your supervisor and come across the street. We're set up for the group meeting now, if you'll follow me.'' He turned to leave, apparently expecting everyone to follow like sheep.

At first the employees just stood and watched Orsi walk across the room. No one moved. The look on most of their faces was of disbelief. I shared their feelings. It now became apparent why there were so many carriers from other stations present. Management had planned all this in advance without our knowledge or involvement. We weren't going to just get help from the temporary carriers, they were going to relieve us of our routes for the full day.

As I moved along with the crowd that gradually edged toward the east doors, I heard grumbling and questions over the shuffling of shoes on the hard tile. The noise drowned out my troubling thoughts and I soon found myself outside in the hot summer morning.

A block from the Post Office, I turned my head and looked back at a sea of blue-gray uniforms behind me. We followed the leader to a church and filed into a large room. Some of the more disgruntled of the group refused to go in, and milled around on the lawn outside. We found seats in folded chairs set up in a big semicircle, but someone had underestimated the crowd size, so many employees stood against the walls. Quiet. A little afraid of what might come next. I felt uneasy and tense with expectation.

Mr. Orsi walked quietly to the center, carrying a microphone, stood silently for a moment, then spoke. He talked about our tragedy, the newness of the difficulties, acknowledged that we'd been through a devastating time, and told us that a time of adjustment was our next step. We had lost our friends and close working associates, he said, and now we must consider the pain of those around us. The mental anguish would not go away quickly. It was okay to cry, it was okay to talk to each other. He knew it would be hard to begin, or to say anything now, but assured us that it must come sooner or later. To start now would be helpful. The death of our fellow workers would fill our thoughts for some time; but would eventually ease as the days passed. No one could reach out and shake the pain away. We, within ourselves, would ultimately grasp the life we still had and pull through. He asked us to re-evaluate ourselves and see that we were still a part of the overall group at the post office.

"Would anyone of you like to say a few words?" Mr. Orsi glanced around expectantly.

John, the SPO, stood, walked quietly to the center, and took the microphone. He spoke in a monotone at first, then his voice quivered and he wept. He forced his words through his obvious pain, and continued to speak. I had never known John to show such emotion.

Finished, John stood silently weeping with his arms at his side, still holding the microphone in one hand. For some reason, I stood up and walked toward him, took the microphone, and started to speak. "I feel like I have to say something. I don't know what to say, but I feel like I have to get up here and say that I know what you're all feeling. I've been studying psychology at Central State University for quite some time now, hoping to learn how to help others. Now, I'm puzzled at my own actions. I don't understand any more than you do about how this whole thing could have happened to us. I'm like you, I can't figure out why. I've asked myself if this is a dream. I want to believe I'll wake up soon and find that it can all be forgotten and be happy again, relieved that it didn't really happen. But when I woke up again this morning, it was still real."

The tears flowed down my face while my voice quavered and broke. "I, too, want this thing we are living to go away. I want our friends to be at work tomorrow and for us to be like we were before. But I have this big fear that it will never be any different. I know now I'll go to the Post Office as I did each day and my friends won't be there. I love you guys. I know you'll be there and I can see you."

Mr. Orsi stood at my side. He put his arm around my shoulders and took the mike. I walked back to my chair and somehow felt stronger. I thought to myself that it did help to say something.

Our temporary supervisor had taken the microphone to say, "Please check out at the office before you leave to go to the funeral this morning. You're free to leave now."

Roger rode with me to the church for Mike Rockne's funeral. The Catholic services lasted a long time with a great deal of dignified ceremony. Later, at the graveside, after a flag was folded and delivered to Mike Rockne's wife, we all filed by the closed casket to say our personal goodbyes. Mike's brother walked slowly to the casket trying to keep his composure. Tears filled his eyes as he stood next to the casket and he cried out, "I'll see you, buddy." He patted the casket, and walked slowly away.

Many of the postmen and friends of the family could no

longer contain their tears, and most of the crowd cried. I had to walk a few feet away to wipe my swollen eyes, trying to get hold of myself. I knew I couldn't go to any more funerals like this. The whole thing cut deep into my emotions. I began to question if I was really one of the lucky ones. Did the living really have it better, or did the dead?

When I finally left, I joined two friends. All three of us hoped we could recover from the grief by getting some food in our stomachs. We still had to go to Jerry Pyle's funeral.

We had a quiet lunch, then arrived at the First Christian Church at about 2:30. In a quiet chapel, we waited for the service to begin. Jerry Pyle was lying in an open casket placed at the altar.

Jerry was a nice man, usually soft-spoken and reserved, and well liked by the whole team of carriers. He worked hard on his rural route, drove an old Volkswagen to work. He always volunteered to make sure coffee was available in the break room. Always willing to help anyone. The coffee he made warmed us on many cold mornings. Now he lay dead from a bullet fired by Patrick Henry Sherrill.

Day Four:
August 24, 1986. 7:00 A.M.

Sunday morning I woke with the hazy remnant of another dream still drifting around in my conscious mind.

I remember lying in my bed for hours last night dreading sleep, holding out for as long as I could before closing my eyes. Each night my fear of dreaming, the fear of what my subconscious would drag up to replay again, now kept me awake until the early-morning hours.

The horror of the massacre and the days that followed had changed my life. No longer did I enjoy the company of friends or life itself. Thoughts of why I was spared from sudden death were at first only passing glimpses of reality. Now, I thought about it seriously. I couldn't believe I had been spared when others had died. I searched desperately for an answer. I grasped at one reason, then another, discarded both and searched for a new one.

My telephone rang. I have a son in the Navy, and the call was to inform me that he had just learned of the massacre while at sea. He had nearly panicked when he heard that a victim named Gene was shot. From his ship, he had reached some of our family by radio patch to finally hear that I was not the wounded man. The caller relayed the message that my son would call me when he reached port.

It must have been a shock for him, being hundreds of miles out to sea. I knew what that was like.

That afternoon, I went to a mass memorial at the Central State University stadium. I sat with Roger in the bleachers near the top. A platform had been set up on the grass below. Fourteen rows of seats were closed off below us, one for each of the 14 dead victims. The remainder of the stadium was nearly full of mourners and good-hearted citizens of Edmond. The huge crowd sat silently under the unbearably hot August sun. A parade of speakers gave condolences and prayers. Everyone sat silently, hoping for answers. Each person in the crowd had the same question. Why?

After an hour or so of speeches, Janice McMillan, one of our carriers, walked to the podium and began reading the names of the 14 victims in a loud clear voice, slowly, one by one, pausing between each name. I felt goosebumps on my arms. As she called out each one, a shock wave of pain surged through the crowd. When the name of a loved one rang out, the families cried aloud. The people sitting close to the relatives were overcome by the pain they saw and cried along with them. By the time all 14 names had been read, the jammed stadium echoed with moans and sobs in a unified voice of sorrow.

Janice stood at the podium expressionless as she stared out over the stadium. It was almost as if she was paralyzed and shocked at what she had done by calling out the names. Finally, she trudged back to her chair, sat down, held her head in her hands, and cried.

At that moment, an entire stadium of sobbing, heartbroken

people was more than I could bear. I had only one thought, "Get out of here."

I stood, turned toward the exit, and said, "Rog, I can't take any more."

"Okay, Gene, I'm coming too." We made our way through the crowd. All the way out to the parking lot, we could hear the mournful wail of the crowd.

Day Five:
Monday, August 25, 1986, 7:30 A.M.

I walked into the break room to sit with Mike and Roger. We discussed a coworker who seemed to be struggling with his emotional reactions more than any of us. Somehow, I felt a distance growing between my friends and me. I was drawing away from them, wanting to be alone. But today, we had one more funeral to attend, for Betty Jarred, and agreed to go together.

"I think this is the last funeral I can take," I said. "I want to pay my respects to her. After going to Rockne's funeral, I wanted to cancel out today, but I'm going to make it."

We sat near the back of the church and could see her casket up front. I remembered Betty for her happy demeanor and friendly smile. The service for her was different than the others. The minister did his best to ease the grieving crowd of friends and loved ones. His message included the Bible passage, "To be absent from the body is to be present with the Lord ..." I knew that verse and it comforted me. When the services concluded, we watched the clerks who had worked with Betty carry her casket to the hearse. The long, black vehicle pulled out, followed by an endless line of cars in the sad procession.

I lingered for a while, standing in the silent parking lot alone, feeling the warm breeze blowing on my face. A peace settled over me as if someone wanted me to know it was over. Now I could start putting my life together, and go on.

* * *

Sitting back in my old comfortable chair at home, I opened the paper. On the front page were pictures and an article covering Patrick Sherrill's funeral. "What a joke," I said, out loud. Why did the press think anyone would care to even read such a thing? I read it, and couldn't believe what it said. So much of the information was wrong. One picture showed a kneeling woman who was supposedly a customer on Sherrill's route. "Hell, he didn't even have a regular route. He was a part-timer, a substitute carrier," I yelled out loud.

I threw the paper across the room. "You rotten piece of shit," I screamed.

My anger mounted. I stomped across the room, picked up the paper and threw it again, and again, yelling, "You son of a bitch. You killed my friends. You got away without even being punished. Dying was too easy for you. I wish I could get you for what you did to my friends."

Exhausted, I sat down on the couch and cried uncontrollably. I cried for a long time. When I finally fell asleep, there were no dreams.

Chapter 11

"I Fear an Incident Similar to Oklahoma"

Boston, Massachusetts
June 29, 1988

Sexual harassment in the workplace had been treated with winks and snickers for decades before being taken seriously in the 1980s. Women had endured everything from double entendre remarks and sly groping to outright propositions upon which their job continuity or opportunities hung in the balance. Gradually, victims of such treatment fought back by dragging lascivious bosses and colleagues into court. Ballooning punitive financial awards by judges and juries staggered many employers and caused them to enact programs of intolerance toward sexual mistreatment. Some organizations installed effective policies and procedures, while others gave lip service to the issues, and failed miserably at curbing the misbehavior.

In East Boston, Massachusetts, Lisa Bruni faced the age-old dilemma. One of her coworkers in the USPS Incoming Mail Center simply wouldn't leave her alone. She had tried everything from subtle demurral and angry refusals to totally ignoring him, but nothing seemed to work. Dominic LuPoli seemed obsessed with her.

LuPoli, age 40, seemed completely insensitive to Bruni's continued resistance. She couldn't understand why he ignored all of her signals of rejection. Alone at night in her Revere neighborhood apartment, not far from Wonderland Park and the State Beach, Bruni fretted over the uncomfortable problem. For months, almost since the day LuPoli started in January 1986, he had been steadily driving her nuts with his sexual innuendo, crude jokes, and disgusting proposals. She didn't regard herself, at age 32, as one of the world's great beauties, but knew that a fair share of men gave her more than one glance of approval. At work, though, she tried to appear as plain as possible, especially around LuPoli. How in the world, she wondered, could he find her attractive in that gray, shapeless uniform? She had certainly done nothing to encourage his barrage of unwanted attention. On the contrary, she'd been downright rude to him at times.

Because his behavior had grown gradually from mild annoyance to constant aggravation, Bruni had been reluctant to complain to managers at work, trying instead to discourage LuPoli on her own. But as his persistence grew, Bruni began entertaining thoughts of reporting him, or trying to escape the whole thing. Although she liked the neighborhood in which she had worked since May 1984 as an operator of the letter sorting machine, Bruni even considered requesting a transfer away from the location she shared with her salacious suitor.

By December 1988, Bruni realized that her individual efforts to repel the obsessed LuPoli had failed. She made an official complaint to her supervisor. Now, she hoped, the weight of management would stop LuPoli's constant harassment.

It didn't stop anything. Dominic LuPoli continued to express his unabated desires for Lisa Bruni. If anything, his campaign intensified.

Within a few weeks, weary and discouraged, Bruni requested a transfer. And waited. She told a Revere neighbor that she hoped the assignment to a new location would come through soon. In the interim, she wondered if a change of shift would help. Bruni and LuPoli both worked 10 P.M. to 7 A.M. If she requested another shift, at least she wouldn't see the ardent suitor every night.

Winter and spring slipped by with no letup by LuPoli. Instead of backing off, his relentless attention to Bruni changed in an ominous way. Where before his intentions seemed amorous or sexual, they now became mean spirited, taking on the form of intimidation and implied threats. Bruni's concern doubled, now tinged with growing fear.

In the last week of June, on a Tuesday evening, Bruni sat down at home and wrote a three-and-a-half-page letter. She entered the date, June 28th, began with *"To Whom It May Concern,"* and noted that copies would be sent to her supervisor, the postal inspection service, and her union representative. Her purpose, she stated, was to notify post office management, along with union officials, of the difficult situation she faced, and to ask for help.

Dominic LuPoli, Bruni wrote,

> *for whatever reason, has singled me out for an outlet for his extreme and bizarre behavior. . . . He has made comments that his seniority will increase due to my 'demise.' He has outlined his abuse of sleeping pills to other employees. He has on several occasions threatened me & my safety.*
>
> *The latest incident of this type was tonight. He has threatened to 'take care of me.' These threats, delivered in an extremely emotional & irrational manner has [sic] caused a great deal of fear & apprehension on my part.*
>
> *I have attempted to resolve this personally by means of conversation. This was three weeks ago. Mr. LuPoli stated at that time some unusual rhetoric about jealousy & his father's jealousy and temper. I wish to state clearly that Mr. LuPoli and I have never had any kind of personal relationship. He has stated to others & myself that I 'led him on.' When asked for specific examples of this, he has said 'You know.'*
>
> *He stares while I talk to anyone else & if I should laugh, always assumes I am laughing at him. I have tried*

ignoring him. I have tried being nice to him. I have tried being rational with him—all to no avail.

I personally have taken quite enough of this abuse. It has escalated to the point of real fear now. I feel that I am entitled to work in what I believe to be a safe work environment. This, I feel, does not exist here. I fear Mr. LuPoli quite capable of physical abuse because of his obvious pattern of repeated threats against me.

Bruni added more details of her concerns, then continued with a foreshadowing reference to an event that had darkened the lives of every postal worker across the nation 22 months earlier. Bruni wrote,

I greatly fear an incident similar to the one in Oklahoma is possible here at the IMC. I am not the only employee here to make this sad observation. . . . I request strongly action be taken before the Postal Service's neglect of a dangerous situation results in real harm to me and others.''

Lisa Bruni could not have been more explicit in her prescient warning. She made it clear that she and other employees saw the potential for more disaster. Could managers be completely blind to the signals?

Before she left for work the next night, Lisa showed the letter to a friend in her apartment.

At the Incoming Mail Center, at 10:15 P.M. on a humid, warm Wednesday, employees heard the alarming bursts of gunfire outside in the parking lot. The closest workers rushed out to see what was going on. They saw a sedan screeching out of the lot, and found Lisa Bruni crumpled in a heap on the pavement close to her car, unconscious and bleeding from several wounds. An ambulance responded within minutes to an emergency call and whisked her to Massachusetts General Hospital. Bruni died shortly after arriving.

Fortunately, one of the observant employees had noted the description and license plate number of the car seen leaving the parking lot. The police put out a radio BOLO (be on lookout) for the vehicle. A pair of uniformed metropolitan police officers spotted the car an hour later parked on Revere Beach Boulevard, not far from Lisa Bruni's apartment. In the darkness, they could make out a figure sitting in the driver's seat. Cautiously, the officers approached.

The flash of a muzzle blast flicked bright orange inside the car, accompanied by a single explosion. The figure slumped over in the seat. Dominic LuPoli died instantly.

As they launched an investigation, postal service officials immediately erected a stone wall between themselves and media reporters. They refused to acknowledge receipt of Lisa Bruni's letter. Her grieving friends, startled to hear the denial, angrily confirmed its existence. A union official who had received a copy of the letter said that it had been forwarded to the superintendent of the tour Bruni worked. Pressed for a statement about Dominic LuPoli, a USPS spokesperson finally said no records could be found of any complaints about the alleged killer, from Lisa Bruni or anyone else.

A flurry of activity by postal officials followed two other reports of sexual harassment in Boston area postal facilities. Managers expedited corrective action, quickly transferring the accused offenders to other locations. As usual, crisis intervention teams were made available to employees at the Incoming Mail Center for counseling. The USPS spokesperson, reticent about information related to the tragedy or the sudden transfers, said, ''A mutual decision was made by the director of human resources and the top managers, who felt it would help employees deal with the emotional impact.''

It fell to the local union president to report on the issues at stake. He told reporters that discussions about methods to deal with sexual harassment complaints were receiving management attention, and meetings would be held between union officials and representatives of the Boston postmaster's office.

In Washington, D.C., media relations executives hoped the awful specter of postal workers killing each other would stop.

Twenty more employees had died from bullets since Perry Smith shot his boss in Johnston, South Carolina, nearly five years earlier. The USPS image tarnishing problem kept popping up. Maybe they could get through the rest of 1988 with no more incidents.

If that's what they hoped, they were to be sadly disappointed.

Chapter 12
"I Wanted to be Killed"

New Orleans, Louisiana
December 14, 1988

The Big Easy! *Laissez Les Bon Temps Rouler* (let the good times roll). New Orleans, Louisiana—home of the French Quarter, Mardi Gras, pirogues on the bayou and paddle wheelers on the Mississippi, jazz, Creole gumbo, and the huge Superdome where ten Super Bowls have been played.

Just a short walk from the domed stadium, down Girod Street to Loyola Avenue is the massive L-shaped federal building which also houses the city's main post office.

Warren Murphy had worked in the bustling mail sorting room of the USPS for several months after having served six years as a mail carrier. His performance record reflected adequate abilities and behavior, with no serious marks against him. To coworkers, he seemed reasonably even-tempered and cheerful. Sometimes, Murphy spoke proudly of his two sons and how one of them was turning out to be a pretty good football player. Murphy told his colleagues about attending one of the games and sitting in the bleachers next to Police

Superintendent Warren Woodfork. The two men had chatted amiably about their sons' football skills.

To his friends, Murphy seemed to maintain his good humor despite a few personal troubles. But as Christmas approached in 1988, his coworkers saw him sink into a blue funk. Murphy's wife had left their Verbena Street home more than six months earlier and taken both of their sons to Maryland. The thought of Christmas without the kids depressed Murphy. At age 39, he didn't want to be by himself.

Murphy's wife felt she had good reason to leave. He had made too many threats, she later reported, and was insanely jealous. Shortly after their 1972 marriage, she said, he started beating her up and yelling at her. At one of her son's football games, she worked in a concession stand. Murphy cornered her there, accused her of having an affair with the coach, grabbed her by the hair, and pulled her out of the stand. On a Mother's Day, when she invited some friends over to play cards, he lost his temper about some trivial thing, and threatened her by pressing a pistol to her temple. She hoped that her move to Landover, Maryland would put enough distance between them to prevent him from causing her any more trouble. But she found out that 1,000 miles wasn't nearly enough to keep him away.

First, Murphy called his sons, ages 7 and 14, and convinced them to give him their address by saying that he needed it to send some Christmas presents.

Then, on December 7th, the police came rushing to her residence to investigate a report from Murphy that she had killed the two boys. Embarrassed and furious, she showed the officers that her sons were perfectly healthy.

Three days later, Murphy himself stood outside, pounding on her door, angry as a wounded alligator, yelling for her to come out. "I was scared to death," she said. She huddled in a locked room with the boys, and refused to answer the door. After several minutes she heard his bellowing subside and his car roar off into the distance. Her pounding heart had barely slowed down when she was stunned by Murphy returning with two uniformed police officers. "He told them there was child

abuse in the house." Once again, nearly speechless with outrage, she made it clear to the officers that her children were
safe and sound. When she asked them for advice on how to
protect herself from Murphy, they recommended she move to
another address because they had no legal way of preventing
his return.

That same evening, December 10th, according to the wife,
Murphy made a telephone call to her family in which he threatened to kill her and take the boys with him. But after a while,
he backed off, she recalled. "He told my family that he was
not interested in the children." When she arrived at her job
after taking a day off to recover, she found that he had left a
message which, she said, was a death threat. "That's when I
called his supervisor [at the New Orleans post office] to find
out if he was in New Orleans or still here so I could know if
I was safe."

The supervisor to whom she spoke could not say for sure
where Murphy was. Sounding somewhat apathetic to her plight,
he turned the call over to a secretary to make a record of the
complaint. The following day, a family member tried to help
by calling the New Orleans post office again, and reached the
same secretary. The relative described the conversation: "I told
her that Mrs. Murphy was so scared, she was seeing a psychiatrist and the doctor felt from her description that the man was
homicidal." The secretary would not give any information
regarding Murphy's whereabouts. Her boss took no action to
notify anyone that Murphy had been called "homicidal."

A postal inspector, asked later about the events, said that
spousal complaints are not uncommon. "If we have any indica-
tion that an employee's conduct reflects poorly on their job
performance, we would investigate." The relative who had
called wasn't the least bit interested in Warren Murphy's job
performance. The family wanted some assurance that authorities would investigate the possibility that Murphy might explode
and go on a rampage of violence.

Even though Warren Murphy missed his wife and children
after they moved out in the spring of 1988, he spent as much
time as he could with his girlfriend, Shantelle Graham, who

was also a coworker. Graham and Murphy's ex-wife had been friends, and still held each other in high regard. Mrs. Murphy thought that Warren behaved better in Graham's presence, so she demanded that Graham be at the Verbena Street house when the sons visited. The demand was easily met since Graham had moved in with Murphy not long after his wife left. She and Murphy even talked about getting married in November.

The same pattern of behavior that had driven Murphy's wife away soon chipped away at his relationship with Shantelle Graham. She saw his intense jealousy flare up. He developed a suspicion that she was too friendly with men in the section where she worked, so Murphy transferred closer where he could keep careful watch on her. Graham submitted a bid for and won a change from the afternoon shift to the day shift. Murphy, moping and pouting, begged her to forego the change, but she refused. His obsession with Graham became so intense that he once hid in the trunk of her car to spy on her and see where she went. When Graham stopped at a gas station, she discovered his hiding place.

Angry and disenchanted, Graham began to withdraw from Murphy. She tried to sever their relationship, but he begged, then threatened in order to persuade her to stay. His pleas worked for a while, but eventually Graham realized she had to get away from him. It disturbed her deeply when Murphy would threaten to kill any man who made a pass at her. She later reported, "He told me a lot of times he was going to come into the post office and kill them, and have me watch while he did it." She didn't know if he was serious. "He said it a lot. It got to the point I didn't believe him because he said it so often."

Whether Murphy was serious or not, Graham decided she had enough of his strange behavior. A couple of months before Christmas 1988, she packed her things and left his house.

Shattered by the loss of his wife and sons, then his girlfriend, Murphy's job performance tapered off and his supervisors let him know about it. Their criticisms rubbed his emotional wounds into raw anger.

On Thursday, December 15th, Murphy walked into the post

office with a stiff-legged limp. He went into the men's restroom on the second floor then came out and approached Shantelle Graham, at about 8:15 that evening. He said he wanted to talk to her. Graham said no, she had nothing to say and didn't want to hear anything he might tell her. Supervisor Leonard King witnessed the argument, stepped in, and ordered Murphy to stop talking to Graham. Murphy glared at King. His face a mask of fury, Murphy disappeared into the restroom again. Within a few seconds, he emerged carrying a shotgun. Before Leonard King even had a chance to react, Murphy raised the gun's muzzle toward him, squeezed the trigger, and shot King in the face. The scattering birdshot also wounded two other employees.

Shantelle Graham froze in fear as Murphy approached, then tried to duck low and twist away from him. It was too late. He grabbed her hair. As other employees scrambled out of range of the gun, he pulled the trigger, reloaded, and pulled it again. Each shot missed the terror-stricken workers who scattered in all directions trying to escape. The wounded supervisor, King, and the other two injured men managed to struggle to an exit. All three were taken to hospitals for emergency treatment.

Threatening to kill Graham, Murphy led her downstairs. On the main floor, he herded a group of employees out of the coffee break room, forced his hostage inside, and barred the door.

Large groups of the approximately 400 employees who had fled the building gathered outside on LaSalle Street, chattering frantically. The hubbub caught the attention of shoppers at the adjacent New Orleans Center, drawing them into the excited crowd. Calls to 911 summoned police and medical personnel, accompanied by news media reporters. Because the melee took place on federal property, officers from the FBI joined New Orleans Police Department cops and the SWAT team. They had to use extreme caution because about 30 employees remained in the building, either hiding or afraid to move. The army of officers moved carefully, trying to avoid endangering anyone still inside.

Gradually, the police infiltrated the post office. They crept from room to room searching for Murphy and his hostage, Graham. As the hours slipped by, most of the nervous employees were found and brought out. None of them knew that Murphy had moved from the coffee break room.

At about 1:00 A.M., as agents approached the closed door of a storage room, Murphy fired two bursts of birdshot through the thin paneling. The spray of pellets caught FBI Special Agent Raymond Fiveash in the wrist and forehead, but inflicted only superficial wounds.

Now they knew Murphy's location, but couldn't attempt an arrest while he still held Graham. They summoned a hostage negotiation team which included a police officer cousin of Murphy. One of the team threw a telephone through a window to Murphy, but he destroyed it with another blast from the shotgun. Through the remainder of the night and early morning, efforts to convince Murphy to surrender were unsuccessful.

At dawn, Police Superintendent Woodfork arrived, the same man who'd sat beside Murphy at their sons' football game. His own boy had heard news reports of the standoff and told Woodfork that it must be his teammate's father. When he arrived on the scene, Woodfork mentioned the passing acquaintance to the FBI agent in charge, who thought Woodfork should take over the negotiations.

Using a bullhorn at first, Woodfork convinced Murphy to use another telephone they tossed into the room. Speaking in more friendly terms, the police Superintendent reminded Murphy of the time they'd chatted at the game. "Look," he said, "we watched our boys play football and we tried to develop them into disciplined and responsible men . . . and now we ought to try to be men ourselves." Murphy responded by describing his loneliness brought on by not having his sons available during Christmas, and that he worried about their safety in Maryland.

"I just tried to appeal to him as a father," Woodfork later recalled. "I assured him I would look into [his children's safety] . . . I told him if he was really concerned about his kids he ought to be a responsible parent."

After 13 long hours, Murphy at last asked Woodfork to meet

him halfway to the door. The officer agreed on the condition that Murphy would throw out the shotgun first. Murphy's only demand was that all reporters and cameras be kept away from him. At 9:00 A.M., Murphy walked out, his hands clasped over the top of his head. Shantelle Graham followed, unhurt but in shock.

With his hands cuffed, and surrounded by armed officers, Murphy said that he was "happy to get the attention of management" at the post office. Agents quoted him as saying, "I didn't have the courage to commit suicide but I wanted to be killed."

All of the injured employees survived, but supervisor Leonard King lost his right eye as a result of the shotgun wound.

Held on a charge of assault with intent to commit murder at a government installation, Warren Murphy faced a possible 20-year stay in federal prison if convicted. A judge ordered extensive psychiatric testing to determine if Murphy was competent to participate in legal proceedings. When psychiatrists pronounced him legally sane, prosecutors charged Murphy with the more serious offense of kidnapping and assault with intent to commit murder, which could imprison him for life.

At the February 1989 trial, Shantelle Graham testified that during the post office siege, Murphy asked her several times to kill him. Her statement was corroborated by a tape officers had made when they interviewed Murphy. In it, he said that he threw the shotgun on a table and invited her to shoot him. He also said he was "disgusted and aggravated" with management at the post office.

Murphy's public defender attorney said, "Our defense is he had no intention to kill anyone else ... The only person he wanted to die that day was Warren Murphy." The defendant did not testify in his own behalf.

In March, the jury filed into their box while Murphy sat motionless showing no reaction. They convicted him of the charges. As he walked out, flanked by armed bailiffs, one of his aunts rose from her chair in the gallery and moaned, "Please forgive them. They know not what they do."

Murphy turned his head toward her and ordered her to stop it. "Don't do that. Don't let them see you do that."

As her family led her from the courtroom, the aunt sobbed, "I can't help it. He's never done anything wrong."

Leonard King didn't agree. With a patch over his sightless eye, he said, "If it took this long to get justice, it was worth the time. If he gets ninety-nine years, then maybe justice was done."

At the sentencing hearing months later, U.S. District Court Judge Veronica Wicker ordered Murphy to spend 200 months in federal prison. He was also sentenced to 260 more months on additional charges, but the judge ruled the extra time would be served concurrently. So Warren Murphy faced 16 years behind bars. The 5th Circuit Court of Appeals subsequently upheld the verdict and sentence.

Chapter 13

"An Unfortunate Incident"

Poway, California
March 25, 1989

"By the time you receive this, I should be dead," Don Mace wrote in a letter to local newspapers in March 1989.

After more than 10 years with the USPS in Poway, California, Mace had endured all the pain and stress he could take. Even though he lived and worked in a sylvan foothill community north of San Diego, surrounded by picturesque canyons and upscale housing developments, Mace's life had fallen apart. Every person has a level of tolerance for coping with problems. When everything turns sour, including health, money, relationships, and the job, the mind can sink like a foundering ship, unable to find a ray of hope in despairing darkness.

Things turned bad for Don Mace in 1979 when he had the accident. In a grinding automobile crash, Mace sustained injuries that would cause him to permanently live with excruciating back pain. Ironic, he thought. He'd survived the hell of Vietnam, only to be shattered in a car accident.

The struggle to live a normal life received a brief shot in the arm three years after the crash when Mace's girlfriend agreed to marry him. During their courtship, and into the first few days of the marriage, his new wife was blissfully unaware that problems had developed in Mace's job with the USPS. Gradually, she learned of the tension that would eventually tighten his nerves to the breaking point. She later recalled, "Mace and I had a happy marriage until the pressures of the post office were more than he could cope with." Her first exposure occurred just two weeks after they married.

The couple had agreed to meet at home for lunch. Within a few minutes of Mace's arrival, after they had taken the first few bites, Mrs. Mace glanced out the window and noticed something odd. In a subsequent statement, she said, "Standing outside in the driveway was a man clocking my husband." She asked her husband what the heck was going on.

"Oh, he won't bother you," Mace said, with a forced smile. "They're just checking up on me. They're playing silly little games."

She tried to accept his reassurances, but still felt a sense of distress. It seemed odd to her that the postal service would go to so much trouble to make sure that an employee didn't exceed his lunch break. She later learned that the incident was just a sample of the supervision techniques under which Mace worked. In the following weeks, she recalled, "They told him in writing that he was to go to the bathroom on his own time, not their time. . . . I was absolutely appalled. I could not believe that in this society this was existing."

As sometimes happens, such stress can cause a man to turn against his loved ones. Mace fell into the trap of lashing out at the person closest to him. In an explosion of frustration one evening, he lost control and began smashing furniture. He picked up a small wine rack and heaved it through a sliding glass door. One of the bottles tumbled to the floor, breaking and spilling the red liquid over the carpet. His reasoning ability distorted by rage, he picked up the jagged bottle neck, grabbed his wife by the hair, and threatened to slash her throat with the broken glass. The marriage ended in 1986.

The costs of a shattered marriage and wrecked health drove Mace to the edge of bankruptcy. Then, his employer discovered they had overpaid him by almost $1,500. To recover the money, they began deducting $122 out of each biweekly paycheck. One of Mace's relatives would later comment, "We figured out somewhere along the line that between his bills and losing that money . . . he was living on eight dollars a day."

When he felt he could take no more, Mace wrote to the news media, complaining of his problems and harassment by his bosses at work. His physical pain, he said, combined with job stress, made his life unbearable. In the remarkable document, he pinpointed the place and time of his planned death. After dropping the letters in a mailbox, Mace dressed in his postal uniform on March 25, 1989, and drove to the Poway Post Office. With the calm and dignity of a man at peace, he walked inside, put a .38-caliber revolver to his temple, and pulled the trigger. Don Mace's problems had ended forever.

A USPS spokesperson called the suicide an "unfortunate incident," then launched into a damage control speech seemingly designed to exonerate the USPS. "His problems continued through three different officers in charge of that post office," the speaker said, adding that Mace had a "disciplinary history." The details, he said, were not a matter for public knowledge.

Mace's family felt betrayed. One member said, "The post office is trying to push the fact that he was crazy . . . When Don first started, he loved his job. But it got to the point he had so many pressures on him . . ." Wiping away a tear, the relative noted that Mace had gone to the post office dressed in his uniform to make a point.

If he did wish to make a point, it apparently escaped the people for whom he'd worked. The San Diego postmaster sent a letter to the family in which she expressed regrets about "the unfortunate circumstance of the death of . . . Donald Mace." She wrote, "Please accept my sincere sympathy on behalf of the postal service." A certificate accompanied the letter. It was dated March 25th, the day he died, and imprinted with the words, "To Donald Martin Mace, in grateful appreciation of 22 years of dedicated service to the government of the United

States, given posthumously by the United States Postal Service.''

Stunned and disappointed, Mace's family went public with their questions and criticisms. They even contacted their representative in the United States House of Representatives, Congressman Jim Bates. The complaints gained momentum when other USPS employees and ex-employees put their grievances in writing. Bates read them with growing concern, and invited Mace's family, along with a dozen postal workers, to a meeting two weeks after the suicide. He listened as the group told him that Mace had killed himself to protest working conditions. Among the problems they described were reports of harassment, unfair firings, and improper denial of disability claims.

Afterwards, the Democratic congressman said, ''I think there is validity to their cases.'' He added, ''I'm sure [Mace] committed suicide because of job-related stress . . . Maybe he had a low tolerance, but I'm sure it played a part.'' Bates announced plans to start the ball rolling for a congressional investigation into USPS practices.

The posture taken by a spokesman for the postal service seemed defensive. Refusing to discuss specific details about allegations of harassment suffered by Mace, citing confidentiality, the official countered the family's comments by saying that Mace had been cleared by a doctor to perform his job.

Donald Mace was not the first postal worker in the country to commit suicide. He wasn't even the first one in Southern California. Not even in San Diego County. In the previous five months, three other USPS employees had taken their own lives, two in the coastal towns of Encinitas and Pacific Beach, and one 20 miles inland, at El Cajon.

It's reasonable to assume that most suicides are not the result of one incident or problem. More likely, self-imposed death comes as the result of a whole complex of real and imagined difficulties. Work-related stress can certainly play a major role, though. Four suicides, within such a short period of time, by people working for the same employer, might very well be a signal of something terribly wrong.

Chapter 14

"I Want an Airplane . . . Now!"

Boston, Mass
May 9, 1989

One of the most bizarre incidents of a postal worker turning to murder did not happen in the post office.

Boston, Massachusetts, had nearly recovered from the news that Dominic LuPoli had sexually harassed Lisa Bruni before pumping several bullets into her body in the Chelsea Incoming Mail Center parking lot, after which he committed suicide. Not quite 11 months later, the city would reel again over another story of a man's alleged obsession with a woman and the tragic consequences.

Alfred J. Hunter III stood before Judge David Doyle on Tuesday, May 9, 1989, accused and convicted of assault and battery against his ex-wife, Elvira Hunter. Considering the appropriate sentence, the judge examined Hunter's criminal record to see if there'd been any prior convictions. He found none. Looking down on the stocky, 42-year-old, mustachioed man, Judge Doyle sternly ordered Hunter to serve one year of probation and to stay away from his ex-wife. It would later be revealed that Hunter was the recipient of an extremely lucky break that day. Someone in the court system had made a clerical error in the preparation of the documents containing Hunter's criminal record, omitting a previous conviction for the same offense, assault and battery. A representative of the district attorney said the error "would have certainly had an effect on the judgment." The judge probably would have put Hunter behind bars if he'd known Hunter was a repeat offender.

Sometimes, the most minor of errors can have tragic long-term consequences.

It wasn't the first time Hunter had sidestepped the consequences of that same criminal record. A few years earlier, he'd acquired a firearms identification card (F.I.D.) which gave him legal authority to purchase a rifle or shotgun in Massachusetts. The law, however, stated that the holder of such a card must relinquish it if convicted of a felony or of alcohol-drug abuse. Hunter's record slipped through the cracks and his card was never revoked.

Hunter had always been interested in firearms, but his passion was aviation. While growing up in Lynn, just a few miles up the coast from Boston, Hunter enviously watched his father pilot small planes and longed to follow in his footsteps. After high school graduation, Hunter enrolled in LeTourneau Technical College, Longview, Texas, intending to earn a degree in aviation. He fell far short of his goal and dropped out. In 1967, at age 20, he enlisted in the U.S. Army with the same goal in mind. This time, Hunter hoped to learn the skills of piloting a helicopter. Once again he failed, lasting only a few weeks at the Fort Rucker, Alabama, flying school. The Army transferred the disappointed Hunter to Mississippi to become an air traffic controller, but that plan aborted as well. He ended up taking medic training at Fort Sam Houston. Next stop: Vietnam.

Even though he never piloted a Huey over the hellish jungles, Alfred Hunter rode at the open-side hatch of the noisy choppers, ready to leap out to rescue wounded soldiers. Now and then, in flight, he would spray targets below with automatic rifle fire. For years after that, he'd relive the experiences by describing his exploits to any willing listener. And he continued to fanta-size about being a pilot. He'd learned the fundamentals by observing his father, from some training at college and in the Army, and by watching the men at the Huey controls.

After Vietnam, Hunter returned to stateside duty and tried to settle down with a new wife. Like many of his previous commitments, this one also failed, ending in divorce. He reenlisted in 1975 to serve tours of duty in Germany and Korea as an armored reconnaissance specialist. His travels took him to the Philippine Islands where he met a bright attractive young woman, Elvira Sanchez. A whirlwind courtship of the quiet, conservative Filipina, 11 years his junior, convinced her that she had a future with Hunter. In her hometown of Anquilar, the couple stood side by side while the town's mayor presided over their marriage ceremony.

As soon as his enlistment period grew close to expiration, Hunter brought his bride back to Massachusetts, to Ipswich, where they lived in a motel cottage owned by his father.

In 1979, Hunter was arrested and charged with assault and battery after an altercation with two men. He escaped serving time behind bars, but the conviction would be on his record.

Acquaintances thought that Alfred and Elvira Hunter were happy, especially when she bore him a son in 1984. One friend observed that "Elvie" seemed very subservient to her husband, but described the union as apparently a good one. "She was real sweet. When she first [arrived] she didn't speak much English. She was real deferential to him . . . doing everything for him. A real housewife."

Elvira Hunter adjusted well to life in the Boston area, an extreme contrast to the semi-tropical Philippine environment. With a degree she'd earned in accounting, she landed a book-keeping job. Her boss characterized her as "a lovely, hardworking person." But Hunter complained to a coworker that his wife "became too Americanized" and he didn't like that. So he had to seek "other companionship." According to another acquaintance on the job, Hunter not only talked of his passionate attraction to Asian women, but he brought amateur pornographic videotapes to the workplace to show selected colleagues. They featured Hunter cavorting with various women from the Far East. Hunter claimed he had traveled to the Philippines and Thailand to seek out ladies who would perform in his videos. In Massachusetts, the coworker said, Hunter would get tired of one girl then move on to another. But he didn't want to divorce his wife because he'd have to pay too much money.

Behind the public facade of compatibility, Hunter's relations with his wife grew increasingly strained. They moved to a houseboat at the Danvers Yacht Club, north of Salem, but the relocation didn't calm the troubled waters. She would later request court protection, saying that "he had caused her physical harm and placed her in fear of imminent physical harm." Hunter responded by complaining that Elvira held a red belt in martial arts and accused her of physically abusing him. Once, he charged, she kicked him for asking her not to change the television channel.

The troubles with his wife didn't prevent Hunter from pursuing his continued fascination with aviation. He built an ultra light plane and spent hours flying it even though he never acquired a pilot's license. In January, he renewed his other interest by purchasing an AK-47 rifle in a Salisbury gun store. Ironically, he bought the weapon on the same day that a young man named Patrick West used a similar weapon in a bloody massacre of five children in a Stockton, California school before killing himself. A man who worked alongside Hunter would divulge a strange comment made by his acquaintance. Hunter reportedly said about the tragic assault, "I really like what happened there. I need a gun. I really want one." The tipster recalled that Hunter would subsequently take the weapon up to New Hampshire and practice with it in the woods.

Halfway through 1988, the Hunters' marital struggles came to a head and the couple filed for divorce. Elvira's attorney would later say that she made no demands for money or property. "She came to me and just said, 'Get me a divorce.' She told me not to worry about child support or any of these things. She just said, 'Get me a divorce.'" He did, and it became final in November. Even so, the estranged couple gave their damaged relationship one more try a few months later, and moved into an apartment in the north shore town of Beverly. By this time, Hunter had been employed with the USPS at Boston's South Postal Annex for nearly eight years as a mail handler.

Again, the Hunter's attempt at reconciliation fell apart. On the last day of 1988, Elvira lodged a new complaint against Hunter charging him with punching her in the face, pulling her hair, and throwing her into a bedroom. Judge David Doyle renewed a restraining order he'd previously issued, ordering Hunter to stay away from her for a full year. When Elvira returned to court a few weeks later to complain that Hunter had violated the order by assaulting and threatening her, the judge filed criminal charges against Hunter and scheduled a hearing for May 9th. In April, Elvira moved out again to an apartment in Danvers, a safe community in which there hadn't been a homicide reported for 20 years.

At the May 9th hearing, Judge Doyle could very well have ordered jail time for Hunter, if the pre-sentencing documentation had reflected the previous conviction for assault and battery. But Hunter walked out of the court with nothing but probation.

At 9:45 that same evening, Danvers police responded to a call of a domestic disturbance on Lummus Avenue. Fire department vehicles also showed up at the scene having been alerted by a smoke alarm in the apartment. A neighbor reported hearing noises that sounded like gunshots, seeing a gray van fleeing the scene, and talking to a preschool child in front of the apartment. The little boy had cried that his father came with a gun. "My mother's dead," the child sobbed. Officers entered the home and were stunned to find Elvira Hunter's bullet-riddled body in the hallway. She'd been shot seven times in the head and chest. Smoke from the weapon had apparently activated the fire alarm.

At the same time police discovered the body in Danvers, Alfred Hunter allegedly began, but has not been convicted of a bizarre train of events Bostonians wouldn't soon forget. After driving his van south on Route 1, the Newburyport Turnpike, he has been accused of pulling off into a restaurant parking lot and trying to carjack another vehicle. The owner ignored his threats and jammed the accelerator, squealing away into the nighttime traffic. Hunter allegedly returned to his van and sped south again, to Peabody. There, he allegedly stole a car at gunpoint near a Chinese restaurant.

From Peabody, Hunter would have had to reverse directions and head northeast again to arrive back in Danvers, outside the office of the Beverly Municipal Airport at 10:20 that night. The darkened facility was closed for the night, but Hunter allegedly exited the stolen car and entered the building. Part-time flight instructor, Robert J. Golder, was inside alone. Jamming his AK-47 rifle barrel into Golder's face, Hunter allegedly demanded the 21-year-old college student lead him to a plane with an ample supply of fuel in the tank. "I want an airplane and I want it now," Hunter allegedly ordered, adding that he didn't want to hurt anyone. The nervous young man pointed at a red-and-white two-seat Cessna 152 which had a half tank of gas. Hunter allegedly threw a green duffel bag from his car and a metal ammunition box, aboard the aircraft. "Don't do anything stupid," Hunter allegedly ordered. "Don't use the phone. I know who you are." After threatening Golder not to interfere, Hunter was accused of taxiing down the dark runway and ascending into the star-studded springtime sky. He probably winged northward, then wheeled to the south along the coast past Boston. The plane was spotted over Duxbury at 10:20 P.M.

Nearly an hour later, a pedestrian on Newbury Street in Boston heard sounds like firecrackers coming from above. He glanced up and saw a low-flying red-and-white plane swooping down toward the Charles River from the direction of the venerable old baseball stadium, Fenway Park. When bullet casings fell from the sky and landed within a few feet of him as the plane passed overhead, the frightened walker hurried to find a police officer. He said, "The plane was flying very low and all the lights were out . . . Then it started popping again. At that point, it was so low I thought it was about to crash. But when I saw all the shell casings lying around I realized what was going on."

A few minutes later Boston police watched in amazement as the plane maneuvered over the USPS Annex near Boston

Harbor where a famous tea party had once taken place. The pilot appeared to be emulating a combat dog fight, plunging toward the ground, repeatedly buzzing the post office building, then zooming skyward again. At least one bullet hole was later found in the structure.

Boston Deputy Police Superintendent Robert E. Hayden would comment, "I've had some busy, crazy nights . . . but this was the most unusual night I've had as a police officer in twenty-two years." He arranged for night-shift officers to continue working, ordered a special unit to surround the South Postal Annex, and dispatched a fleet of ambulances to the neighborhood. Police blocked off all streets in a two-block radius. Hayden hoped the pilot didn't plan a suicidal kamikaze attack. "We felt that [the Annex] might be the place he decided to end it all and crash." Approximately 1,200 employees inside the building were advised to evacuate if possible or to seek safety in the heavily reinforced basement.

The plane disappeared from the airspace over the Annex for a short time, during which a tugboat operator in the harbor noticed an unlit plane flying very low directly overhead. He heard popping noises and thought the pilot was dropping fire-crackers on the boats below.

After reports came in of the aircraft being seen as far south as Duxbury, 25 miles south of the harbor, it returned to attack the USPS Annex again like a mad wasp in flight. 911 calls poured into the emergency reporting center from all over the city. Air traffic controllers across the harbor entrance at Logan International Airport watched the Cessna on radar screens and occasionally caught sight of it in the night sky. Their attempts to contact him on the Cessna's radio frequency were futile.

"We were helpless," Hayden said. "We were totally out of our element. We were bound to the ground . . . trying to go where we thought he was going to deploy out men and ambulances. Within a minute, he'd be over Winthrop, or over Duxbury."

At a couple of minutes after midnight, observers watched

with mouths agape as the pilot zoomed the plane underneath the Tobin Bridge, a span rising 200 feet over the inner harbor. Then the air traffic controllers at Logan gasped as the Cessna headed directly for the tower, swerved off at the last second, and repeated the stunt four times. After another repetition of the death-defying maneuver, officials ordered the controllers to close down all air traffic and evacuate the 20-story glass-enclosed tower.

Employees of Continental Airlines scattered at the sound of gunfire, and reported that windows in one of the jetliners were shot out. Nearby office windows also shattered from gunfire as the Cessna circled above. A police van and a motorist's car were struck by bullets during the incredible sorties in which the pilot wove a flight pattern between downtown skyscrapers and dropped to within a few hundred feet of the ground.

The red-and-white plane had been flying for well over two hours when someone called 911 from a Howard Johnsons to report that a box had been dropped from the plane. It would never be recovered, but police have speculated it was the metal ammunition box.

Nervous officials worried about the potential destruction the pilot could inflict on the city and still feared that the pilot planned to end his wild odyssey with a spectacular crash. They braced for the possibility of the Cessna slamming into the Prudential Tower, where he'd already fired shots into the sky-walk atop the building. Maybe his target would be one of the bridges, or the cluster of large gas storage tanks on Morrissey Boulevard. Deputy Police Superintendent Hayden said, "We kind of thought he was not only going to commit suicide but that what he was doing was so spectacular that anything he did less than crashing in a big way would be anticlimactic."

It appeared that the drama was coming to an end at about 1:00 A.M. when the pilot came in for a landing at Logan. But as he taxied along the runway with police vehicles in hot pursuit, he veered off to another runway and rose again into the night.

Finally, at 1:15 A.M., the Cessna came in for a final landing at Logan. Alfred Hunter allegedly switched the engine off, stepped out, and surrendered to a small army of uniformed and armed police officers. He allegedly tossed the AK-47 out of the plane, perhaps into the harbor waters, because searchers never found it.

Within a short time after arresting Hunter, authorities transferred him to Bridgewater State Hospital to undergo psychiatric evaluation. They learned that the postal worker-pilot had been undergoing psychiatric treatment at a Veteran's Administration facility in Bedford where he'd been hospitalized two years earlier. In 1988, he'd also been treated on an outpatient basis, and had been taking prescription drugs to control anxiety disorder symptoms.

In June, doctors from Bridgewater State Hospital concluded that Alfred Hunter was not mentally competent to stand trial. Dr. Wesley Profit, director of forensic services at the institution, confirmed a recommendation that Hunter be committed for treatment. At a court hearing late in June, Judge Charles Black of the Brockton District Court, accepted the doctors' recommendations and ordered Hunter hospitalized until found able to understand the charges against him and to interact with lawyers appointed to defend him. Hunter, the judge said, would remain in custodial care until able to stand trial for murder and armed robbery. Subsequent hearings weighed the issue of Hunter's competency until March 1992, when he was cleared to stand trial. A jury convicted him of first-degree murder and Judge Barbara Rouse sentenced him to life in prison. Two years later, an appeals court overturned the verdict. As of February 1997, a new trial was still pending.

Postal officials had little to say about the Alfred Hunter case. He hadn't been accused of murdering any supervisors or coworkers, but his alleged strange aerial attack on the South Postal Annex where he worked would certainly raise questions. They wouldn't comment on whether or not they had knowledge that the employee was undergoing psychiatric treatment. If the allegations were true that Hunter brought pornographic videos to the workplace to show to coworkers, shouldn't USPS officials have been concerned? Once again, media relations executives chose to say as little as possible. No other postal employees had been injured or killed.

If that was the rationalization for failure to comment on the case, it wouldn't work in a tragedy that would occur exactly three months later.

Chapter 15

"They're Trying to Set Me Up"

Escondido, California
August 10, 1989

The massacre in Edmond, Oklahoma remained fresh in the memory of USPS employees even though three years had passed. USPS officials certainly still felt the raw embarrassment of it, and postal workers hoped desperately there would be nothing like it again. But many of them sensed that pressures on employees still might set off another bloody disaster.

In a rural Southern California town, a mail carrier's calm exterior fooled everyone, and effectively hid an inner turbulence ready to erupt at any moment.

The comparisons would be inevitable. Both tragedies happened in small towns, both in the month of August, both by quiet, uniformed mail carriers who had served in the U.S. military as Marines, both shortly after 7:00 A.M., and both ended with the same self-inflicted punishment. The separation between the two massacres existed primarily in time and distance: three years and 1,200 miles, the span between central Oklahoma and southern California. Escondido, like Edmond, offered the clean, peaceful environment and security of country living where the last thing residents expected was an angry rampage of gunfire and murder.

Like Patrick Henry Sherrill, the Oklahoma killer, John Merlin Taylor harbored a festering grudge that would take its toll at his place of employment, the USPS. The two men even bore a faint resemblance to each other, both with high foreheads, square chins, deep vertical lines etched in the cheeks, and full mustaches. Sherrill, though, was regarded as reclusive, while Taylor was a sociable family man. And the Oklahoman, at age 44, had worked for the USPS only 16 months, while John Taylor, 52, had reached the portal of retirement after 27 years as a postal worker.

An event early in Taylor's life may have planted a seed that eventually led to the calamity in Escondido.

Taylor entered the world in Mokane, Missouri, a tiny hamlet on the northern bank of the river after which the state was named. Fewer than 300 farmers and merchants lived in Mokane, situated in the "Kingdom of Callaway," so called because Callaway County had actually seceded from the United States during the Civil War. The Taylor clan settled on rich bottomland to farm and raise cattle. By the 1950s, John's father, Joseph Milligan Taylor, still ran a small farm but supplemented his income by working as a heavy-machine operator. He needed the extra money to support his wife and eight children. Soon after graduation from the local high school, John Taylor became the only one of his siblings to leave their hometown. He enlisted in the U.S. Marine Corps.

Letters from home kept John informed about his family. He flushed with pride when he read the good news that his younger sister, JoAnn, was the high school homecoming queen and class valedictorian. The next communique from his family had just the opposite effect, slamming into the young marine like cannon shell.

For several years, townspeople had whispered dark gossip about the Taylors. Old Joe, they said, would guzzle too much booze, stagger home, and take out whatever ailed him on his wife, Mildred, by giving her a terrible thrashing. The kids cowered in fear while their father threatened to kill the whole family. It all came to a head on the night of June 12, 1958. Still bearing yellowing bruise marks from a recent beating, Mildred hid in a closet when Joe came home drunk, bellowing his anger.

JoAnn, the homecoming queen, heard him slurring his venom. Her heart pounded with dread that he might carry out his threats. When Joe collapsed on the bed, she desperately searched her soul for the power to intercede and prevent the inevitable violence he would inflict on her mother. Still trembling, JoAnn dug out a hidden .38-caliber revolver, walked over to the bed, and blasted three bullets into Joe's head and body.

At the trial, attended by John Taylor who was home on an emergency leave, JoAnn testified that she couldn't stand to see her mother beaten again. "God helped me pull the trigger," she said. Mildred Taylor corroborated the stories of physical abuse. On the advice of an attorney, JoAnn accepted an offer to change her plea to guilty of manslaughter. A sympathetic judge sentenced her to three years in prison, but granted an immediate parole. JoAnn Taylor would not have to serve time behind bars, and townspeople rallied in her support, but the traumatic scars would remain with the family.

With the terrible events in Mokane behind him, John Taylor returned to complete the last year of his hitch with the Marine Corps. When he left the service in 1959, he chose not to settle in Missouri where the rest of his family remained. Instead, he married and selected Southern California as his home. In 1962, he joined the USPS.

Like his parents, Taylor liked the idea of a large family. He and his wife had five children. But another alleged similarity to his father emerged, as indicated by documents later filed in a Vista, California court. Mrs. Taylor asserted that her husband was "extraordinarily violent" and "frequently drinks to excess." She also noted, "He threatened my life on many occasions, physically struck, battered and beat me to the ground."

The strained relationship reached a divorce court in 1977. John Taylor's attorney disputed the allegations of spousal abuse by his client. "There was no showing of physical violence," he scoffed. "It was an extremely quiet, placid and pleasant separation. There was no real drinking or abuse and that petition is just the kind of typical garbage we lawyers put in there." The judge granted a dissolution of the marriage and awarded custody of the five children to the mother.

After more than a year of living the single life, Taylor stopped in a Kmart one day and struck up a conversation with a cute, full-bodied divorcee whose lilting German accent and toothy, sparkling smile riveted his attention. He asked Leisbeth McMullen if she would like to go dancing sometime. She wondered about the drawling man who looked about 40 in his faded jeans and a plaid shirt, but thought his tan, mustachioed face handsome enough. His manner seemed gentle, he stood a full head taller than she, and he was about the right age to go with her 38 years. She accepted the date.

That evening, Taylor learned that Liz was born in Germany a few years after the end of WWII, had married an American soldier stationed near her hometown, and had mothered four children after moving to Southern California. McMullen divorced the soldier in 1977, the same year John Taylor's marriage ended. Enthralled with each other, Taylor and McMullen danced and talked the night away, then made arrangements for future dates. The romance blossomed. He nicknamed her "Boopsie" and she responded by calling him "Schnookie." After they were married, he moved into her Escondido home on Begonia Street to take over stepfather duties with her brood. His new family lived just a few blocks from the home Taylor had shared with his ex-wife and five children.

With a new name, the former Liz McMullen would joke with customers in her new job, selling jewelry at Montgomery Ward. As she wrapped the merchandise, she'd laugh, "Now you can tell everybody that you've bought a diamond from Liz Taylor."

There was no lingering rancor between John Taylor and his first family. His kids would often spend time with his stepchildren. Naturally, a certain amount of friction developed and jealousies flared, but it didn't seem to damage the new marriage. Taylor told a coworker, "They're her children. She loves them and I love her." Rumors would develop that some conflict developed between one of the older sons and his stepfather, but the Taylors shrugged off such speculation. The couple continued to go out as they had while dating, usually to dance at various night spots in the community. She sometimes wore her native German dirndl, with the colorful flower-embroidered bodice, white peasant blouse, and apron-covered full skirt. A musician at one of the dance clubs became acquainted with the couple and expressed his affection for them. "They were the nicest people you'd ever want to meet."

Other friends and associates expressed the same sentiments. "He was just a real friendly guy," said one. "He'd come out and say, 'Hey, how you doin' today?'" A next-door resident would recall, "They were very friendly, a nice couple. They had a lot of friends . . . went out dancing and they had people over." The neighbor looked back into his memory for a moment, and added, "I know they loved each other very much."

About Mrs. Taylor's congeniality, a friend said that Liz loved to chitchat. "You're talking to her outside and you're there for twenty minutes. . . . But she was a real nice lady."

At the Orange Glen Post Office, where Taylor had worked since the facility opened in 1974, his coworkers held him in high esteem. He usually arrived there early to join buddies Richard Berni and Ron Williams at a picnic table on the loading dock for morning coffee and cigarettes. The three would chat about their social lives and job issues. Williams, four years older than Taylor, until recently had been president of the local branch of the National Association of Letter Carriers (NALC). He willingly listened to any job problems his colleagues wanted to discuss, and had a reputation of being a leader among the mail carriers. The third member of the trio, Dick Berni, who had spent 10 of his 38 years with the USPS, liked to boast about his son and how well the boy had performed as a pitcher on the Little League team. For all three men, the morning coffee sessions were an indispensable start to the workday.

Other coworkers also would express admiration for John Taylor. "John was a happy-go-lucky guy, always. You could never make him mad," said one of them. Another observed, "Nobody was more conscientious about his job than John. He always had a smile. I looked up to him." A fellow mail carrier and 20-year colleague said, "John Taylor was an outstanding mail carrier. He never created any problems. He was always smiling, always laughing . . . well liked and respected by his coworkers, and, as far as I know, his managers."

If awards reflected Taylor's reputation among managers, the coworker was correct. In 1986, Taylor was the recipient of an award for excellent job performance. In addition, supervisors singled him out several times to be given a quarterly performance award. On the most recent occasion, Taylor had declined it with a smile, and suggested that someone else receive the honor, along with the corollary bonus, because he'd already won it so many times. Even the San Diego area postmaster, Margaret Sellers, said about the Orange Glen facility and John Taylor, "This is a model station, and he was a model employee."

His conduct on the job may not have been affected by it, but something troubled John Taylor in the late summer of 1989. On Wednesday evening, August 9th, he made an odd statement to a colleague who later spoke of it. "When [John] went home, he made some comment about how there's not enough mail here. But he was being sarcastic, because there was a ton of mail in there." That wasn't like him at all.

Another coworker and friend said that Taylor seemed to be worried that management was investigating him for possibly stealing mail. Taylor had mentioned to the pal that someone was apparently planting dollar bills in mailboxes on Taylor's route. "They're trying to set me up," Taylor had complained to his friend, "to see if I'll take the money."

Physical pain had been bothering Taylor for some time. His back, shoulders, and heels had been giving him trouble, so he had accepted a motorized route which wouldn't require so much walking. But he reportedly felt a great deal of job pressure. According to a fellow employee who worked with Taylor for 15 years, the problem became apparent in July and August. "The word was out among the guys that he was very disgruntled with the way things were going at work. The pressure was there—keep doing better, do more, do more."

That same week, in a discussion with one of his coworker friends, Taylor brought up a topic still painful to postal employees. When the two men shared some concern about the possibility that another fellow worker might break under the ongoing pressure, and resort to violence, Taylor frowned. Almost in a joking manner, he said he hoped there would be no repetition of the horrible massacre in Edmond, Oklahoma, that had taken place three years ago.

Just after sunrise on Thursday, August 10, 1989, John Merlin Taylor arose from bed, and began getting ready for work. His 23-year-old stepson nodded a "Good morning" to his stepfather before departing the house. A few minutes later, Taylor quietly retrieved a Sturm Ruger .22-caliber semiautomatic pistol from its hiding place and gave his sleeping wife, Leisbeth, one last look. Then he aimed the barrel at her head and fired two rounds, killing her instantly.

After dressing in his mail carrier's uniform, Taylor placed a box containing 100 rounds of ammunition and two loaded magazines on the seat of his 1974 Plymouth Duster. As the sun climbed, and the temperature rose, he drove to the small Orange Glen station, where he followed the usual routine of meeting Ron Williams and Dick Berni at the picnic table on the loading dock. But instead of sitting down for coffee and a smoke, he raised the pistol and pumped a barrage of slugs into each man, killing both of them.

As he entered a side door into the building, employee Paul DeRisi happened to glance over his shoulder from where he was seated behind the customer service counter in the front lobby. DeRisi described it: "I was just working at the front window and went around to where Patricia Washington was. We were saying good morning. I noticed John Taylor come in behind me at the side door. I thought he was waving at first.

The first shot missed me. The second one hit, but I didn't realize I'd been hit until I saw the blood.'' The wounded man, bleeding from the shoulder, leaped over the counter and dashed out through the front door. He sprinted across the street toward a coffee shop to get help. Another arriving mail carrier saw DeRisi, beckoned him over to the car, and rushed him to the hospital. From there, he called 911.

Window clerk Patricia Washington who had been standing near DeRisi recalled that she thought the popping noises were firecrackers. But her mistaken notion was soon corrected. ''I saw that Paul DeRisi was shot in the shoulder. I could see the blood [and] realized that it was not a toy gun.'' She hastily made her way into station manager Bob Henley's office and yelled that Taylor was out there shooting at people.

While Washington bolted out through another exit, Henley stepped from his office just in time to see a bleeding DeRisi escape through the front door, then froze as Taylor pointed the gun directly at Henley. He heard Taylor say, ''I'm not going to shoot you.'' But as soon as the words had left Taylor's mouth, he pulled the trigger again. The slug missed. Henley dove back into his office and slammed home a locking deadbolt.

Outside, the owner of an adjacent shop heard the muffled explosions in the post office and the screams of Patricia Washington. ''She was in bad shape,'' the shop owner said. ''She had turned and run the hell out of there. We sat her down in the [nearby] dry cleaners to try and calm her down.''

A few seconds after the first shots, a custodian inside heard someone yell, ''Get down, it's for real.'' The words came from employee Roger Hutchinson who became a hero to several of his coworkers. Hutchinson never left the building, choosing to stay and try to warn others of the danger. He repeatedly yelled, ''This is for real! Clear the building—Get out! Get out!''

The custodian, Reginald Keith, looked up to see Taylor staring at him. ''He saw me. He kind of looked at me. His eyes looked kind of dazed. He walked right by me . . . didn't say anything. There were several employees he didn't bother. He kept walking toward the back of the building.''

One clerk would always wonder why she was spared, but

thanked her lucky stars for it. Taylor aimed the pistol toward her and pulled the trigger. But it clicked, empty. "Thank God," she later said. "He had to reload."

Another lucky soul, Mike Collins, also narrowly escaped death. Taylor took aim at him, but the gun's hammer just clicked. As he started to snap another magazine into place, Taylor dropped the box of bullets, scattering them on the floor.

Bullet casings later found along his path of destruction would reveal that Taylor reloaded more than once.

A part-time mail carrier, Phyllis DiVito, worked only on Thursdays. When she heard gunshots, her first thought was that an angry customer had barged in and was slamming mail onto the floor. Then she heard Roger Hutchinson yelling for everyone to get out and spotted Taylor. "I saw him standing in the doorway," DiVito said. "I saw him putting bullets in the gun." In her mad scramble to escape, she stumbled several times, sustaining cuts and bruises, then fell in the alley outside, fracturing her nose.

To some of the frightened employees, it appeared that Taylor may have been heading toward the work station of his friend and coworker, Jonny Sims. It didn't make sense that Taylor would be trying to kill people he knew and liked, but he'd already shot two of his closest colleagues outside, and seemed to be working his way along the interior toward the spot where Sims would ordinarily be. However Sims hadn't yet arrived at the post office.

As Taylor progressed toward the rear of the building, Roger Hutchinson stood his ground still shouting warnings. His voice caught Taylor's attention. The gunman took several steps toward Hutchinson, stopped near a water fountain, and calmly announced, "Roger, I'm not going to hurt you."

With that, Taylor put the muzzle of the Ruger to his own head and fired a final round. As Taylor fell and dropped the weapon, Hutchinson stepped forward and gave it a kick, sending the gun spinning across the floor, out of reach.

Within seconds, paramedics rushed in, along with Escondido Police Officer Robert Benton. The medics examined the two men outside and found them beyond help. Taylor, though, with a bullet in his brain, still had vital life signs. The technicians quickly loaded him into an ambulance for transport to Palomar Medical Center.

Officer Benton, now aided by additional police arrivals, heard the accounts of witnesses and asked for the home address of John Taylor. Two officers sped over to Begonia Street. When no one responded to their knocking, they circled to the rear of the house and looked through a window. Because they could see a still, silent figure on the bed, they forced entry, and found the dead body of Leisbeth Taylor. As in the case of any obvious homicide, the uniformed officers sealed off the crime scene with yellow tape and waited for investigators to take over.

One of Leisbeth's grown sons had heard reports of the massacre on the radio at his workplace. Shocked and fearing the worst, he rushed to the house on Begonia, only to find a flurry of police activity, and the devastating news that his mother had been killed.

Another radio listener felt her heart race as she heard the news of the post office shootings. She waited in her home for her husband, Ron Williams, to call and inform her of the details. When he didn't, she drove to the Orange Glen station, where other concerned friends and relatives had gathered trying to find out what happened. As the crowd thinned out with relieved people taking stunned employees home, Arlene Williams heard the unimaginable. A police officer spoke softly to her as he explained that her husband wouldn't be coming home.

A man who had already known the pain of losing a relative who worked for the USPS also tensed when he heard the news. He had worried for almost five months that something terrible would happen, ever since his brother-in-law, Donald Mace, had committed suicide in the post office where he had worked. Angrily, the relative spoke out. "This is another message, and I hope the post office is listening this time."

If USPS officials were listening, they weren't saying much. The first announcement from a spokesperson stated that employees of the Orange Glen station would be allowed to take the rest of the day off. "If there is a problem," the speaker said, "and a person needs more time off, we'll be very sympathetic.'' He also announced that a counseling service would be made available.

Management brought in cleanup crews that night to scrub blood off the linoleum floors so the post office could be opened on the following morning. Workers arriving on Friday morning could see white paint covering bloodstains on the concrete below the picnic table. While all 48 of the scheduled letter carriers dutifully reported to work, a squad of volunteers from other stations also showed up to help sort and deliver the backlog created by the one-day closure. All of the employees spoke in quiet, somber tones, still dazed by the horror.

Reporters attempting to question them were sent away by a guard. A USPS spokesperson said that officials would review the events to evaluate the need for policy changes. But he thought it unlikely that security would be tightened at post offices. "How can we do that?" he asked. "We're not Fort Knox, we're not the CIA. . . . You have to make it a pleasant place to work. You have to have trust."

In the Palomar Medical Center, John Taylor still clung to life by the slender thread of life-support systems. Family members who traveled from Missouri, plus his children, conferred and decided that if he died, they would offer his organs for donation.

Late on Friday night, doctors declared his life at an end. Unfortunately, none of his internal organs met medical requirements for transplanting.

On Thursday, the bleak day after the murders, Postmaster General Anthony Frank spoke to a gathering of postal employees in Atlanta, Georgia, the site of two postal murders in 1985. He expressed bitter resentment against anyone who criticized USPS policies in a manner suggesting faults that might have contributed to the Escondido tragedy. He accused critics of making "political hay" out of John Taylor's rampage. "Obviously," Frank said, "it's a matter of great moment to me. But when you shoot your closest friends and your sleeping wife, is it fair to blame work on that? Is that the fault of the postal service?"

To make his deep concern even more clear, Frank flew to

California on Saturday. He met with 60 postal workers at the Orange Glen station, then spent some time with the grieving families of Ron Williams and Richard Berni. In a written statement, Frank said, "I am deeply moved and impressed by the dedication and caring of these postal people. They all feel a deep sense of grief over the loss of their friends. Yet they all maintain a firm commitment of service to this community. This is a tragic loss for the families, the victims and the entire postal family across the nation."

The postmaster general also told reporters that he was satisfied with San Diego Postmaster Margaret Sellers's handling of the situation and her administration of service in her area. Soon after the murders, she initiated a program she called "quality circles" to allow employees to meet with supervisors for the purpose of airing complaints. Anthony Frank blessed her efforts by saying, "As near as I can tell, she's awfully good. Of course, I don't work with her day after day . . . but in terms of attitude and performance, I would say San Diego is one of our top divisions."

A memorial was placed at the base of the flagpole in front of the Orange Glen station to honor victims Ron Williams and Richard Berni. The cost would be shared by the USPS and the employees.

Shortly after Donald Mace and John Taylor died, postal employees complained not only to their Congressman, but also sent bundles of letters to a major San Diego newspaper, complaining of job pressure and stress. The USPS spokesman couldn't provide any answers. Sometimes, managers saddled with the duty of reporting to the media are caught between a rock and hard place. If top level executives are unwilling to promise analysis and corrective action, the spokesperson is reduced to offering nothing but vague suggestions or politically correct rhetoric. The individual who dealt with the deluge of complaints following Mace's suicide said, "I think it's too early to determine what will come of all this. . . . I don't know what to tell you about these incidents." The media wanted more, so he continued by pointing out that USPS personnel in the San Diego area were not being subjected to anything different from employees in other sectors. "The objective in San Diego is the same as postal workers' all over the country. We try to provide service at the best possible price. As far as the number of employee complaints about management go, I know that nationally there were a higher number of grievances resolved this year than any other. The postmaster is addressing the labor issue."

To questions from reporters, his response sounded somewhat defensive. "How can a carrier's job really be that stressful? They're out on the street for four-and-a-half hours a day in the sunshine. If it's that stressful, why are there hundreds of people lining up like crazy to get post office jobs every time there are openings?"

Patrick Henry Sherrill, 44, killed 14 of his coworkers at the Edmond, Oklahoma post office on August 20, 1986. (*Photo courtesy of AP/Wide World Photos*)

Sherrill's continued participation in the National Guard sharpened his skills with the Colt .45 semiautomatic he used on his rampage.

Gene Black, mail carrier at the Edmond, Oklahoma post office, who witnessed the murders. (*Photo courtesy Gene Black*)

USPS logo on the Edmond, Oklahoma post office. (*Photo courtesy Don Lasseter*)

The monument erected in memory of the Edmond, Oklahoma victims is called "The Yellow Ribbon." (*Photo courtesy Don Lasseter*)

After shooting his wife to death, John Merlin Taylor, 52, drove to an Escondido, California post office where he murdered two coworkers on August 10, 1989. (*Photo courtesy AP/Wide World Photos*)

Victim Ron Williams, 56, shared coffee and cigarettes every morning on the loading dock outside the post office with coworker Taylor. (*Photo courtesy National Association of Letter Carriers, Branch 2525*)

The Orange Glen Post Office in Escondido, California and its memorial to Taylor's victims. (*Photos courtesy Don Lasseter*)

MAY THE FLOODWATERS OF FORGIV
WASH AWAY THE TEARS AND THE SU
AND CLEANSE THE MEMORIES OF OU
BROTHERS

10 AUG

On October 10, 1991, while wearing a Ninja-style uniform, Joseph M. Harris, 35, killed his supervisor with a Samurai sword, shot and killed her boyfriend, then drove to the Ridgewood, New Jersey post office and executed two coworkers. (*Photo courtesy AP/Wide World Photos*)

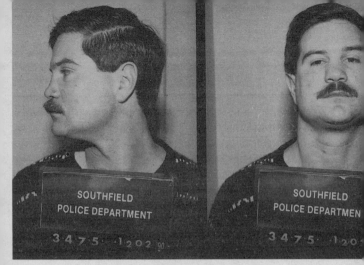

Dissatisfied with the outcome of a 17-month arbitration over his termination, Thomas McIlvane, 31, killed four with a sawed-off semiautomatic rifle at the Royal Oak, Michigan post office on November 14, 1991. (*Photo courtesy Southfield, Michigan Police Department*)

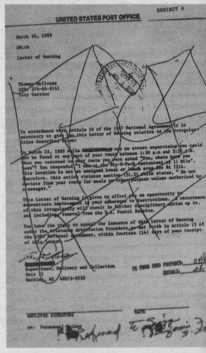

March 24, 1989 USPS Letter of Warning to McIlvane which he defaced with an obscenity.

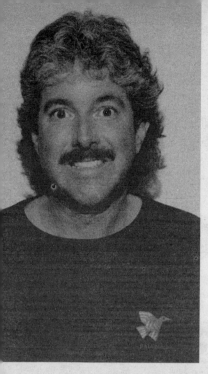

Mail carrier Mark Hilbun, 38, was the subject of a county-wide manhunt after murdering several people on May 6, 1993.

Hilbun slit the throat of Golden, his mother's spaniel, so the dog would not warn her he was in the house.

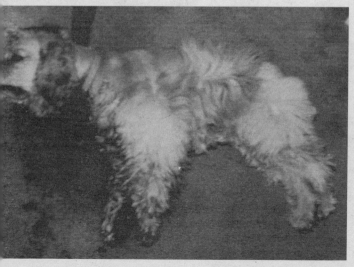

After waking his mother, Hilbun repeatedly plunged a knife into her so that she wouldn't have to face the destruction of mankind he believed would happen on Mother's Day.

The mail sorting station where Hilbun shot and killed his friend and coworker Charles Barbagallo.

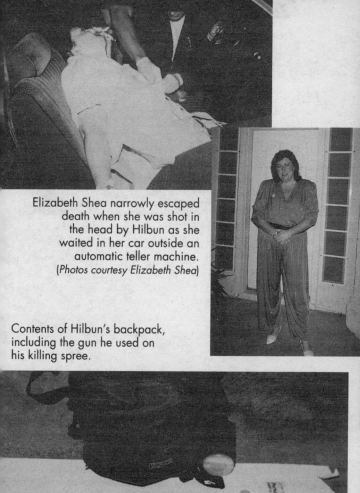

Elizabeth Shea narrowly escaped death when she was shot in the head by Hilbun as she waited in her car outside an automatic teller machine. (*Photos courtesy Elizabeth Shea*)

Contents of Hilbun's backpack, including the gun he used on his killing spree.

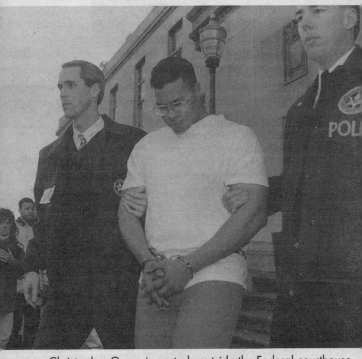

Christopher Green in custody outside the Federal courthouse in Newark, New Jersey. A former postal employee, Green was convicted of having shot two coworkers and two customers while robbing the post office on March 21, 1995. *(Photo courtesy AP/Wide World Photos)*

Congressman John McHugh, chairman of the House of Representatives Subcommittee on Postal Service. He is currently working with the USPS to make changes in the workplace.
(Photo courtesy John McHugh)

Congressman William L. Clay was the chairman of the House of Representatives Committee on Post Office and Civil Service. He headed up an investigation after the tragedy in Royal Oak, Michigan.
(Photo courtesy William L. Clay)

Dean Brewer, president of American Postal Workers Union, Oklahoma City Area.
(Photo courtesy Dean Brewer)

Don Landis, president of the Oklahoma City branch of the National Association of Letter Carriers.
(Photo courtesy Don Landis)

Ed Dunne, president of the
Escondido, California
National Association of Letter
Carriers, Branch 2525.
(Photo courtesy Ed Dunne)

(Right to left) Art Hunter,
president, and Charlie
Williams, executive
vice president, of Garden
Grove, California National
Association of Letter Carriers,
Branch 1100. (Photo courtesy
Art Hunter and Charlie Williams)

Orange County, California
Sheriff's Investigator Mike
Wallace heard Mark Hilbun's
bizarre confession.
(Author collection)

Deputy District Attorney
Christopher Evans
prosecuted Mark Hilbun.
(Author collection)

Chapter 16

Executed With a Samurai Sword

Ridgewood, New Jersey
October 10, 1991

A dark secret troubled Joseph M. Harris. He had carried it in the recesses of his tortured mind for nearly two years, unable to share it with anyone. Perhaps it caused the odd behavior noticed by coworkers on his job at the Ridgewood, New Jersey post office, where he sorted mail on the night shift. They whispered among themselves about his brooding, sullen behavior and his short temper. A maintenance worker who often brushed by Harris described him as "rebellious." Harris refused to associate with any of them and always seemed tense, close to the breaking point.

Carol Ott, the night-shift supervisor, gritted her teeth and suppressed the urge to tell Harris just what she thought of him. Sick of the man, his work performance, and his stubborn resistance to her directions, Ott had reached the end of her patience. As hard as she tried, Ott couldn't avoid letting the conflict with Harris bother her, and even took it home to discuss with her 36-year-old live-in boyfriend, Cornelius Kasten, Jr. Ott sometimes wondered if the three years Harris had served in the Navy had caused him to resent working under the supervision of a woman, especially one who was five years his junior. At 35, Harris should have matured enough to shed such attitudes, she thought, but some people never grow up. The friction between Ott and Harris didn't go unnoticed among the work force, either. One of the employees described the ongoing trouble in clear terms. "They were like oil and water. They just didn't mix. He just had something against her."

Whatever it was that Harris had against Ott, she decided he had carried it beyond acceptable bounds. His verbal abuse and threats to harm her had gone too far. On a frigid morning in February 1990, Ott marched into the Ridgewood Police Department and filled out a report. In it, she simply stated that Harris had been harassing her on the job. She declined to give any specific details about his abuse. Asked if it was of a sexual nature, she shook her head in the negative. The officer in charge inquired about Ott's wishes to file a formal criminal complaint against Harris. Ott thought about it for a few moments, mentioned the possibility of obtaining the services of a lawyer, then fell silent again. The threats by Harris had, after all, been verbal and had never resulted in any physical contact. Finally, Ott stood and said, "I don't want to do that." She thanked the officer for his patience, donned her coat, and left the police station.

Within a few days, Ott took the first step toward an administrative solution of the problem with Harris. USPS policy allowed a supervisor to set in motion procedures to require an employee to submit to physical or psychological examinations for the purpose of measuring ability to perform their job duties. Ott called Harris into her office and requested that he make an appointment with a doctor and undergo a battery of examinations that would determine his fitness for duty.

Harris glared at Ott in fury. His fists clenched and his jaw tightened. He unequivocally refused to go to any doctor. He'd been performing his job for nine years, he said, and could continue to do so without any examinations. "I'll get you," he growled as he stood to his full height, 6 feet two inches, with every muscle in his 175-pound body tensed, and stalked out of her office.

The outright refusal gave Ott the ammunition she needed. She immediately initiated the steps to fire Harris. He was terminated in April 1990.

When informed that he'd been dismissed, Joe Harris, an African-American, became convinced that the underlying reason for his job loss was racially motivated discrimination. Yet, he chose not to seek help from the American Postal Workers Union when it was offered. The local president would later say, "Mister Harris refused the local grievance procedure. He said he would take care of things his own way."

Now, the desire for revenge had been planted, and it would be nurtured for the next 18 months.

Life had always been a struggle for Joseph Harris, from the time he was born in Trenton, in March 1956. It had been a constant scrap to survive among 10 brothers and sisters, even though he was the second oldest. After the family moved north to Paterson, he strained to manage passing grades at John F. Kennedy High School. His photo in the 1975 yearbook was accompanied by notations that he participated in boxing, karate, and the rifle club. A commentary noted that Harris "despises people who talk too much. Hopes to be wealthy and happy."

Immediately after high school, Harris joined the Navy where he learned to repair mechanical and electrical equipment. After mustering out in 1977, he struggled to find a career which would utilize his skills. Unsuccessful, he finally landed a job sorting mail with the USPS in 1981. Fellow employees found him strangely quiet and uncommunicative. The only time he spoke, it seemed, was to criticize one of them or to offer some rude comment. He received a supervisory reprimand in 1984 for harassing coworkers.

That same year, Harris became involved in a transaction that would have tragic results. Somehow, he'd managed to acquire a considerable nest egg of cash. He spoke about it to a coin dealer, Roy Edwards, in Montville, west of Paterson where Harris lived. Following the conversation, Harris made the decision to invest $10,000 with Edwards. It looked like a sound way to earn handsome returns on his money without sinking it into the risky stock market or tying it up in a conservative interest bearing account which would produce minimal income.

Unfortunately, his plans didn't work out the way he expected. The big profits never developed. Instead, Harris received not one cent of return on his money over the next few years. Then, disaster struck—Roy Edward's company went bankrupt.

Livid with fury, Harris confronted the man and demanded full restitution. But Edwards claimed he was flat broke and couldn't refund any of it.

Harris found an immediate solution. His actions would haunt him for years.

Two years after the end of his investment trauma, Carol Ott fired Harris. The loss of his job at the post office continued to eat away at Harris's psyche. Months slipped by and his anger grew. He'd sit alone for hours in his tiny second floor apartment on the east side of Paterson, fuming and thinking of vengeance. Remaining unemployed, he eked out a living by any means he could. Never married, Harris spent most of his time as a loner, but now and then interrupted his solitude by hanging out with a male cousin who was close to his age. The relative observed some of Harris's disturbing interests. "[Joe] was always fascinated with martial arts. He was always fascinated with explosives. He always liked guns, but he never hurt anyone. . . ." Those habits, the cousin said, dated back to Harris's high school days.

Despite having no identifiable source of income, Harris managed to acquire the ingredients for a bomb, including explosives and an ether-based can of automobile starting fluid, along with a 9 millimeter Uzi semiautomatic, a .22-caliber pistol equipped with a silencer, and several hand grenades. The weapons were supplemented by a gas mask and a bulletproof vest. He even collected apparel to match his arsenal, assembling a uniform of black combat boots, black military camouflage clothing, and a black silk Ninja-style hood to mask his face. The whole outfit was set off by a menacing samurai sword three feet long.

On the night of Wednesday, October 9, 1991, while the nation watched or read news about confirmation hearings for

Supreme Court nominee Clarence Thomas and the statements of a woman charging that he had sexually harassed her, Joseph Harris reached a culminating point with his inner turmoil. A woman in power had ended his career, much like the threat against Clarence Thomas. He would have his revenge.

Harris sat in his apartment scrawling a two-page letter, addressed to no one in particular, in which he complained about USPS authorities and bitterly described the "unfair treatment" to which he'd been subjected. He wrote of his need for vengeance. Someone had to pay. Harris also wrote about the massacre in the Edmond post office three years earlier. Patrick Henry Sherrill had settled the score there. Now Joseph Harris would find his revenge.

Leaving the letter on a table, Harris donned his uniform, and bundled up his weapons along with plenty of ammunition. Before stepping out of the apartment, he rigged a bomb to his front door, set to explode if anyone tried to enter. He drove west to Wayne, about ten miles away, where he had no trouble locating the beige split-level house he'd scouted previously.

With the sword strapped to his side, and the .22-caliber handgun holstered, Harris quietly picked the lock and slipped inside. Seeing no one, but hearing some muffled sounds from downstairs, he descended to a basement recreation room. In the dim glow of a flickering television set, he could see a man asleep in an armchair. Padding softly and slowly to a position behind the chair, Harris eased the pistol to the ready position, aimed it at the back of the sleeper's head, and fired once. Cornelius Kasten slumped forward, lifeless, with blood oozing from a wound behind his right ear.

Harris glanced around the room. His primary target wasn't there. He crept back up to the entry and moved silently up the carpeted stairs.

Carol Ott stirred from a deep sleep and suddenly snapped awake in horror as Harris entered her bedroom. Terrified, her eyes grew wide as she saw him pointing the weapon within a foot of her face. Clad only in a T-shirt, she clutched the covers to her chest just as Harris pulled the trigger. The gun misfired. Frightened and whimpering, Ott begged Harris not to shoot again, but he continued to squeeze the trigger. The gun failed to fire two more times.

In a fit of furious disregard for the woman's pleas, Harris pocketed the handgun, drew the samurai sword, and swung it in a wide arc. It struck Ott on the left shoulder, opening a gaping wound. He struck again, and again, slashing at his victim. Then, Harris wielded the deadly blade in both hands, and drove it forward like a spear. The stab wounds drained the life from Carol Ott.

Revenge against the supervisor who had fired him did not satisfy Harris. He hurried from the bloody scene and drove to Ridgewood.

At 2:15 A.M., a truck driver from Paterson carrying a load of mail to be sorted and delivered, rolled to a stop at the rear loading dock of the post office on Ridgewood Avenue near Maple. Something seemed wrong to him. The whole place was dark. Normally lit up for the night shift, the change caused the hairs on his neck to bristle. The driver, although feeling nervous, got out of his truck and entered the building at the basement level. From out of the dark a black-clad figure emerged and fired a shot in the driver's direction. Adrenalin took over and he raced back to his idling truck. Within moments he braked in front of the local police station.

Two uniformed officers arrived at the blacked-out post office by 2:20 A.M. Sergeant Robert Kay, accompanied by Officer Pete Tuchol, cautiously moved into the back entry, calling out for the intruder. Once again, the shadowy figure stepped forward. This time he lobbed a hand grenade toward the two cops. They scrambled away in time to avoid injury. Moments later the surrounding area swarmed with emergency vehicles, blue-and-red lights pushing back the predawn gloom. Officers prevented arriving postal workers from entering the building.

Attempts by the police to contact the black-clad intruder by telephone failed. For nearly three hours, until the sun appeared over the eastern horizon, continued attempts to establish communications with him failed. Shortly after 6:00 A.M., SWAT team negotiators entered the building through a side door.

Inside, at last, the armed man responded to officers' appeals to talk to them. Joseph Harris insisted on several conditions before he would surrender. First, he wanted to be able to wear his Ninja mask when they brought him out. He also insisted that the toilet in the jail cell where he'd be kept be equipped with a seat. Twenty minutes later, they brought Harris out.

Inside, a search revealed more tragedy. In one of the women's restrooms, they found the bodies of two postal workers who'd been on duty, waiting to unload mail trucks, when Harris invaded the building sometime after midnight. He'd herded Johannes VanderPaauw, 63, and Donald McNaught, 59, into the restroom, forced them to lie facedown on the floor, and coldbloodedly executed them with gunshots to their heads.

A bomb squad searched the entire post office building before workers could be allowed inside. Another team went to the apartment where Harris lived and disarmed the booby trap he'd planted. They found the two-page document he'd written, along with a letter penned three years earlier to coin dealer Roy Edwards. In it, he advised Edwards that if he, Harris, ever died in combat, that he might return as a ghost.

The letter to Edwards hadn't been mailed for a very good reason. The coin dealer, whose business had collapsed costing Harris $10,000, had been murdered three years before, in 1988. Apparently, Harris had settled the score with Edwards for losing his $10,000 investment. The letter would provide evidence linking Harris to Edwards' death.

That same morning, family members discovered the bodies of Carol Ott and Cornelius Kasten. It didn't take long to connect Joseph Harris to the savage murders.

After officers jailed the suspected killer, a judge charged him with four counts of homicide and imposed bail of one million dollars. Harris would also stand trial for killing Roy Edwards.

Anxious to keep the mail moving, just as they had done in Edmond, Oklahoma, a few years earlier, USPS officials hurriedly had the blood mopped up and reopened the workplace. In a questionable show of sensitivity, they taped a handprinted note to the front door.

"Thank you for your condolences. In this difficult time,
Please do not ask the window clerks any questions regarding
the events of yesterday. Thank You."

There was no signature, no expression of sorrow over the
terrible loss of the employees. Outraged postal workers who
had known Joseph Harris spoke of him with sharp criticism.
"He was a troublemaker," proclaimed a veteran custodian.
Another worker said, "They extended themselves to help him.
He didn't want it. He resented authority." Officials from headquarters refused to discuss the case with reporters. A spokesperson did say that Harris had rejected the orders to take fitness
examinations in early 1990 because he felt he was the object
of racial discrimination.

As usual, justice moved at its slow pace. It would take nearly
five years for Joseph Harris to face a trial for his grisly crimes.

A jury in Hackensack, New Jersey found him guilty on four
counts of murder, but they were dismissed before they could
begin deliberations to recommend a penalty. Harris had sent a
note to the judge complaining about the racial imbalance of
the jury, demanding more African Americans. A second jury
was impaneled to decide if Harris should die for his crimes.
When they filed back into the jury box after hearing all the
evidence, they astonished court officers and gallery observers
with their sentencing recommendations.

Yes, they said, Harris deserved the death penalty, but for
only one of the murders! The killing of Cornelius Kasten, Carol
Ott's boyfriend, had no mitigating circumstances, the jurors
said, so Harris should die by lethal injection for that murder.

For the other three slayings, they recommended terms of life
imprisonment. If lawyers and court watchers were caught off
guard by the jurors' reasoning, USPS executives must surely
have gnashed their teeth. Part of the reason Harris shouldn't be
executed for killing Carol Ott, Donald McNaught, and Johannes
VanderPaauw, the jury said, was *because the U.S. Postal Ser-*
vice should have done more to keep Harris from boiling over
into a murderous rage!

While distressed that Harris hadn't been sentenced to die

for murdering Carol Ott, one of her siblings expressed his satisfaction that Harris would go to death row to await execution. The brother, also a postal worker, made his contempt for Harris amply clear when he told a reporter, "I just can't wait for the day I can piss on his grave."

A different jury had already sent Harris to death row for killing coin dealer Roy Edwards, so little chance existed that he would ever escape the spectre of execution.

From the time Joseph Harris went on his murder rampage, it would take only five weeks for the occurrence of another outburst of deadly violence in a post office.

Chapter 17

"If I Lose, I'll Blow People Away"

Royal Oak, Michigan
November 14, 1991

The automobile manufacturing industry roared onto the American scene during the infancy of the 20th century, primarily around Detroit, Michigan. As it grew, so did trouble between management and organized labor. Friction reached flashpoint in the 1930s when oppressed employees of the burgeoning automobile plants rebelled against tyrannical management policies that sought to constantly improve production schedules. At Chrysler, 65,000 assembly-line workers went on strike. Dearborn's Henry Ford announced he would *never* recognize the United Auto Workers Union. In yet another flare up, police and hired thugs used tear gas to route harried strikers. The ebb and flow of labor wars overflowed to other industries as well, eventually seeping into the USPS.

Labor strife and turbulence was not unexpected in the industrial zones of Detroit, but somehow, such unrest didn't seem to fit in the suburb of Royal Oak. Located just a 10-minute drive from the center of Detroit, or from the shores of Lake Erie, the town had slept quietly for decades. Established as a bedroom community in 1921, Royal Oak spurted with growth in the early 1940s, then fell on hard times, becoming according to one observer, "a doughty doyen of Oakland County conservatism—a boring collection of 1940s store fronts with little to amuse a visitor." That all changed when local business owners brainstormed a way to revitalize their 11.9 square miles of historic homes and comfortable tracts housing 60,000 residents. They hit upon the idea of keeping stores open until 11:00 P.M. It worked magic. Crowds began strolling the streets at night, filling up the tables at restaurants, and patronizing newly opened shops. Eclectic assortments of colorful visitors chose to gather along Main Street and around Farmer's Market to browse the antique stores, galleries, and boutiques. Royal Oak gained a reputation of *avant garde* funkiness, a mecca for chicdom, and was dubbed the Greenwich Village of Michigan.

By contrast, over in the huge post office at 200 West Second Street, covering a full city block, trouble brewed behind the fortress-like walls. A simmering pattern of anger and friction threatened to explode among the 1,500 employees who processed over a million pieces of mail annually. In the latter half of 1991, the growing labor/management and operational problems, combined with customer service complaints, escalated all the way up to U.S. Senator Carl Levin. He launched a two-month investigation of post office operations and summarized the results in a staff memorandum dated September 10, 1991. The report documented "patterns of harassment, intimidation, cruelty, and allegations of favoritism in promotions and demotions . . . [and] testimony relating to wide-ranging delivery and service problems."

Such a hotbed of difficulty, it would seem, should have drawn immediate and vigorous corrective action by USPS executives. If they responded at all to the senator's criticisms, it apparently had no preventive effect. Another tragedy was waiting to happen.

A cold wind blew off the lakes on Thursday morning, November 14, 1991, sweeping autumn leaves along West Second Avenue and threatening rain. A furious 31-year-old man parked his Jeep Wrangler in the adjacent lot, lifted out his semiautomatic .22-caliber carbine rifle, which had the barrel sawed short, and headed for the entrance. His flat-nosed boxer's face twisted in fury, he marched into the post office Management Section Center (MSC) bent on revenge. He'd been fired from his job as a letter carrier over a year earlier, and had anxiously awaited the outcome of grievance and arbitration procedures, hoping to be reinstated. When he learned that he had lost the arbitration, Thomas Paul McIlvane decided to make good his threats.

Other employees had heard McIlvane make increasingly frequent references to the 1986 massacre at Edmond, Oklahoma. If he didn't get his job back, he growled, he'd "make Edmond look like a tea party." He certainly appeared tough enough to back up his threats. Standing 5 feet 11 inches, a solid 175 pounds, he moved with the grace and power of an athlete, and was an accomplished kick-boxer. He kept his black hair no more than a couple of inches long, matched by a trim beard outlining his square jaws and a mustache protruding from his upper lip. A flattened, broken nose punctuated his menacing look.

Like two of his hell-bent-for-killing predecessors, Patrick Henry Sherrill and John Merlin Taylor, McIlvane had served in the U.S. Marine Corps. His own father, Richard McIlvane, had been a tough, chain-smoking marine. The younger McIlvane, after enlisting in January 1979, took basic training at Perris Island, North Carolina, a swampy military base famous for turning out hardened young leathernecks. He qualified as an expert with the M-16 rifle and as a marksman with the .45-caliber pistol. In June, the Marine Corps transferred McIlvane to a tank battalion with the 3rd Marine Division in the desert at Twenty-Nine Palms, California. Twelve months later, McIlvane violated the Uniform Code of Military Justice and carved the first notch in his long history of transgressions against authority. A naval petty officer spoke to McIlvane in a manner that ignited his short-fused temper and the marine shot back with, "Fuck you." It cost McIlvane $100, restriction to the "B" Company area, and 14 days of extra duty.

A few months later, on September 16th, a young lieutenant chewed McIlvane out for "nonmilitary performance in company formation." Once again, his temper flared. He said, "I'm not going to argue one bit because I don't give a shit." The company commander ordered 14 days of extra duty and restriction, which he generously suspended, but deducted $138 from McIlvane's pay.

If the leniency was aimed at teaching Lance Corporal Thomas McIlvane to keep his mouth shut, it failed. Only eight weeks passed before he found himself facing a special court-martial on six charges of disrespect to a superior officer and failing to comply with orders. When a lieutenant commanded McIlvane to take his hands out of his pockets, button his jacket, cover his head, and stand at attention, the rebellious leatherneck barked, "Fuck off, you fucking asshole." Found guilty on three of the more serious charges, McIlvane lost his Lance Corporal stripes, gave up three months pay, $690, and served time in the Camp Pendleton brig from January 21st until April 5, 1982.

Chastened, McIlvane managed to stay out of trouble until the following January, at which time his commander charged him with careless driving, in a manner of speaking. Apparently McIlvane decided it would be a good idea to drive an M-60 tank over a car, crushing it like an empty beer can. The exact charge stated, "Willfully operating an M-60 tank in an improper and unsafe manner, crushing an unattended automobile that was intended to be a fire department training aid." He also destroyed the asphalt pad upon which the car was parked. His stunt cost him one month's pay, $114, and another two weeks of restriction with extra duty.

The Marine Corps decided Thomas McIlvane might fare better as a civilian. On April 12, 1983, he received a discharge termed "general under honorable conditions" along with "RE-4" reenlistment code, which would bar him from being accepted into the Marine Corps again, or from joining a military reserve unit. McIlvane's permanent file contained a reference to a psychological evaluation he'd undergone, which noted a tendency toward violent behavior involving cursing and threatening when crossed. But he had subsequently been found qualified to perform ''all the duties of his rank at sea, on land, and in foreign service.'' Officially, his separation from the Marine Corps was related to his misconduct, not a mental or emotional disorder.

Within three months of his discharge, Thomas McIlvane applied for employment at the Royal Oak USPS office. The following year, in March, he took a postal service physical examination which revealed problems from a previous knee injury. For that reason, he was informed by letter of his medical unsuitability to become a letter carrier, and that his name had been removed from the active register of eligibles. McIlvane submitted a written appeal containing a personal physician's opinion that he could climb stairs and walk eight or more miles per day. A USPS regional medical director ''evaluated'' the appeal and reversed the original decision not to hire McIlvane. In November 1984, he began his postal career, initially as a casual distribution clerk. In a short time, he became a mail carrier.

Postal employees are placed on a probationary period during which supervisors have broad powers to terminate them. After that, the procedure becomes more difficult. McIlvane skated through his probation with no reported problems, completing it on April 4, 1985. Two months later, he was involved in a preventable automobile accident after failing to yield the right of way. It was the first entry in a slim folder that would soon fill a file drawer. Letters of warning began to pile up documenting repeated failures to follow instruction, tardiness, misdeliveries of mail, and violations of mail security.

He eventually reverted to his habit of expressing anger at colleagues and bosses with volleys of crude obscenities. In May 1988, McIlvane and a coworker crossed swords in the post office workroom. A supervisor approached and asked McIlvane to leave quietly. Instead, he yelled, ''Go fuck yourself. I'm tired of being fucked with.'' The director of field operations overheard, approached and found himself the recipient of Mc-

Ilvane's wrath, expressed with his favorite word. "Fuck you, man. Don't fuck with me."

For "failing to maintain the requirements of the position," which meant "not to be obnoxious or offensive to other persons or to create unpleasant working conditions," the managers levied a one-week suspension against McIlvane.

Off the job, McIlvane usually lived alone in a two-story house on Majestic Street in Oak Park, directly south of Royal Oak, not far from where he had grown up. His mother had deserted the family while McIlvane and his brothers were children, and his ex-marine father had passed away.

After he worked for the USPS nearly three years, McIlvane bought the brick home which was located about three miles from the post office. The house had been seized from an arrested drug dealer the previous year and put on the auction block. McIlvane paid $35,700 for it. To help pay the mortgage, he rented out spare bedrooms, sometimes having two male tenants. The few people who ever had social contact with McIlvane noted that he kept the place immaculate, but sparsely furnished. "He was always doing things to fix up the house," said an acquaintance. McIlvane showed no interest in acquiring personal possessions or additional clothing, choosing instead to wear the same outfits until they were no longer usable. Besides practicing kick-boxing, McIlvane's only other noticeable recreational activities were bicycling and jogging at Kensington Metropolitan Park, or lying on a lakeside beach.

McIlvane's nightlife appeared to be as dull as his hours at home. When he would venture out, it was usually to a local bar, always alone. A 21-year-old man who later rented a room from McIlvane saw him only once with a woman, who was married. He had picked her up in a bar and brought her home for the night. The housemate thought the woman was also a postal employee.

According to the roommate, McIlvane had trouble relating to or communicating with women, which seemed to cause him a great deal of personal stress. Although McIlvane had the appearance and temper of a tough guy, he surprised the roommate by demonstrating remarkable reading skills. Once, the man said, he brought home a couple of textbooks from night school about police science. McIlvane read both of them, cover-to-cover, in two days. Also surprising was McIlvane's interest in theology. He enrolled in a Bible study class at Oakland Community College.

Principles of religion had no effect, though, in reducing the trouble McIlvane caused for himself on the job. Near the end of March 1989, a female supervisor checking up on her subordinates couldn't find McIlvane on his route. When she finally located him, she asked, "Tom, where have you been?"

With a perturbed sneer, he replied, "I was at the Nip-N-Tuck restaurant on 11 Mile [Road]." He admitted eating lunch at a restaurant outside his assigned area.

The supervisor arranged for the issuance of a warning letter for the infraction, citing a rule which states, "Do not deviate from your route for meals or other purposes unless authorized by a manager." McIlvane refused to sign it. At the end of his shift that day, as he left the workroom area, McIlvane walked past the woman and muttered, "Fucking whore."

The next day, he barged into the personnel office, asked to look at his file, and in the presence of another female supervisor, turned to the warning letter. He reached for his pen and scrawled something on the document. When she examined it, she saw he had inscribed on it in large capital letters the words, "FUCK OFF."

A motorist made the mistake of getting too close to McIlvane's mail delivery van in late April. In the civilian's report to the police, he said that as he drove behind the postal van, it moved into the left lane. The motorist pulled right to make a turn, when suddenly the van made a big sweeping right turn from the left during which the van driver shouted obscenities. After halting, the motorist said, he approached the driver, who yelled, "You punks are all the same, trying to cut me off." With that, the postal employee pushed the motorist to the ground, saying, "I ought to knock your fucking teeth down your throat." According to the motorist, he escaped and drove away, with the van in hot pursuit. They finally went separate ways.

In addition to reporting it to the police, the outraged motorist also told the Royal Oak postmaster.

A postal inspector twice attempted to telephone McIlvane to arrange an interview, but was cut off by hangs ups. When McIlvane finally did answer, as the inspector reported, he said, "Sure, you can come out now, but you'd better have your facts straight when you come out here pal, or I'll knock your fucking head off." The inspector, accompanied by a colleague, drove to McIlvane's home, but couldn't raise anyone.

McIlvane's version of the altercation differed considerably. He said that while making a right turn, the motorist's car had squeezed between him and the curb, nearly striking his van. The two men got out of their cars, and the man grabbed McIlvane's shirt. "I displaced his hand at which point he fell to the ground," McIlvane wrote.

The postal inspector doubted his story, but when McIlvane produced a woman who had witnessed the altercation, some doubt was cast on the motorist's version. She said, "The kid was not knocked to the ground," and when he left, "the kid burnt rubber and ran the next stop sign."

Despite the witness, postal authorities decided to suspend McIlvane for "conduct unbecoming a postal employee." They wrote, "You are hereby notified that you have been placed in an off-duty [without pay] status effective April 21, 1989, and continue in this status until you are advised otherwise." Later, they converted the indefinite period to a seven-day suspension and changed the reason for the punishment. Now, the supervisor said, McIlvane was being suspended for his alleged threat to the postal inspector.

Because the issue became somewhat clouded by the witness's report, which mitigated McIlvane's behavior, he appealed for help from the letter carriers's union. They presented a grievance that reached a settlement in which management agreed to remove the letter of warning providing McIlvane could stay out of trouble for three months. He met his part of the bargain.

In the fall, McIlvane applied for, and received a permit to carry a concealed weapon. Approved by the director of Oak Park Public Safety, the three-year permit was restricted to hunt-

ing and target practice. Within a month, McIlvane purchased
a 30/300/20 gauge over/under rifle-shotgun, which often mal-
functioned, requiring him to return it more than once to the
manufacturer for repair. He also owned a .357 magnum, but
sold it to a friend. McIlvane's third gun was a .22-caliber rifle
he kept hanging on his bedpost, by the sling, usually loaded.
He'd sawed off nearly a foot of the barrel, which made the
weapon illegal.

As 1989 wound down to a close, Thomas McIlvane's troubles
spiraled upward. The supervisors at work had him under a
microscope. They watched each step he took, and documented
everything, in remarkable detail. His slightest bending of any
rule wound up in the rapidly expanding file. Three days after
Christmas, his boss handed him a letter notifying him of a 14-
day suspension for a myriad of violations, neatly categorized.
Under the heading "Safety Violations," McIlvane was cited
for failing to clear ice from the right-side window of his vehicle,
making it "unsafe to drive," for leaving his engine running
while he used the restroom for two minutes, and for doing 31
to 35 miles per hour where the speed limit was 30. Under
"Work Performance," they nailed him for wasting time by
stopping to put 2.6 gallons of gas in his tank, for dividing a
section of his delivery route into 3 loops instead of one, for
engaging a secretary in "unnecessary conversation," and for
arranging a stack of mail in delivery sequence after he'd already
done it once. Also, management had reduced the size of Mc-
Ilvane's route by dropping a segment which they said should
shorten his delivery time by 25 minutes. McIlvane, the bosses
wrote, not only failed to complete his load in shorter time, but
used an extra hour to complete his route that day.

While waiting out the suspension, McIlvane wrote to the
U.S. Marine Corps asking them to change the RE-4 reenlistment
code he'd been assigned which prevented his serving in the
reserves. In January 1990, he received notification denying the
request.

McIlvane returned to work, only to be slammed again with
notice that his next pay increase would be withheld due to
"poor work performance."

On March 8th supervisors accused McIlvane of engaging in unsafe horseplay by riding a mail hamper down the dock ramp. Later that same day two supervisors followed him on his delivery route. Seated in their car at a convenience store parking lot, they beckoned McIlvane and confronted him for stopping to buy a bottle of root beer and a sandwich. He had taken five whole minutes, they said, to drink and eat. McIlvane's temper flared. He leaned into the car and jammed the empty bottle between the legs of one of them. With jaw muscles twitching and eyes sparking, he jumped into his van, jammed it into reverse, and accelerated backwards toward the supervisors's vehicle, screeching to a halt within inches of a collision. Then he sped out of the lot. The outraged bosses followed, one of them scribbling notes that McIlvane continued to drive in an unsafe manner. They put a halt to his deliveries, demanded the keys to his van, and ordered him to ride back with them.

The conflict rapidly deteriorated to a childish level. McIlvane pouted and refused to buckle his seat belt, while a supervisor headed for a phone to call police for assistance in forcing him to buckle up. With the belt snapped in place, en route back to the post office, the two bosses accused McIlvane of trying to shift the car into reverse while traveling 30 miles per hour. And upon entering the building, they were sure that he tried to slam a glass door in their faces.

A three-page letter, dated April 11th, detailed the almost comical fracas. But the purpose of the document wasn't very funny. It informed McIlvane that he was fired.

The cooler heads at the letter carriers's union prevailed, and through the grievance procedure they negotiated a 30-day suspension instead of termination. McIlvane's job was saved, but he was put on notice that his misbehavior would no longer be tolerated.

Meanwhile, as McIlvane and his supervisors waged war, two personnel moves at upper level management took place. A new postmaster, who'd been temporarily transferred from Indianapolis was made permanent in Royal Oak. He immediately brought in some of his own people from Indianapolis, including Christopher Carlisle as the new Branch Operations Manager. A groundswell of grumbling among locally passed-over managers exacerbated an already high level of tensions in the Royal Oak facility.

Given a new lease on his job, one more chance, McIlvane couldn't seem to avoid doom. The new manager, Carlisle, held an impromptu operational meeting for all mail carriers on July 8th. The briefing session delayed all of the carriers, necessitating each of them to fill out a PS Form 3996 to request overtime assistance. According to management, McIlvane didn't submit his form in a timely manner, so they relieved him of duty again and placed him on administrative leave for "failure to follow instructions." He vehemently argued that he'd placed his form on the supervisor's desk at the same time as the other carriers. A few of the other forms, he stated, actually landed on the desk after his, but none of those tardy individuals received punishment. Nevertheless, McIlvane remained on suspension from July 18th to July 30th.

During his time off from working at a part-time job he had landed, McIlvane vented his feelings to his housemate about the problems at the post office. The tenant recalled that McIlvane felt intimidated by his coworkers. But McIlvane, he said, was not the "type of guy you'd want to mess with." And, the tipster said, McIlvane was certain that Christopher Carlisle was "gunning for him." Not a healthy situation, because if McIlvane felt you had "wronged him, he would screw you back." According to the tenant, McIlvane felt that certain people were against him, that there was a conspiracy involved, and that his enemies wanted to ruin him financially.

In the post office, though, at least one person went to bat for McIlvane. His supervisor, Doris Hazard, apparently felt he deserved some reconsideration regarding the suspension, so on July 30th, she recommended that McIlvane be reinstated. "I didn't want him to lose his job," she explained, "only for him to follow instructions." Carlisle approved her appeal.

Anxious to notify McIlvane, Hazard telephoned his home. She got a busy signal, which continued "for a very long time." Hazard's shift would end at 3:00 P.M., and she wanted to give

McIlvane the good news before she went home. So she asked
the operator to interrupt.

According to Hazard's version of the ensuing conversation,
McIlvane cut her off as soon as he heard her voice. His voice
growling with fury, he said, "All right, cunt, what do you
want? Who do you think you are interrupting my phone call,
you stupid bitch?"

Trying to be patient, Hazard said, "Tom, I'm not scared of
you, and what are you trying to prove? I want you to calm
down and be quiet. I want to tell you something."

McIlvane snapped back, "You're just like the rest, a fuckin'
cunt, an asshole."

Straining to hold her own temper, Hazard said, "You'd better
shut up and listen to what I have to say!"

She apparently caught his attention. He started laughing and
said, "Okay, bitch, what do you want?"

"Unless you stop speaking to me this way, I'm not talking
to you at all."

A few moments of silence eased the red-hot anger. McIvane
mumbled, "Sorry." Hazard told him that she'd been trying
hard to work in his behalf, and announced what she thought
would be welcome news, that she wanted him to report back
to work the next morning.

His answer stunned her. "Fuck you. I've got to go to work
at four o'clock [to a part-time job]. You can get hold of my
lawyer. You're nothing but a fucking whore." With that, he
hung up. When Hazard recradled her phone, she felt herself
shaking. She'd never had anyone speak to her in such a vile
manner. And she felt a strong sense of fear.

No more than a few moments had passed before another
supervisor received a call from McIlvane, who demanded, "Let
me talk to that fuckin' Carlisle asshole." When Carlisle picked
up the extension, he later said he heard McIlvane's voice.
"Listen up, you asshole. Here's my attorney's phone number.
You can fuckin' call him because I'm not coming in there."

In Carlisle's documented version of the incident, he wrote,
"I tried to tell Mr. McIlvane I didn't want his lawyer's phone
number. He then stated, 'Listen, you fucking asshole, I'm com-

ing in there Friday to get my check and to see my steward.' I then tried to instruct Mr. McIlvane to report to work, when he started shouting into the phone, 'Fuck you, you fucking dick asshole,' and hung up.''

A ''notice of removal'' letter was issued a few days later, telling McIlvane that he was fired. The decision, they informed him, had been made based on his verbal assault and use of ''crude, offensive, vulgar language which you directed at your supervisors and manager.''

That wasn't the way it happened at all, countered Thomas McIlvane. In the filing for a subsequent arbitration hearing, his representative stated McIlvane's version:

> It was the grievant's testimony that on the afternoon of July 30th he was asleep prior to reporting for work on another job at 5:00 P.M. Some time after 2:00 P.M., he was awakened when he heard his roommate's footsteps on the stairs. The roommate was extremely ''mad'' when he entered the grievant's bedroom and said that 'someone from the post office broke into his [telephone] conversation and asked him to hang up.' The grievant denied that he had received the telephone call from his supervisor on July 30 or that he had called her or the Stations and Branch Manager that afternoon. However, he did call the MSC director at the Royal Oak post office because he ''wanted to know why a supervisor had called.'' According to the grievant, the Director said he would ''check into it and get back to me,'' but he did not do so.

From the time of the formal termination, until the final settlement of the arbitration, over 17 months would elapse, including a staggering 13 months for the processing of the arbitration. While sweating out the long wait, McIlvane took several part-time jobs, most of them for very short periods of time. After Thanksgiving 1990, he joined a manufacturing firm in Wixom and lasted there for over five months. One evening as he was leaving, McIlvane walked out with another employee and casually asked where he was going. The employee replied that he was going to night school. McIlvane asked what classes he was taking, to which the man gave flippant, sexually loaded comment. It infuriated McIlvane who snapped, "Aww, fuck you." The employee responded in kind.

When later interviewed, the coworker said he then went into his "Fred Sanford routine" and said to McIlvane, "Come on, boy, let's go outside." In the parking area, he recalled, McIlvane demonstrated lightning speed with his fists. The coworker found himself on the ground with a split lip. From then on, the two men avoided each other, until McIlvane left the firm in June.

In August, McIlvane found another job with a carpet cleaning service. He told his tenant that he hated it because it wasn't "clean work," and left in October.

The tenant stated that McIlvane had an obsession with his post office arbitration case. McIlvane, he said, expressed confidence that he would win job reinstatement plus a settlement of back pay which he planned to spend fixing up his house. "He set himself up mentally to win. He was waiting for that money. McIlvane talked over and over about his case for several months." It seemed to the tenant that McIlvane cared about nothing else.

McIlvane had no intentions of sitting quietly throughout the long wait or of being docile about it. In September, he telephoned William Kinsley, acting Director of Field Operations (DFO), identified himself as "Leonard Brown," and said, "You are the one who got me fired . . . I'm going to be watching you and I'm going to get you." Kinsley had transferred the previous month from the Royal Oak post office to the Southfield facility, eight miles west. Alarmed, Kinsley contacted the local USPS Director of Public Safety, Jerry Tobin, to file a complaint.

A few days later, supervisor Robert F. Young, who had been present when McIlvane allegedly narrowly missed ramming his van into the manager's car, and who had also transferred to Southfield, happened to be attending a meeting at the Michigan Employment Security Commission (MESC). McIlvane turned up at the office the same day to apply for unemployment compensation. When he spotted Young, he approached and said, "You might win today, but I'm going to get you."

Another executive heard of McIlvane's threats and began to wonder about his own safety. A few months earlier, Robert E. Byrne, Director of Human Resources in the Royal Oak MSC, had been one of several people urging that McIlvane undergo a psychiatric fitness review to measure his fitness for duty. Now, with associates buzzing about the potential danger McIlvane threatened, Byrne wondered if he might be a target. He sought the advice of a postal inspector who brushed him off with, "We're not a babysitting service." Perplexed by the cavalier attitude, Byrne turned to another postal inspector. Not only did he receive no satisfaction, but the inspector would later report, "Mr. Byrne could not articulate any specific threat at this time."

With growing concern, Byrne telephoned Gladys Bryer, Regional Counsel, about the possibility of obtaining a restraining order to bar McIlvane from the Royal Oak MSC. She advised Byrne that he could pursue such a possibility if he chose, but that the region would not initiate it.

No one, it appeared, wanted to take the initiative in trying to prevent McIlvane from carrying out his threats. The prevailing posture seemed to be, "It's not my problem. You deal with it. I don't want to be involved."

The National Association of Letter Carriers (NALC) union officers worked hard to amicably settle the matter. By October, the local president had taken the grievance to the highest level.

Meanwhile, DFO William Kinsley received another strange phone call in his office at the nearby Southfield post office. Someone identifying himself as "Inspector Fixall" said, "Fuck you, you faggot postmaster. I'm going to be watching you, and I'm going to get you." Fearing for his life, Kinsley complained to the Southfield Police Department, explained about the calls and reported having filed a report with postal inspectors. All the inspectors had done, Kinsley said, is to request that he "keep them advised." The Southfield Public Safety Director, Jerry Tobin, asked if the postal inspectors could be convinced to provide some protection. No, Kinsley said, because the inspectors had advised him it was a labor relations matter.

Trying to help, Tobin telephoned the Inspection Service intending to discuss the threats and to offer his help to jointly provide some protection. His call was never returned.

Kinsley figured that the most likely place McIlvane might come after him was the Southfield post office, so he immediately arranged to have a security system installed, including buzzers at the main entry and at the doors to the workroom and offices. He ordered the placement of combination locks on the loading dock gates.

By early November, McIlvane's tension over the long wait for settlement of his arbitration case sent him into spiraling fits of anger. He visited the MESC office again to renew his application for unemployment benefits. Impatient with employees across the counter, he grumbled, argued, and finally screamed at them. Red-faced with rage, he crumpled up the application form, threw it in the face of one of the clerks, and stormed out. They summoned the police and reported serious concern that McIlvane might return and injure someone. An official showed the responding officers a document describing "a history of abusive and dangerous behavior by McIlvane."

While the officer wrote his report, still on the premises, McIlvane called the MESC manager and shouted into the phone, "I'm going to come up there and kill you." When the manager quoted the threat to the police, he was advised to telephone them again if McIlvane returned.

A few miles north of Royal Oak, at the Troy post office, recently promoted Rita Ashburn supervised delivery and collection operations. She had known Thomas McIlvane for some time. On November 21st, at 3 P.M., Ashburn answered the phone, only to hear his familiar voice say, "I can't believe they promote sluts! You had better not turn your head because you'll be dead! I'm going to get you!" After she talked it over with management, Ashburn filed a police report. Her boss telephoned the postal inspectors to advise them of the threat.

McIlvane had made one threat too many. The Royal Oak Police Department asked for and received a warrant for McIlvane's arrest. He turned himself in on December 2nd, was booked, and promptly released on bond. Two months later, despite testimony from four of the threatened managers, a jury acquitted McIlvane. A union official who attended the trial watched the defendant, and later said he was struck by McIlvane's anger. In a short conversation with him, McIlvane referred to Branch Operations Manager Christopher Carlisle as a "snake of snakes."

Within hours after the trial had ended, DFO William Kinsley answered yet another call from McIlvane, who said, "I'm still watching you, you little dickhead." And a few weeks afterward, Kinsley was handed a telephone message memo from "Tom Ecles," which read, "Do you still have a faggot postmaster there? Tell him I'm still going to get him."

A steady stream of worrisome phone calls continued to plague Rita Ashburn at the Troy post office as well. In March, her boss made another appeal to the inspection service. The only response was a cold, "We're well aware of the problem."

Another manager at the Southfield post office, David Hardy, joined the growing list of employees who listened to threatening calls. On April 5th, he signed a statement describing a call from McIlvane, who didn't attempt to disguise his identity, asking Hardy to give DFO William Kinsley a message: "I will be looking forward to seeing the little faggot at arbitration. I will have fun when I get my job back [and] I will get the little faggot and you."

Doris Hazard, the supervisor who had tried to help McIlvane, heard from McIlvane at least monthly by telephone, beginning in January. In April, he called again, not bothering to identify himself. He simply said, "Hello, cunt, how are you?"

Weary and disgusted, Hazard replied, "Oh, this must be Tom McIlvane."

He said it was, and delivered another barrage of obscene, verbal abuse. Afterwards, Hazard contacted the postal inspectors to report the litany of unwelcome, threatening calls. They casually advised her to "write them down" and to mail her notes to the inspection service. Hazard complied, but unfortunately didn't keep copies. When the inspectors failed to respond to her notes, and denied ever having them on file, she was unable to prove that she had sent them. All Hazard could do was document the problems, and send letters to worried DFO William Kinsley.

In mid-April, McIlvane decided to turn the tables on managers who had been denouncing him. He marched into the Royal Oak Police Department, and lodged his own complaint, saying that he'd received two calls earlier that week from an unknown man who said, "not to do it" and "they were going to get him." Expressing grave concern and personal distress over the incidents, McIlvane told the officer that he had to do something about it, and was "contemplating homicide." He added that he owned a handgun and had obtained a permit in Oak Park.

The officer advised McIlvane to arrange for a phone tap to record any threatening calls and warned, "Don't do anything stupid."

As a courtesy, the police called William Kinsley at the Southfield post office and told him of McIlvane's report. Referring to McIlvane's endless spoken hostilities, Kinsley said he thought that McIlvane "is capable of carrying out any verbal threat." The officer, apparently cognizant of the previous failure to convict McIlvane in a trial, advised Kinsley to get a recording device for his phone.

In Southfield, the police department took it one step further. They issued a memorandum to all police personnel describing McIlvane's background, listing the threats, and requesting that all patrols be on the alert. The memo, which included a photo, warned, "Use extreme caution in that McIlvane has mentioned purchasing a handgun."

The ownership of a gun by a man who had repeatedly threatened a number of people finally came to the attention of the Oakland County Concealed Weapons Board, who had issued a permit to McIlvane in 1989. By letter, they advised him of an interim suspension of the permit. Subsequently, they revoked it.

The loss of his license to carry a weapon apparently didn't bother McIlvane. The entire focus of his existence seemed to center on the pending arbitration. Twice, witnesses heard him say, "Someone is going to pay if I lose," and "It will make Edmond, Oklahoma look like a tea party." Confident that he would win, McIlvane even dropped in at the Royal Oak MSC to submit a bid for newly adjusted carrier routes. When an employment manager sent him a letter saying his bid would be honored upon return to employment, he courteously telephoned her to offer his thanks for helping him with the procedure.

In the late summer of 1991, McIlvane's concern about the arbitration heated up. He was heard commenting that, "If I lose this thing, I'm going to go in and blow Carlisle's fucking brains out." A mail carrier on his route met McIlvane, and heard him say, "If I don't get my job back, a lot of people are going to drop. I've been thinking about it for a long time."

The carrier, perhaps trying to lighten the moment, replied with a nervous laugh, "As long as I'm not in the line of fire."

McIlvane said, "Don't worry about it."

Another acquaintance called managers to report McIlvane saying, "If I lose my arbitration, it will be a sad day for Royal Oak."

In late August, McIlvane had been off the payroll for a year, so he was notified that his health insurance coverage was terminated. He stormed into the personnel office and told an official, "If I lose my arbitration case, everyone is going to pay. You understand? Everyone." To yet another witness, he said, "If I lose, I'll make Edmond, Oklahoma look like Disneyland."

It could be argued that McIlvane's threats had lost their sting by this time due to so much repetition. Conversely, it's easy to wonder if too many people acted in a complacent manner, failing to aggressively seek a way to head off the potential disaster.

On October 10, 1991, postal employees across the nation reeled when they heard of another massacre, this one in New Jersey. Newspapers and television reporters told how Joseph Harris had donned his Ninja costume, crept into a home near Ridgewood, killed his ex-supervisor's boyfriend, slashed her to death with a sword, then murdered two mail handlers at the post office. Harris, too, had made references to the slaughter at Edmond, Oklahoma, prior to his deadly foray. If managers around Royal Oak had reason to worry before, it seemed they should be approaching a stage of panic after hearing the terrible news.

Christopher Carlisle was concerned enough to place another call to the postal inspection service and express his worry about McIlvane. He also drafted a two and one-half page letter to the inspectors, then called a meeting of supervisors to discuss the threats. Among them was Rose Proos, a 33-year-old acting supervisor who had also received a threatening call from McIlvane. According to a friend of hers, she had "laughed it off."

People who saw McIlvane in his daily routine noticed some subtle changes. He'd been eating breakfast at the same restaurant for years, usually ordering a special omelette which he doused in ketchup, and then consumed slowly while reading the local newspaper. More recently though, he had replaced the paper with a Bible.

After 15 months of delays, the arbitration hearing on McIlvane's removal finally kicked off on October 21st. Christopher Carlisle had requested the presence of a postal inspector, but none attended. During the three-week process, McIlvane was once again heard threatening, "If I lose this, I'll blow people away." An employee at the Southfield post office reported receiving a call from someone who sounded like McIlvane saying, "I'm going to kill the postmaster."

On November 8th, the arbitration panel made a final decision. Thomas McIlvane would not be reinstated. A copy of the findings was immediately sent to Christopher Carlisle, who reportedly, "knew something was going to happen." An executive suggested he temporarily relocate his office to the Madison Heights post office for safety. But Carlisle, with a weak smile, declined, saying in half-hearted jest, "I'll be the first one he'll shoot. It only hurts for a little while." Carlisle did make one more stab at obtaining help from the postal inspector, only to hear that there was nothing they could do because they didn't have enough available manpower.

From November 8th to 12th, the panelists spent considerable time discussing with each other the possibilities of violent reaction from McIlvane. Several more attempts were made to obtain protection from the postal inspectors, but each thrust was parried with apathetic inaction. During those four days, no one bothered to tell McIlvane of the arbitration outcome. Their procrastination was understandable.

On November 12th, one of the officials from the panel made a decision. He chose to ignore the usual procedure of advising the grievant by letter, and telephoned McIlvane's home. He reached an answering machine, and left a message giving him the bad news.

No one knows exactly when McIlvane learned of the disappointing outcome. His tenant said that McIlvane didn't mention it. On Wednesday, the 13th, the tenant had a few friends over for their regular weekly card game. McIlvane rarely joined the group because he didn't play cards. Late that evening, he called his tenant to the second floor and asked him to turn down the volume on the stereo. He wasn't feeling well, he said.

On the following morning, the tenant heard McIlvane leave the house at approximately 8:30 A.M.

Fifteen minutes later, McIlvane entered the Royal Oak post office through the rear dock area, carrying his sawed-off .22-caliber rifle partly concealed under his raincoat. He also brought along four 25-round banana clips of ammunition, two of them taped together.

Within seconds after he entered the building, McIlvane moved toward letter carrier Rockie McDonald, whom he knew. The colleague glanced up from his work, saw the gun, and yelled, "No, Tom! No!" McIlvane brought the barrel down and squeezed the trigger, just as McDonald dropped down behind some cases. Incredibly, McDonald survived without a scratch.

With cool deliberation, McIlvane moved on, heading directly for the office of Christopher Carlisle, the 33-year-old manager he had threatened so many times. Acting supervisors Rose Proos and letter carrier Sue Johnson stood near Carlisle's office. As soon as Johnson saw the gun-toting intruder, she snatched up the phone and called the Royal Oak Police Department.

Carlisle spotted him, too, and searched for a way to escape. First, he helped a woman squeeze through the window, then attempted to force his own larger body out the narrow opening. Too late. McIlvane opened up with a burst of gunfire. Carlisle slipped from the window and slumped to the floor. Screams filled the air in the offices. McIlvane turned the weapon toward the two women, Proos and Johnson, and pulled the trigger again. Bullets slammed into the chest of Proos and two slugs caught Johnson, one in the hip and another through her ribs into her liver.

His face a mask of determined fury, McIlvane turned and proceeded southeast between rows of carrier stations, firing as he walked. Terrified employees grabbed anything they could find to smash windows and leap out to safety. One carrier vaulted outside, then turned to pull a coworker through the broken glass. "Nobody was safe," he later reported. "I didn't think we had a chance at all."

On his trail of destruction, McIlvane found mail carrier Clark French, leveled the weapon at him, and sent a slug ripping into the victim's abdomen. Despite the bleeding wound, French managed to stagger outside. After he ran a block, he collapsed on the curb of Main Street where a woman kneeled and tried to stem the bleeding. She whispered, "I know this sounds silly, but try and relax." She worked hard to keep him conscious, afraid that if he passed out, he would never awaken.

Still on the main floor inside the post office and continuing his hunt, McIlvane walked east through the corridors, firing into administrative offices. He stopped in the doorway of the Director of Human Resources complex. Glancing right and left, he located the office of the labor relations staff, tried the door, and found it locked. Pausing there, McIlvane reloaded the rifle. While he snapped another clip into place, someone set off the fire alarm, sending a wailing howl throughout the entire building.

McIlvane kicked in the locked office door, and focused his bloodshot eyes on Keith Ciszewski, a 37-year-old labor relations specialist. The frightened man had been struggling in an attempt to squeeze through the narrow, vertical window, adjacent to one through which a woman had just escaped. She made it out, even though the drop to the pavement broke her foot.

But Ciszewski couldn't make it and twisted away from McIlvane when he saw the weapon. The gunman opened fire again, shooting Ciszewski in the back and in the head at close range, killing him instantly.

Turning north, McIlvane made his way into the finance section, forced his way into another pair of offices, and aimed the gun at the head of trembling employee Eileen Otto. She pleaded with him not to kill her. McIlvane stared at her for a moment, said, "You know who I want," lowered the gun, and left the room.

Reversing direction, McIlvane headed back toward Carlisle's office, but made a turn toward a stairwell and climbed to the second floor. He caught sight of a sign marking the Safety Director's office, entered, and turned his gaze on a man and two women: Allen Adams, who'd been temporarily assigned to the safety staff; Joal White, a 46-year-old supervisor; and Mary Benincasa, 32, an injury compensation specialist. McIlvane sprayed all three with a lethal fusillade of lead. He attempted to exit the room through another door and found it locked, whirled around and lifted the gun's muzzle toward Joal White again. As she gasped in pain from a bullet hole in her jaw, she begged him not to shoot her again. McIlvane, with a dazed expression, eased past her, left the room, and walked back toward the stairwell.

At approximately 8:47 that morning, the Royal Oak Police Department 911 board lit up. Officials would later express the belief that the caller was Proos, but she didn't give her name. The caller said, "We need a lot of ambulances at the Royal Oak post office."

"What's the problem?"

"Somebody's in there shooting everybody."

"Can you describe him?"

"His name is Tom McIlvane."

"Tom McIlvane?"

There was a pause. The dispatcher heard voices in the background, apparently in the same room as the caller. Someone cried, "Oh, my God, two people have been shot . . . Rose."

Recognizing the urgency, the dispatcher asked, "Are you

down? He can't get to you. He can't get to you now. Can you describe him?"

"No, I can't. Hurry up, I think I'm going to die."

"Okay."

That call disconnected, and while the dispatcher alerted emergency personnel, the console lit up again. A voice said, "Yes, I need somebody quick here."

The dispatcher replied, "We have everybody on the way. We got to get a description. We don't know who we're looking for."

"You've got to get half the world over here. . . ."

"We got them all on the way."

". . . 'cause this guy is outside my door. He's going to shoot me."

The dispatcher couldn't help but raise his voice. "He's at the postmaster's door. Right outside his door. Okay, we got police cars there now, okay? Are you still there?"

"Yes, I'm still here."

"Your door's locked, right?"

"Yes."

"We got cars there. We're getting a description of him now. We have officers there and fire trucks all there, okay? Just stay with me."

"He's still at my door. He's walking back and forth outside my door."

If McIlvane paced outside the postmaster's office, he must have realized, at last, that his mission of vengeance was over. He entered the stairwell. One last explosion of his weapon echoed through the building, and all fell silent, except for the moans. Then the rushed entry of police and medics. Wounded employees were scattered in various locations. Three of the shooting victims medics found were beyond help.

Christopher Carlisle died on the floor below the window through which he'd tried to escape.

Keith Cszewski, the labor relations specialist also lay dead on his office floor.

Mary Benincasa, who'd been shot in the safety director's office, had also succumbed to her wound.

The medics loaded six wounded employees, including Proos, into ambulances and whisked them away to two hospitals.

Uniformed Royal Oak police officers and plainclothes detectives deployed inside the post office to search for the killer. They found McIlvane where he had fallen, on top of his sawed-off rifle, in the northeast stairwell. His last gunshot had been aimed at his own head. When medics kneeled to examine him, they found vital life signs, and rushed him to a hospital for emergency treatment.

Shortly after midnight on the day of disaster, November 14, 1991, doctors declared McIlvane "brain dead." Six hours later, his life officially ended when they said he was "clinically dead."

Rose Proos fought for her life until the next day, but became the final victim to die from the massacre in the post office.

Three years earlier, doctors had attempted to salvage organs from postal killer John Merlin Taylor to be used in lifesaving transplants, but were unable to use them. When Thomas McIlvane expired, doctors obtained permission to test his organs for the same purpose. The tests were positive, so his heart, liver, and both kidneys were transplanted to needy patients that same day.

Chapter 18
Aftermath at Royal Oak

In the final days of November 1991, some interesting versions of Thomas McIlvane emerged when reporters interviewed relatives and people who knew him.

A man who identified himself as "a lifelong friend of the McIlvane family" said, "I've never known Tom to be bitter. I've never known Tom to be temperamental, unless you did something. If you did something to him, he'd tell you about it." The speaker added, "This is not something that's going to be swept under the rug. We're going to find out what drove Tom to this point, somehow."

In the restaurant where McIlvane always had breakfast, a cook said, "He was not somebody you would say, 'Tom's going to go off the deep end someday and start killing people'."

Nodding her head, the cafe owner added that McIlvane told her about his problems on his job. "[He] used to tell me about how they'd harass him. He'd say, 'I'd wear a pair of shorts to work, and they'd tell me the shorts were too short. I'd put the hem down, and they'd still be too short. They'd harass me to death.'"

At the post office, a coworker observed, "He was an easygoing guy when he first started working here, then the pressure got to him . . . they took his job away . . . he changed.''

An elderly neighbor, shocked over the tragic events, asked, ''Is he the one? Oh, my goodness! Now he was as nice a guy as you'd ever want to meet. I'll be darned.''

Yet another neighbor, across Majestic Street, described McIlvane as ''a very nice guy, never no trouble, and he kept the place up.''

When McIlvane had applied for a handgun permit after Oakland County revoked his license to carry a concealed weapon, his reaction contrasted sharply with his reputation as a fiery troublemaker. The official who notified him that his request had not been approved said, ''He was very calm, didn't get angry, didn't swear. He accepted what I told him, turned, and walked away.''

Perhaps the greatest contradiction could be seen in how McIlvane's treatment of USPS management contrasted with his respect of an instructor and fellow students at an Oakland Community College night class. It was a Bible study course. A classmate said she thought he was an intelligent but troubled man who was seeking some answers. The instructor, a pastor, pointed out that McIlvane was an ''A'' student who took the class very seriously.

Public perception of another man's reputation also changed after the murders. Christopher Carlisle, the first victim to die, had been characterized by some as a heartless manager who was out to get McIlvane. But a sports instructor of Carlisle's said, ''Yes, I know. I read all that stuff and I just couldn't believe it about Chris. That wasn't the man I knew. Chris was soft-spoken, a mild-mannered guy who really enjoyed jumping and bringing other people into the sport.'' The speaker referred to skydiving, and had been Carlisle's mentor. One of the new students Carlisle recently had brought with him to learn the breathtaking adventures was, ironically, one of the four victims who died, Rose Proos.

At the post office, another manager also leaped to Carlisle's defense. ''Some of the workers are trying to make him out the big bad monster and that's not the way he was at all. He was fair. Please believe this. He tried to get the best out of himself every day. . . . He wanted the best out of his people, too. He demanded eight hours work for eight hours pay. But that's fair, isn't it?''

The Postal Inspection Service, who had repeatedly ignored or turned away requests for help to deal with McIlvane's threats by claiming inadequate available staff to provide protection of the frightened managers, suddenly found all the staff they needed to post guards around the Royal Oak facility, *after the massacre.* The top local executive of the inspectors announced that the service had done what it could to prevent tragedy, short of sealing off the post office. In rationalizing earlier decisions to not offer help, he said, "This is a mail-processing facility. There are so many mail carriers coming in and so many vehicles, it's impossible to keep the back of the post office sealed." Yet, that's exactly what happened, after the killings, through the remainder of the year and into 1992.

U.S. Postmaster General Anthony Frank left Washington, D.C. and flew to Royal Oak, just as he had gone to Escondido, California following the bloody carnage inflicted by John Merlin Taylor two years earlier. Addressing an assembly to discuss complaints about poor service and low morale, he announced that he planned to review the background of every employee of the USPS, all 750,000 of them. Also, he said, a hotline would be made available soon to give every employee a place to report threats and potential danger.

But the undercurrent of tension still existed. One Royal Oak employee said, "They rode you all the time. You couldn't even use the bathroom unless it was your break. They sent a guy home for whistling. *For whistling!*" He referred to an incident in which a workroom employee had looked at a towering pile of mail, and started to whistle, *It's Beginning to Look a Lot Like Christmas.* The man was suspended for "disrupting the mail room."

From a retired postal worker came the comment, "There's no morale and it doesn't help when my supervisor said, 'morale's not in my dictionary'."

After Frank ended his speech by saying the postal service

would try to avoid dangerous situations in the future, some other government officials in Washington, D.C. decided to examine the problems.

The House of Representatives, cognizant that Senator Carl Levin had recently presented his findings of labor-management problems in Royal Oak, not long before the savage raid by McIlvane, decided to launch a full investigation by the Committee on Post Office and Civil Service. Missouri Representative William L. Clay, chairman of the committee, directed the probe.

The objective of the investigation, as stated in official documents, "was to determine as best it could what happened on November 14, 1991, and the days and month leading up to that tragic day, and to identify any changes in practice that any of the participants could implement to reduce the likelihood of a recurrence." The optimistic attitude continued by saying, "This tragedy, like every other, has lessons to be learned and not to be ignored. It is the committee's hope that the postal service, its employees, and employees' representatives will profit from any lessons learned."

With those noble goals, the committee launched into a series of visits, examinations of documents, and interviews through December and into February. Bolstered by help from the FBI and Secret Service, they scrutinized operations, attitudes, and policies. Noting that the Royal Oak incident was the ninth in a series of "violent happenings involving present or former postal employees to occur since 1983," and that it followed by only one month the "shooting incident in Ridgewood, New Jersey," the committee criticized USPS management. It said, "In recent years the personnel management and labor relations activities in the postal service have been repeatedly reviewed by the committee. These oversight activities repeatedly revealed an autocratic management style within the postal service, a style both admitted to and regretted by Anthony M. Frank . . . Postmaster General . . ."

By the time the committee released its full report on June 15, 1992, Anthony Frank's tenure in the office had almost expired. On his departure, he revealed that he had some regrets about his inability to improve the "corporate culture" in the

USPS. Noting that the agency "seems to have a paramilitary character," Frank said that if a worker asked, "Why do I have to do that?" the answer too often given by a manager would be, "Because I told you to."

Frank expressed the hope that improvements had been made, but was concerned about too many supervisors adopting the unfortunate attitude that, "I ate dirt for twenty years, now it's your turn to eat dirt."

The final report also criticized the response by the Postal Inspection Service to requests for information. After complimenting the Royal Oak Police Department for promptly responding to a letter which asked for documents, the report noted some apparent reluctance to comply by the chief postal inspector. A letter from the committee chairman, dated December 12, 1991, requested "certain documents and records in the possession of the Postal Inspection Service." Eight days later, the chief inspector responded with a "preliminary investigative report."

In diplomatic language, the committee expressed dissatisfaction. "The chairman renewed his request for certain documents . . . and records by letter of January 31, 1992. There was not a complete response to the chairman's request. The Inspection Service did not have all the documents requested. This failure was, in part, due to improper protection of evidence at the crime scene."

Even when the Inspector's office finally submitted more information, they wanted to keep it from the public. With a tweak of petulance, the committee ". . . decided to abide by the Inspection Service's request. However, the committee believes the report should be released immediately."

The 350-page booklet was released in June 1992 by the Committee On Post Office and Civil Service, House of Representatives, titled, *A Post Office Tragedy: The Shooting at Royal Oak.* It included a section dealing with management changes and labor relations problems. Observing that many of the supervisors and managers at Royal Oak had been brought in from

Indianapolis, the committee referred to the April 1990 investigation by Senator Levin which quoted a GAO audit of the Indianapolis post office, dated April, 1990:

> *It was found by the GAO that the Postal Service's management style caused tension between it and its employees and their union. This tension was blamed for heart attacks suffered by three employees and numerous physical confrontations by supervisors. Many of these supervisors have been brought to Royal Oak by (the MSC Postmaster). The GAO report also found that in a two-year period, the Indianapolis division issued 2,700 disciplinary actions against a work force of 4,000. The materials in this package show that these patterns are taking place in this region since the arrival of (the MSC Postmaster), which was a promotion.*

Christopher Carlisle was one of the transfers from Indianapolis. Employees and supervisors at Royal Oak told committee interviewers that they were troubled by the influx of Indianapolis personnel, especially since qualified local people were passed over for promotions.

Other employees complained about the "insensitive, autocratic management style in Royal Oak." According to one union official, management became especially "authoritarian" beginning in 1990, particularly regarding employees who requested representation from their unions or assistance in pursuing collective bargaining rights. These people, he felt, were selected by management as targets for discipline and harassment.

There were allegations, the report said, that supervisors were trying to use fitness-for-duty examinations including psychiatric evaluations to retaliate against these employees. In addition, according to one supervisor, "Some supervisors purposely tried to 'set up' certain letter carriers, one of whom was McIlvane, to make examples of them."

One case was cited in which "a female carrier who was six weeks pregnant was given a letter of warning for falling down

on the cement which resulted in her losing the baby.'' A memorandum excoriated Royal Oak management, saying, ''All the
material here shows an intent on the part of the MSC management to manage through the use of threat, fear, intimidation,
demotions . . . and sometimes physical confrontation.''

Not only craft workers complained. The committee took
notice of an article written for the National Association of
Postal Supervisors (NAPS) by Jim Collins, the regional vice-
president of the organization. In it, he was highly critical of
the management style in Royal Oak. Collins wrote that he had
personally tried to talk to, or meet with, the postmaster about
a series of complaints. Several weeks after Collins had publicly
criticized an unidentified manager in the NAPS magazine, he
ran into the postmaster at a public event. The executive
''spewed forth a torrent of abusive and provocative language
toward Collins, including profanity and a challenge to 'step
outside'.''

Later, a NAPS group unanimously voted for the postmaster's
removal.

According to the committee report, there were ample advance
signals that a disaster loomed. At least 21 firsthand accounts
of threats by McIlvane were related to committee staff interviewers. ''At one point, in the spring of 1991, two local union
officials discussed their belief that McIlvane had a list of five
people he would 'get' if he lost the arbitration. . . .'' Employees
had been so alarmed, taking the threats seriously, they'd been
planning escape routes in the event McIlvane showed up. The
repeated attempts by managers to obtain help from the Postal
Inspection Service also came under close committee scrutiny.

The report stated that the Postal Inspection Service is empow-
ered to investigate postal offenses and civil matters. During
the investigation, an inspector-in-charge was queried as to the
responsibilities his office had for the protection of employees.
The executive acknowledged receiving a number of calls
requesting protection, but offered his opinion that ''inspectors
are essentially investigators and they should not be considered
a first response unit in emergency situations.'' In other words,
they were not a babysitting service. His men, he said, are

instructed to advise postal complainants to first call the local authorities. Regarding threats, he said there are no "adequate local or federal laws in this area."

Taking a different point of view, the committee report said, "Although Detroit Division Inspection Service personnel may not view employee security as a primary responsibility of the service, official postal policy guidelines and regulations suggest otherwise." It quoted the USPS policy, as stated in a manual, "The Chief Postal Inspector is designated as the Security Officer for the U.S. Postal Service."

To reinforce this opinion, the committee said, "The Inspection Service publicly touts its security work. . . ," and quoted from a semiannual USPS report:

> *Uniformed Postal Police Officers provide security at postal facilities where a combination of risk, vulnerability and history has demonstrated the need.*

> *The Postal Inspection Service has the obligation to maintain a safe work environment for employees . . . Postal Inspectors ensure the safety of postal employees through the investigation of work related threats and assaults against employees while on duty*

> *We view protection of our employees as a very important responsibility.*

Pointing an accusing finger at the Inspection Service, the committee wrote, "[They] also failed to investigate any criminal record on McIlvane once informed of his verbal threats. If such a check had been made, the inspectors would have known that the Southfield Police Department considered him potentially dangerous because he was 'contemplating homicide.' A check with the Southfield Police Department would have led them to his concealed weapons permit. A records check is standard investigative procedure at most law enforcement departments including both the FBI and Secret Service."

Taking one more poke, the committee noted, "After the

shooting, the Inspection Service sealed off areas of the Royal Oak MSC to preserve evidence. . . . However, in their search the inspectors failed to immediately examine and secure data on Carlisle's computer. Committee staff was told that the 2 ½ page letter to [an inspector] recounting McIlvane's threats most likely was saved in Carlisle's computer files. Last December and January, the computer was found being used in another area of the Royal Oak facility. Unfortunately, Carlisle's computer files could not be restored.''

Finally, the report said, the Inspector-in-Charge ''has instituted new procedures at the Detroit Division.'' The next statement raises all kinds of question marks. ''The Inspection Service chose not to inform this Committee of any specifics on the new procedures.''

Another important issue addressed by the committee was the long delay in hearing McIlvane's grievance and in completing the arbitration. They concluded, ''The grievance procedure took almost 13 months from the time a step 3 grievance was filed until McIlvane was informed of the arbitration decision. That is too long. During that year, McIlvane's anger festered. A decision on a removal when an employee is in a non-pay status should not take a year to be issued.''

The extensive report summarized its findings and listed seven recommendations:

1. The Postmaster General institute preemployment screening procedures which require investigation of previous employment if information in an application indicates a history of violence, belligerence or difficulty accepting intense supervision.

2. The Postmaster General require the Inspection Service to implement the procedures of the FBI and U.S. Secret Service for handling reported threats and to modify the performance evaluations of Inspectors so that investigations of threats is no longer discouraged.

3. The Postmaster General clarify that the role of the Inspection Service is to protect not only postal finances and the mail, but also postal employees. This could be accom-

plished, in part, by severing the audit function from the duties of the Inspection Service.

4. The Postmaster General establish procedures at all postal facilities for the handling and reporting of threats to employees and for the appointment of security control officers, and that the Postmaster General publicize the procedures.

5. The Postmaster General study the security measures at private sector warehouses and trucking facilities to prevent the entry of unauthorized personnel in the dock area and study whether the Postal Service has adequate personnel to increase security.

6. The national employee organizations should establish procedures for all locals so that threats made by members being represented in grievance proceedings will be reported in the manner established by mutual agreement with the Postal Service.

7. The Postal Service through negotiations with employee unions and organizations establish a reasonable time standard for completing a grievance arbitration proceeding on a removal (such as 6 months), and provide that, if a proceeding extends beyond that reasonable period, the removed employee should be placed in a pay status until the decision is issued.

Finally, the Committee requested that the Postal Service report within six months their responses and actions taken to implement the recommendations.

Chapter 19

"They're Getting Away With Murder"

Sacramento, California
June 3, 1992

Twelve days before the House of Representatives committee released their report on the tragedy at Royal Oak, Michigan, a California postal worker sank deeper into depression.

Sixty-year-old Roy Barnes had been working regularly at the post office of a northern suburb of Sacramento. Classified as a "limited-duty" employee due to a chronic lung condition which followed his contracting pneumonia as a letter carrier, Barnes feared the USPS wanted to get rid of him entirely. His bosses had reassigned him to full-time letter sorting, but recently had embarked on a campaign to once again change his status, this time to "light duty" which would allow them to keep him off the job if they so chose. Even if he worked, there would be no guarantee of 40 hours per week. Without the assurance of a set number of hours, he could not depend on earning the minimum income his family needed to survive. Barnes felt sure that management had singled him out as a target for forced retirement.

A coworker agreed, saying, "All the employees in our post

office are pressured to work hard, but Roy in particular was being pressured heavily by management. Roy had been injured, but the management felt his injury was not as serious as he said it was. . . . Management was always on him. They were always riding Roy, telling him to work faster, faster. It was obvious he was working with pain and doing the best he could.''

Barnes's own adult son complained that his father's employer had attempted to push him into early retirement, despite more than nine years of faithful service. Senior workers, the son said, were vulnerable and should beware of the treatment given his father. "Prepare for your older years," he warned, "because obviously the post office won't do it for you."

At the beginning of June, Barnes's supervisor handed him a form and requested him to sign it. With a sense of dread, Barnes looked over the document, a waiver giving up full-time classification and accepting limited duty. Without a word, he shoved it in his pocket.

The following day, it got worse. Barnes examined the work schedule for the following week and found that his work hours had been scratched out. Also, his designated parking spot had been reassigned to someone else. His coworkers tried to comfort Barnes, but didn't know what to say. They could see the hurt in his eyes, but heard no complaints from their soft-spoken colleague.

Shortly after lunch, Barnes returned to the post office. He stood up on the workroom floor in full view of several coworkers, pulled a .22-caliber pistol from his pocket, aimed it as his own chest, and pulled the trigger. Paramedics rushed him to a hospital where he was declared dead at 1:14 that afternoon.

Managers closed the post office for the balance of the day, but reopened it promptly the next morning.

When a coroner's investigator examined Roy Barnes, he found a bloodstained piece of paper in a pocket, upon which the deceased man had scrawled a message. He had written that he'd signed the form assigning him to light duty, but under protest. In another pocket, they found the wadded work schedule from which Barnes's next five shifts had been crossed out.

Barnes's grown daughter sobbed uncontrollably, and later

said she felt partly responsible. Earlier that spring, she had seen his sad depression after his bid for a job assignment had been denied. The daughter had wanted to help, so she contacted the USPS general manager in Sacramento and asked for a meeting to discuss the reasons her father hadn't been awarded the position. After he agreed to hear her appeal, for reasons the executive chose not to reveal, he reversed the local manager's decision and gave Barnes the slot. It appeared to be more than coincidence that Barnes suddenly found himself subjected to extreme pressures.

His grieving wife said, "Every single day my husband would come home nervous and upset over the way they were treating him. It was a daily thing and it was a lot of pressure for all of us to live under."

Bitter and angry, Barnes's heartbroken son commented, "They think that because they're an agency of the federal government, they can do whatever they want. They're getting away with murder."

A spokesperson for the Sacramento Division of the USPS said, "We're totally shocked about what happened. We don't know why it happened."

But some of Barnes's coworkers thought they knew, and pointed directly at their postmaster. Said one of the 135 workers at the facility, "This was a smooth-running post office until our new postmaster took over."

"Yeah," another chimed in, "The postmaster is lacking communication skills. Overall, [he] is a devil, and we as employees are dealing with a devil."

Several of the outspoken employees thought that Barnes hadn't been treated fairly.

The USPS spokesperson put up a defense. "Mister Barnes had not been harassed. It's absolutely not true that any employee would be singled out for harassment. I cannot substantiate those kinds of statements." Despite the postmaster's denials, he accepted management's offer to put him on administrative leave as of June 5th, two days after the stunning suicide. "It was given as part of the healing process," the media relations folks claimed.

A letter carrier expressed his sentiments, while some of his associates nodded in agreement about the postmaster's departure. "There was applause. Most people are fairly pleased that he's been placed on administrative leave. He's a mean-spirited manager and we're hoping he won't be back."

Barnes's widow put it in stronger terms, saying she was very pleased that the postmaster "was suspended." She added, "But I'm disappointed that my husband had to die to get this man out of the post office."

While a labor relations manager defended his colleague, saying that the postmaster was "just as shaken up as anybody else," the official spokesperson gave a little ground. She said a crisis intervention team had heard information that would preclude her from completely denying the existence of any problems at Citrus Heights.

It was worse than that, charged Barnes's widow. She revealed that her husband had gone to the trouble, with the help of his union representatives, to obtain a "restraining order" from upper level management to keep the postmaster off his back. But it had little effect, she said, since the postmaster "continued to harass my husband."

Roy Barnes's daughter, still feeling that somehow she had contributed to the events leading to her father's death, wanted to know more about the job conditions that caused him so much depression. She requested information from the postal investigator's inquiries, and received their usual stonewall refusal. Relying on the Freedom of Information Act, she escalated her demands to L'Enfant Plaza, the Washington, D.C. headquarters of the USPS. Weeks passed. After she made some calls, the generous executives complied with her requests for information about her father's employment by sending 51 pages, mostly photocopied clips from various newspapers. For some reason, they included an article forecasting job losses if the post office continued to lose business to competitors. The few pages of post office forms containing any information about Roy Barnes had line after line blacked out. An accompanying letter from a Postal Inspection Service executive explained in cold terms that confidentiality and privacy requirements prohibited revealing any more details.

Ostensibly, there was some slim hope expressed by postal officials who said that if the daughter could convince local managers involved in the case to authorize release of information, it would be provided. She soon found herself in an endless circle of frustration, discovering that those same local managers had apparently been ordered not to cooperate with her.

The sensitivity of postal officials was demonstrated by some additional material they sent to Barnes's widow. She hadn't been allowed to view her husband's body at the scene of his death. Sheriff's deputies had been concerned that the sight of her husband, lying in a pool of his own blood, would cause her too much grief. But postal officials, who would provide only minimal printed information, graciously included gory photos of Roy Barnes lying on the floor of the post office. "I hadn't seen those pictures," the widow cried. "I didn't know they existed, and I certainly didn't send for them. There was no warning on the envelope, and to open it up and just find them. . . . I just can't understand the insensitivity. It was terribly upsetting. I really feel that's what they intended to do—upset us like they did."

Because the USPS failed to provide any meaningful information, Mrs. Barnes turned to her late husband's union. A NALC steward collected statements from people who'd seen the progressive mistreatment of Barnes, and turned over full reports to the widow. Armed with that information, she sought an attorney to pursue a claim for worker's compensation.

Sympathizers wished her luck, hoping to see at least some good come out of the tragedy of Roy Barnes's death.

Without admitting any culpability or fault on the part of the postmaster, Sacramento Division officials announced in September that he would not be returning to Citrus Heights. The postal service gave him a new assignment as a delivery retail analyst in another community. The field operations director who ordered the change explained it. "I made this decision based on what I perceived to be the best interests of [the individual], the Citrus Heights employees, and the post office in general.'' Even better news for his former subordinates, the reassigned manager would no longer have supervisory duties.

Another manager making his exit just one month after the death of Roy Barnes came from the peak of the postal pyramid. U.S. Postmaster General Anthony M. Frank, who'd taken office on March 1, 1988, cleaned out his desk and departed on Independence Day in 1992.

The new head man, Marvin T. Runyon, hoped that the tragic string of murders would fade into history. His massacre-free period would last exactly 10 months.

Five months into his job, Runyon responded to the House of Representatives investigation of the Royal Oak tragedy. On June 15, 1992, the Committee on Post Office and Civil Service, with Missouri Representative William Clay as chairman, had requested a response within six months to its seven-point recommendation. Three days after the deadline had passed, Runyon signed a cover letter transmitting the USPS answers. Over his signature were the words, ''The Postal Service is committed to providing a safe working environment for all its employees and I appreciate your interest in helping us achieve that goal.'' Under the cover letter, eight-single spaced pages of text addressed the issues raised by the committee.

Regarding the suggestion that the USPS should do more thorough preemployment screening to identify each applicant's history of violence, belligerence or difficulty accepting supervision, the response said, ''This recommendation reflects our current policy.'' The USPS agreed, however, to do a better job in training personnel office employees and provide them with a comprehensive directory titled *The Guide to Background Investigations*.

On the matter of better security, the response recognized ''the need to enhance the training of . . . managers and supervisors relating to their responsibilities as security control officer.'' It also noted that ''the Inspection Service is finalizing a national review of security needs at postal facilities.'' One of the committee concerns was that inspectors should be trained to understand that protection of employees is one of their first duties. The response said the Inspection Service ''has always affirmed that providing a safe and secure workplace ... is one of its most important roles.'' The training for inspectors would be ''supplemented.'' All threats would be recorded in a national database.

Thomas McIlvane's arbitration had taken an ''unconscionably long'' time, and the committee suggested such intervals should be reduced to an objective of no more than six months. The USPS response agreed to ''discuss with the unions ways to improve the arbitration procedures and reduce the time it takes to get through the process.'' Improved procedures were currently ''being tested.''

The response also dealt with corollary labor-management problems, disciplinary procedures, and other related matters.

It would remain to be seen if the language of the response accurately reflected real changes to be implemented, and if those measures would have any significant effect on reducing incidents of violence in post offices by postal employees.

Chapter 20

"I've Got A Silver Bullet With Your Name On It"

Dearborn, Michigan
Thursday, May 6, 1993

Just when USPS managers thought they could finally take an easy breath after an 18-month hiatus from in-house murders, the dreadful trend slammed into them again with the force of a lightning bolt. As with lightning, the only way to avoid being struck is to use common sense and take intelligent precautions. Incredibly, the new outburst happened within 15 miles of Royal Oak, Michigan, where Thomas McIlvane had slaughtered four people before taking his own life, and where the spotlight of publicity had focused with the investigation by the House of Representatives Committee.

The committee had made seven optimistic recommendations from that probe. Their report concluded with a request for a USPS response within six months describing what actions would be taken to prevent recurrences. The committee's proposals included several methods to report and handle threats to employees. Procedures for handling such threats, the committee said, should be established at all postal facilities and should be well publicized. Also, the postmaster general should appoint security control officers in addition to making the Postal Inspection Service responsible for not only protecting finances and the mail, but employees as well.

If any of these recommendations were implemented, they had no effect on the events in Dearborn, Michigan, on Thursday, May 6, 1993.

In that Detroit suburb, which boasts the University of Michigan campus and the Ford Motor Company research-engineering center, USPS employee Lawrence "Larry" Jasion brooded over a personnel move he regarded as blatant sex discrimination. With 24 years of service, much of it maintaining the fleet of vehicles, Jasion couldn't believe it when he discovered that managers had not selected him for an assignment he'd sought for more than a year. At age 45, Jasion didn't want to wait any longer to become an administrative clerk. Built like a fireplug at 5 feet 10 inches and 250 pounds, with a solid, unlined face that brought to mind movie actors who portray Mafioso soldiers, Jasion could look tough, but also had a disarming smile. The grin faded rapidly on December 3, 1992, when managers gave the opening to another employee, June Collins.

It wasn't fair, Jasion complained. He suspected that she was getting special treatment because of her sex. Why should a woman get the job he'd been dying for? She didn't have nearly his seniority, he complained, ignoring the fact that she had performed for several years the required duties of the administrative clerk job. Instead, he bemoaned his observation that Collins had been granted three-day weekends while he was being forced to work overtime. He felt that she couldn't perform the full range of duties. And he was forced to overlap her job to make up for her shortcomings, he complained. In a documented statement, Jasion wrote, "When I asked when she was going to do all the work the man before her did in that same position, the manager made me keep doing her work."

It had to be because she was a woman, Jasion rationalized. He believed it was a clear-cut case of sex discrimination. That idea formed in his mind and gained momentum until Jasion convinced himself that he should seek relief through a full-fledged complaint to the U.S. Government. He filed a sex dis-

crimination complaint to the Equal Employment Opportunity
Commission (EEOC). While he waited for a decision, his frustration and anger seethed inside him. Jasion became a bomb
ready to explode at the slightest touch.

The grisly events at Royal Oak had shocked and saddened
postal employees across the nation, especially in the Detroit
area. The memory of it lodged in Larry Jasion's brain like
a minuscule tumor that would grow and metastasize, unless
someone discovered and treated it.

If there were any characteristics in common among the 13
USPS employees who had killed and wounded coworkers, or
committed suicide, they might have been identified as:

1) male employees
2) loners, many of whom were never married
3) owners of guns who showed unusually strong interest
   in them
4) generally anti-social behavior, including difficulty
   accepting authority
5) traumatic event, usually early in individual's life
6) employees who often makes references to previous post
   office massacres
7) military veterans who often dressed in combat boots and
   camouflage garb
8) collectors of warfare or paramilitary magazines
9) employees with a growing pattern of disciplinary action
10) employees who made threats against supervisors or
    coworkers
11) employees who appear increasingly tense and angry, or
    engage in bizarre behavior in the weeks before they
    exploded in lethal rage.

It's important to realize that all individuals who fit these
descriptions, whether with a few of the traits or with all of
them, are not necessarily going to cause trouble. But the characteristics did apply to many of the thirteen, and could possibly
serve as indicators for management to consider.

Did Lawrence Jasion fit any of these criteria? If he did,

was management or the Postal Inspection Service aware of his problems and potential for violence?

Born Lawrence Jasionwicz in 1948, Jasion would later legally shorten his Polish name because, as he told an associate, he thought its tongue-twisting pronunciation was difficult for most people. Among his few friends, it was thought that he wanted to hide his east-European background. Jasion's father, though, who toiled in the Detroit automotive industry, actively participated in organizations and events celebrating his ethnic heritage. Jasion's mother worked for the postal service all day, after which she cooked dinner and cleaned their modest brick home in Dearborn. In addition to having a twin sister, little Larry doted on his younger sister, Cynthia. In 1954, Cynthia died in a tragic accident, leaving the parents and the twins devastated. Everything changed in the dark days afterwards. Children who had socialized with Larry found him withdrawn and silent. Mr. and Mrs. Jasionwicz grieved for years.

After attending St. Barbara's Catholic Grade School and Dearborn's Fordson High School, Jasion received his "Greetings" from Uncle Sam at age 19. In 1967, for the first time in history, Americans watched daily full color television news reports of their countrymen at war, and got a close-up view of combat in the green hell of Vietnam. Bloody battles and body counts motivated a wave of protest in this country. Young men publicly burned their military induction cards and scores of draft-age candidates sought refuge in Canada. Not Larry Jasion, though. He dutifully reported for his physical and spent the summer of 1967 in basic training at Ft. Knox, Kentucky. Fortunately for him, he was never sent to Vietnam. The Army made him a supply clerk and sent him first to Germany, then to California.

Two years later, without ever having seen one minute of combat, Jasion gladly accepted a discharge. In June, he used his veteran's status to help win employment with the postal service. Apparently, managers there thought he had automotive maintenance skills, so they assigned him to repair the delivery trucks.

A fellow USPS mechanic, Tom Gordon, could see some

good sides to Jasion, and some alarming hints about him. Both men periodically spent off-duty hours tinkering with cars, and sometimes worked on old junkers together. Jasion angered his neighbors by using his front yard as a storage and work area, keeping it littered with greasy auto parts, tools, and trash. One of the things that disturbed Gordon when he visited Jasion's home on Bennet Street, in Dearborn, was that Jasion had covered his windows with a thick layer of white paint. Jasion explained that he wanted to be sure that "nobody will be able to look at me."

The small, rectangular house had belonged to Jasion since June 1973, when he bought it. He had been the sole occupant for 20 years. Other than Gordon, few people ever visited or saw the inside of Jasion's home. No one could ever recall seeing him date or bring a woman to his residence. In a neighborhood of well-kept homes and tidy lawns, Jasion's shabby yard and scabrous house didn't seem to fit, and other residents grumbled about the eyesore. But many of them felt intimidated by his physical appearance and reclusive attitude. An elderly neighbor, though, expressed compassion for him. "I really feel sorry for him," she said. "He always acted like he didn't have anything to look forward to." She recalled one of the few conversations she had had with Jasion.

The neighbor had asked, "You working much overtime?"

"Yeah," Jasion had said. "I filed a grievance."

Trying to cheer him up, she had chirped, "You're lucky to have a job." That had ended the brief exchange. He had switched her off with the same disdain he might have given a television commercial and had walked away.

A coworker agreed with the woman's assessment of Jasion. "He was a very unhappy person," said a mail carrier. The wife of Tom Gordon, Jasion's colleague, felt the same way. She had tried to help by cooking a whole turkey for Jasion on Thanksgiving, and delivering it to him. He had responded in his usual inept way, just as he usually demonstrated at work, with ragged social graces. "Oh, that's just Larry," Gordon rationalized.

One of the few things about which Jasion showed any enthusiasm when talking was his guns. No one knew exactly how many he owned, but he admitted to having registered 26 firearms with the Dearborn police.

A comment Jasion made involving one of his weapons ended his friendship with Tom Gordon. That, and Gordon's promotion to supervisor. A cold distance grew between the pair as soon as Gordon joined the management team, as Jasion's boss. Gordon would later say that Jasion rejected all authority with obvious contempt. "He didn't want anyone telling him what to do," Gordon said. As the friction heated up, Jasion began making subtle threats to Gordon. To provoke Gordon, Jasion would point a finger at him and imitate the sound of a machine gun. Concerned about his safety and his family's, Gordon alerted the postmaster and postal inspectors. He couldn't believe their apathetic reaction. To him, no one in the hierarchy seemed to take the threats seriously.

Finally, Jasion told the man who had once been his friend, "I've got a nine millimeter pistol you're going to see someday. I've got a silver bullet with your name on it." Not long after that, in 1987, Gordon retired and moved away.

At about the same time, Jasion's job troubles escalated. He couldn't seem to please his new supervisor. After several disputes, he found himself demoted from his regular job and assigned as a mail sorter. Jasion took his grievance to the union and won an arbitration, which restored him to his duties in the vehicle maintenance garage.

Jasion withdrew into himself even more. Coworkers often heard him mumbling to himself, and he spent breaks and lunch alone. Within days after the November 1991 massacre at Royal Oak, just a 15-minute drive north on the freeways, postal workers at Dearborn found a hand-lettered sign in the men's restroom. The scrawled words suggested that something was going to happen in Dearborn that was "going to make Royal Oak look like Christmas."

If Larry Jasion was angry at management, he wasn't the only one. Dearborn union officials would later point out that trouble had been brewing for two years at the post office. They singled out supervisor Harvey Kruger as the center of unrest. "We've had problems with him,'' said the union local president. ''He has a dictatorial management style.''

Those words echoed with haunting similarity the comments of the report from the House of Representatives Committee that had investigated the Royal Oak shooting. An ''autocratic management style,'' it said, had been ''repeatedly revealed.'' The report was issued on June 15, 1992.

Among the problems employees complained about was the heavy workload forcing excessive overtime. For months on end, workers spent 50 or 60 hours each week on the job. ''It's pretty bad working out in Dearborn,'' said a mail carrier. 'They'll go to any extreme to get their mail out.'' Others agreed that working conditions had deteriorated and that management didn't seem sensitive to the growing frustration.

In the autumn of 1992, Jasion told a coworker he'd befriended that his problems at work were becoming serious. The confidante approached the former postmaster of Dearborn, Robert Carpinski, who had established a reliable reputation as an independent consultant regarding labor problems. When Carpinski probed deeper, he found that Jasion appeared to be having the most trouble with supervisor Harvey Kruger. It might help, the consultant advised, for Jasion to keep a diary of his complaints against Kruger.

Unfortunately for Jasion, the only man he singled out as a friend and confidante transferred out of Dearborn to Ann Arbor. It struck Jasion a severe blow. Carpinski noted that Jasion no longer had an outlet to express his fury. He ''had absolutely no one else there to be a support person for him.''

As the head butting between Jasion and Kruger escalated to dangerous heights, Jasion seemed to become more interested in his guns. At work, if he ever spoke to anyone, it was about his arsenal and articles in the military magazines he collected. When anyone who knew him saw Jasion off duty, they noticed he always wore ''cammies,'' the military uniforms colored in camouflage designs.

Some coworkers regarded Jasion as a harmless eccentric, but others worried about his potential for violence. ''He was constantly in trouble, and they wouldn't let up on him," commented a fellow employee.

"Yes," agreed another. "[Jasion] felt a lot of intimidation by upper management. That's the way they motivate you at work. It's a prehistoric era there, really." Filing grievances didn't seem to satisfy the disgruntled Jasion.

When management gave June Collins the assignment Jasion wanted, he sank deeper into his anger, and focused it on her. He filed the complaint with the EEOC and waited. On February 26, 1993, a judge ruled that no violation of the federal laws had occurred. The manager who informed Jasion offered counseling, which Jasion accepted. It apparently did little good.

After being denied satisfaction, Jasion really didn't say much to Collins, but his dark, furious glances at her gave her the creeps. And when he would get her attention, he would point to guns pictured in a military magazine he held, making sure that she could see it. The gesture left no doubt that he was threatening her life, so she sought advice from postal inspectors. They suggested she write a letter to document her fears. On March 17, 1993, Collins wrote to postal officials informing them that she was afraid of Jasion.

As a result, the postmaster, accompanied by a postal inspector, paid a visit to Jasion and interviewed him. The region's chief of the Inspection Service would later say, "The inspector's impression and the postmaster's impression at the time was that [Jasion] was very stable, that he was not making any threatening remarks or was not engaged in any threatening behavior."

The Detroit executive of inspectors chimed in. He noted that Jasion acknowledged owning guns, but said "he would not take any violent action. The meeting went well."

The officials decided to chat about Jasion with the Dearborn Police Department and inform them that Jasion acknowledged owning guns. That came as no surprise to the officers, since Jasion held 13 legal permits for the weapons which he had obtained over a period of eight years.

Incredibly, the postal inspectors did not bother to check with any other employees and did not visit his home. Later explaining those decisions, the region chief said, "Quite frankly, there would have been, I'm sure, complaints of harassment against us, or intimidation, or violation of his rights."

Jasion continued working, sharing duties in the post office maintenance garage with coworker Gary Montes. The 34-year-old mechanic talked excitedly with fellow employees about his new home in Sterling Heights. Beaming with pride, he gave his friends all the details of how he'd acquired the place and the thrill of moving his wife and three children in. Montes's other main topic of conversation was the church, which he attended without fail.

The ebullient mechanic's chatter didn't interest Jasion. His thoughts centered on the escalating difficulties with their supervisor, Harvey Kruger. Jasion knew that the 43-year-old Kruger had three daughters, but lived alone. Ex-postmaster Robert Carpinski noticed that Jasion had tapered off his expressions of anger about losing the coveted assignment to June Collins, and growled more often about "unfair" treatment by Kruger.

A letter carrier would later comment that managers in Dearborn had made very little change from their authoritarian style after the shooting at Royal Oak.

Perhaps USPS managers couldn't see it coming, but a union newsletter writer could. In a September 1992 issue of *The Communicator,* Reginald Brown, Sr. wrote his observations: "Can Royal Oak happen again? The warning signs are there, the tension is there, and bad management is there . . . Let's pray that I'm wrong, but we in Dearborn feel that the situation is like a time bomb going tick, tick, tick . . . Management, are you listening? Do you care? Stop playing games with people's lives!"

On a sparkling spring day, Thursday, May 6, 1993, Lawrence Jasion showed up on the job at his usual time. Dressed in his usual blue jacket and trousers, he carried a doughnut box which he wielded as if the contents were made of lead. Sometime that morning, he also carried a larger parcel in, unnoticed.

Coworker Glen Gay, 49, would later say that he mentioned to Jasion it would be a good idea to clean the garage floors before the morning break at 10 A.M. Jasion nodded and headed toward a stockroom apparently to find a broom. But it wasn't a broom he came out with.

At 8:45, Jasion strode into the garage area carrying a shotgun in one hand and a pistol in the other. He said nothing. Instead, he started pulling the triggers of both weapons.

Slugs tore into the body of Gary Montes, who fell mortally wounded. He would never go home to his wife, three children, and their new house.

"It's time to educate the supervisors," Jasion shouted, and headed toward the garage offices. Glen Gay made a dash for the exit. Feeling sharp chest pains, he stumbled and injured his hip, but escaped the gunfire.

Jasion found June Collins and unleashed another hail of lead. One bullet ripped into her face and two more into her body.

Harvey Kruger stood at his telephone, shouting into the mouthpiece. He'd called the adjacent main post office to warn managers about the violent attack underway. Jasion saw Kruger, took aim, and caught the supervisor with three more slugs.

Letter carrier Larry Nagy, 40, was close enough to hear, but not witness the onslaught. "I didn't see it," he later reported. "I heard a couple of shots and . . . started running for the back door. I started running around the corner and saw my boss . . . He told me, 'Get out! . . . I'm thinking to myself, damn, this is for real. Somebody could be coming from the front, somebody could be behind me. I was thinking about my kids and . . . about my wife at the time."

A couple of lives may have been saved because Dearborn Fire Department personnel happened to be conducting a training session in the fire station next door, and responded to a 911 call from a woman inside the post office. The fire captain described the quick deployment of his emergency team. "They went in and immediately encountered a victim [Montes]. In fact, they had to step over him to get to the other injured parties. It was apparent he had not survived the shooting." Both Kruger and Collins lay on the floor in pools of blood. "They quickly found two others and pulled them out. The woman could only squeeze their hand. She was conscious but in very bad shape and couldn't talk. The male victim was coherent and talking though he had also been shot."

Collins, who was severely wounded and would require extensive surgery, would survive. So would Kruger. Montes, who had absolutely nothing to do with the disputes, lost his life.

When Jasion surveyed what he had done, he placed the pistol's muzzle to the bridge of his nose and fired. He became the fifth postal employee killer to take his own life. Police investigators found the doughnut box he had brought to work that morning. In addition to the shotgun he carried, and the pistol, they discovered two more handguns in the box. From Jasion's pocket, they retrieved a silver-tipped bullet. A subsequent search of Jasion's home turned up an incredible arsenal. Dozens of weapons and boxes of ammunition, including full clips, lay among the clutter. Investigators turned up books and magazines about guns, bomb construction, and warfare in general. The police chief said, "It is obvious this house was fortified. For what, I don't know."

Afterwards, the chief postal inspector made an astonishing comment. "We had no information that he'd ever made any threatening remarks or anything else."

Larry Nagy had heard the whole thing, and suffered haunting afterthoughts. It would be painful, he said, to return to the job. He wondered who was at fault, commenting that Dearborn management had not changed its authoritarian style after the Royal Oak massacre. "There are a lot of questions in my mind about what's going to happen. After Royal Oak, I thought that was going to be the last. I just wonder if this is going to be all in vain, like Royal Oak."

Neither Nagy nor USPS management would have long to wonder. Exactly *four hours* after Lawrence Jasion put a bullet in his own head, a disturbed postal worker in Southern California went on his own rampage!

Chapter 21

"I Love You . . . I'm Going to Kill Us Both"

Dana Point, California
May 6, 1993

Employees knew they were in trouble when Mark Hilbun showed up at the post office wearing his green underwear on the outside of his pants. A disgusted supervisor demanded he change the outlandish clothing arrangement. Hilbun quickly complied. He stripped off the shorts and promptly fitted them onto the top of his head. The bizarre acts were not the first indications that Hilbun might be dangerous, nor would they be the last.

One of Hilbun's fellow mail carriers, Sue Martin, had already learned that Hilbun could be a nuisance. He'd been harassing her for months, obsessively pursuing his compulsive efforts to have a relationship with her. But she wanted no part of him. Martin, a few inches over five feet tall, slim, blue-eyed, with light blonde hair, already had a steady boyfriend. Even if she hadn't, she wouldn't have been attracted to Hilbun. His fanatic pursuit of Martin at first just gave her the creeps but eventually frayed her nerves to the breaking point. Gradually, her discomfort turned to fear.

Even when Hilbun's vacation took him out of town, he still tormented Martin. He sent a postcard to her featuring a leering photo of himself. Hilbun wrote, "Who me crazy? Nah, just horn doggy."

Most of his colleagues went out of their way to avoid Hilbun, but he did have one good friend at the huge post office in Dana Point, California. Charles Barbagallo felt embarrassed for Hilbun. He knew how much the strange fellow craved attention, especially from Sue Martin, but also saw warning signals in the odd behavior. Barbagallo tried to understand human frailties, much as the flower children of the sixties had, and espoused compassion instead of castigation. His personal appearance reflected his philosophies. He still wore a full, bushy mustache, oversized wire-rim glasses, parted his long hair in the middle and pulled it back into a pony tail. Barbagallo could usually be seen wearing faded jeans, sometimes with bell bottoms and a tie-dyed T-shirt, like a latter-day hippie. Described by neighbors as an easygoing, laid back, gentle person, Barbagallo had no trouble making friends, including customers along his mail delivery route. Originally from Hampton, New York, he'd served as an altar boy and attended the New Paltz campus of the State University of New York. He transplanted to the sunshine of Southern California in the seventies, and bought a house in San Clemente.

Residents living close to Barbagallo knew that he liked music from the sixties because they could hear it from his open windows on soft summer nights, drifting along with cool Pacific breezes. Sometimes, Barbagallo invited Hilbun to attend concerts with him to escape the daily grind at the post office, and hoping that music might distract Hilbun from his obsession with Sue Martin.

If Hilbun had been able to conduct himself in a more conventional manner, some women might have found him attractive. At 38, he stood six feet tall and weighed a trim 160 pounds. His smooth face was unlined but he often covered the soft features with a full mustache and curly beard, salt and pepper in color like the curly hair that reached his shoulders. His dark hazel eyes could be warm, but had recently taken on the round, intense look of a lunatic.

Born on May 9, 1954, in comfortable affluence, Hilbun grew up in a wealthy Southern California coastal community. His parents owned two homes, several rental properties, and a partnership in a private airplane. They drove their BMW and Cadillac to a posh country club where they held membership. Hilbun, though, unlike his sister, had trouble with social adjustments from early childhood all the way through high school. Most of his interests centered on "loner" activities. He liked to dabble in electronics, alone, and often avoided contact with people by seeking solitude on camping trips, by backpacking, or kayaking on a secluded bay, always alone. Aimless in his youth, he finally joined the U.S. Air Force in December 1976. After basic training at Lackland Air Force Base (AFB) near Dallas, Hilbun attended military police training on the island of Guam. He stayed there 15 more months before being reassigned to March AFB in California to serve his final 18 months.

Early signs of mental disturbance showed up during his Air Force service. Records reveal that Hilbun received treatment for manic depression during that time. Nevertheless, Hilbun managed to complete his full four-year tour, rising to the rating of sergeant, and left the Air Force in December 1980 with an honorable discharge.

Utilizing his skills in electronics, Hilbun found employment with two Irvine firms until the latter part of 1984, when he joined the USPS as a mail carrier in Dana Point. He reported to the big post office building at the corner of Del Prado Avenue and the exotically named Street Of The Violet Lantern. Dana Point is famous for its spectacular cliffs and colorful history. In the early part of the 19th century, ranch workers threw dried cowhides from the heights to the crashing surf 300 feet below. Sailors pulled the hard sheets of leather from the water and rowed the cargo out to four-masted sailing vessels for transport to rich markets. Richard Henry Dana chronicled the events in *Two Years Before the Mast,* and settlers eventually named the cliffs and the town for the seagoing author.

Hilbun's parents' marriage ended in 1982. Sporadically, he

lived with his mother, Frances Nell Hilbun and her blonde cocker spaniel, Golden, in a posh coastal town aptly named crown of the sea, Corona Del Mar. He kept a pair of rabbits as his own pets. A neighbor learned of Hilbun's odd personality when her nine-year-old son tried to trim some tree branches overhanging from the Hilbun yard. The boy's mother later said that Hilbun raced outside and threatened to kill the youngster if he didn't stop. He shouted that he would also kill the family's pets. The woman's discomfort with Hilbun increased when she caught him peering through her windows at night.

During the early part of his tenure with the post office, Hilbun performed his job adequately. But his behavior began to change with the new decade. When he met Sue Martin and decided she was the only woman in the world for him, he found new ways to manifest his eccentricity. He sent mail with obscene suggestions. He annoyed her with frequent and unwelcome phone calls. He became a major irritant in her life.

In June 1992, the simmering unrest in Hilbun's psyche boiled to the surface. He had consumed a few too many drinks and his driving showed it. A highway patrolman pulled him over for driving 70 miles per hour in a 55 zone. When the officer undertook the first steps of administering a sobriety test, Hilbun bolted back to his pickup truck and jammed the accelerator to the floor. As he sped out, he clipped the officer's leg. Subsequently arrested again, Hilbun faced a September trial for driving under the influence and resisting arrest.

In the early part of September, free on bail while waiting for his court date, Hilbun showed up at the post office with his green underwear worn outside his pants. When he placed the shorts on his head, the boss, Don Lowe, sent him home. According to witnesses, Hilbun was defiant, flippant, argumentative, and laughing. He was quoted as saying, "I don't care. I do what I want around here. I've had it up to here with Mr. Lowe." Later, he returned carrying a burlap sack containing his two pet rabbits. He told coworkers that it was okay if they skinned and ate the rabbits. He found no takers.

Hilbun turned his attentions again to Sue Martin, making suggestions to her that she found repulsive. She decided she didn't have to take that kind of treatment. When he refused to stop calling her, she requested help from her employer and the police. While Martin and her boyfriend took a vacation trip to escape the tension, Hilbun found himself in custody. A judge ordered that he be given a psychiatric examination. After a 72-hour battery of tests, doctors diagnosed manic-depression, extended his stay in the mental clinic to two weeks, and prescribed lithium treatments. Temporarily, the drug seemed to help.

For the previous drunk driving and resisting arrest conviction, the court assessed a hefty fine plus a year of probation. In addition, Hilbun was sentenced to serve 350 hours of community service in the harbor at Dana Point, near the post office where he worked. He had plenty of time to do his community service, because the USPS placed him on administrative leave in the middle of September.

The free time gave Hilbun even more opportunity to harass Sue Martin. On the last day of November, his telephone call sent her spinning into a vortex of fear. He made all kinds of threats suggesting that he couldn't live without her, and hinting that maybe they should both die.

Hilbun's harassment of Martin was the final straw for his employer. They fired him on December 8, 1992.

But Hilbun continued his pursuit of the woman he had selected for his mate. For months, he left phone messages, sent letters, followed her on her delivery route, and pestered her constantly. At one point, he left flowers and a package at her apartment. The parcel contained a book titled, *Secrets About Men Every Woman Should Know.*

Martin telephoned the police again in the last part of April, twice. She told her bosses at work. Dana Point Postmaster Don Lowe alerted his employees to be cautious if they noticed Hilbun lurking about the place. He also ordered that doors and gates of the post office were to be securely locked when not in use.

Nonetheless, at the public entrance to the building, no one thought of posting guards or installing any security devices. The rear loading dock was also vulnerable to unnoticed entry.

Considering the recent history of violence by disgruntled employees in post offices across the country, whether their anger was directed at management or coworkers, it seems that someone should have taken measures to tighten security and protect the workers.

During the last part of April, Sue Martin read a note Hilbun had sent her, and shook with rage. It said, "I love you. I'm going to kill us both and take us both to hell." She had to get away. Martin took a two-week leave of absence to give herself relief from Hilbun's smothering attention, his persistent stalking, and now threats of death. She would return on Thursday, May 6th.

In Martin's absence, Hilbun went on a shopping spree at a sporting goods store, purchasing hundreds of dollars worth of camping and survival gear. He stored it in his mother's garage.

Remarkably, Hilbun's attack caught many people by surprise.

In the early morning of Thursday, May 6th, Mark Hilbun parked his blue pickup in the alley by his mother's home. The bed of the truck had been equipped with a camper shell and Hilbun had strapped a kayak on top. He wore a T-shirt emblazoned across the chest with the word "Psycho." His beard and mustache had been shaved off, and his hair trimmed to a conservative length. Making as little noise as possible, he entered the residence and crept silently up the stairs. The blonde spaniel, Golden, met him, barked protectively, then howled a greeting, and wagged a stubby tail in recognition. Leaning over as if to pet Golden, Hilbun calmly slit the dog's throat.

In total silence, he slipped into his mother's bedroom, and approached the sleeping woman. She stirred, and looked groggily at him. They exchanged a few words about Mother's Day coming up shortly. Without warning, Hilbun leaped on her and repeatedly plunged a knife into her body. She would never wake up again.

After loading the pickup with camping supplies and provisions, including candy bars and junk food, Hilbun drove the 10 miles from Corona Del Mar to the Dana Point post office. At 9:30 A.M., he parked near the adjoining escrow office and walked the full length of the USPS building exterior, through the parking lot, noticing that Sue Martin had parked her car in its usual spot. He entered, unchallenged, through the rear loading dock. Inside, he spotted his friend, Charles Barbagallo, and asked where Martin was. Barbagallo, fearing danger for the woman, refused to tell Hilbun that she was, indeed, in the building. Hilbun raised a pistol to his friend's face and shot him between the eyes. Barbagallo died instantly.

Stalking through the building and calling out for Martin, who was hiding in a supervisor's office, Hilbun saw another coworker, postal service clerk Peter Gates, 44, and fired again. The bullet grazed Gates's head, leaving a painful but superficial wound.

Pursuing his hunt, Hilbun spotted Postmaster Don Lowe, who ducked into an office and locked the door. Hilbun pumped one round into the wooden barrier. Unable to find Martin, he walked calmly back across the work area, out the side door, through the employee parking lot, and returned to his pickup. Squealing out of the parking place, Hilbun ran the red light at Del Prado Avenue, and raced away.

Nearly one mile from the post office, a retired Los Angeles probation officer worked at some unfinished chores in his open garage. John Kersey, 65, had moved from Burbank to seek a quiet, serene environment close to the ocean, where he could live his golden years in safety. He looked up and saw a young man approach wearing a baseball hat with "Pink Floyd" lettered on it. Without warning, the intruder pointed a pistol and said, "This is a holdup. Get down and kiss the ground." Kersey decided to obey, and had just kneeled when the gunman struck him on the head with the pistol. Even though the retiree had shown no signs of resistance, the intruder pulled the trigger, sending searing metal into Kersey's right hand and forearm.

Inexplicably, Hilbun spun around and sprinted away without taking anything. In making his exit, he dropped the Pink Floyd hat. Kersey called 911 and was transported to a hospital for emergency treatment.

Still searching for Sue Martin, Hilbun drove up and down her mail delivery route, stopping periodically. At one of her customer's homes, he left the pickup, broke into the house, and paused long enough to guzzle beer from the refrigerator. Back outside again, Hilbun unstrapped the kayak from his pickup, hid it in the resident's garage, and drove away.

Six hours slipped by. In Newport Beach, 15 miles up Pacific Coast Highway from Dana Point, businesswoman Patricia Salot, standing a few yards from her parked van, saw a curly-haired man lifting magnetic placards from the side of her vehicle and sticking them on a blue pickup. She ran toward him demanding he return the signs. He jumped into the pickup and raced up the street. Salot, determined to recover her property, started the van and sped after him. Her two dogs in the backseat jumped into the front and squeezed against the backrest to keep their balance. The male mini-schnauzer, Georgee, and the female Lhasa apso, Harri, seemed to sense the danger. Ahead of Salot, the arrogant thief skidded to a halt and yelled, "If you follow me, I will kill you!"

Undeterred, Salot chased him. He wheeled to the curb and she braked behind him, putting the transmission in neutral while the engine idled. Hilbun jumped from the pickup, trotted to her open window, pointed the handgun, and squeezed off six rapid shots. At least three of the "snake-shot" cartridges sent metal fragments into Salot's face, neck, arm, and hand. She slumped forward trying to remain conscious, and somehow managed to scrawl the assailant's license number on a scrap of paper using her own blood.

Salot didn't want to give up, but she felt the dark shrouds closing in, and the world fading away. The nudge of Georgee's wet nose under her forearm brought her back just enough to put the shift lever into drive. The van lurched forward, toward a United Parcel Service (UPS) driver who had just parked, and emerged from his truck to witness the whole incident. He saw the van moving in his direction and rushed quickly to Salot's aid. The UPS man hailed another Samaritan who brought a towel to apply pressure to Salot's bleeding wounds. One of the men used a cell-phone to call for help. Salot couldn't speak, but she would always remember the evil of something she saw. Her assailant had circled the block, and sat watching paramedics working feverishly to save her life.

When the news hit radio and television stations that evening, all of Orange County braced in near panic. A madman was on the loose along the coast. A brutal assailant who attacked at random. When a photo of a wide-eyed, bearded Mark Hilbun was released, fear rose like thermometers in Santa Ana winds. Imagined sightings of the fugitive were reported everywhere within the San Diego-San Francisco-Las Vegas triangle.

Postmaster General Marvin Runyon, who had flown to Dearborn, Michigan in response to the murder and suicide by Lawrence Jasion, couldn't believe how quickly the next tragedy had come about—a mere four hours! Just four short hours after Larry Jasion had put a bullet in his own brain, Mark Hilbun invaded the Dana Point post office and murdered a coworker. The nightmare just kept growing. Runyon caught a quick flight to California, but refused to grant interviews.

Postal inspectors now found enough resources to put full-guard service around the Dana Point post office. They inspected every item entering the building, including bouquets and notes sent by sympathetic customers.

The Orange County Sheriff's Department spearheaded the search for the killer, but had no idea where to look.

By Friday morning, Patricia Salot lay in critical condition in an emergency room ward. The retired probation officer, John Kersey, was expected to be released from a hospital after recovering nicely from his wounds. The postal employee who was grazed by Hilbun's bullet returned to work the following day. On the orders of USPS management, he declined to speak to reporters.

Orange County remained on fearful alert for Mark Hilbun. Some citizens hoped they would encounter the fugitive and have a chance to collect the $25,000 reward news reporters had announced.

Meanwhile, Hilbun rested in a comfortable Garden Grove motel, 35 miles north of Dana Point.

Just before midnight Friday, Mike Heath stood in front of a Garden Grove Automatic Teller Machine (ATM). The aspiring baseball announcer needed some quick cash. From out of the darkness, a man walked to within two feet of Heath, aimed a handgun at his head, and demanded money. Heath hadn't yet used the ATM, and showed the robber that he had none. With no hesitation, the gunman pulled the trigger. Nothing came out but a loud click. A jolt of adrenalin and fear raced through Heath like an electric charge. Twice more the would-be robber squeezed the trigger, and the gun misfired both times. Confused at the moment, Heath would later report, "I thought he was some jerk. I thought maybe it wasn't a real gun . . . just a joke."

The gun wielder shrugged, said it was a joke, and vanished again into the dark. When Heath later saw Hilbun on the news, he realized he'd escaped death by the thinnest of margins.

Twenty minutes later, at a Wells Fargo ATM in nearby Fountain Valley, a couple stopped to make a withdrawal. Elizabeth Shea waited in the car while her boyfriend went to the machine. Just as it had happened with Heath, a figure emerged from nowhere and pointed a gun through the window at Shea. She wasn't as lucky. Without a word, Hilbun sent a bullet spiraling into her head. When her boyfriend rushed to her aid, he too was wounded by a hail of lead.

Film at 11:00, on all television news reports, was accompanied by hair-raising reports of the postal worker's rampage. Mark Hilbun's photo showed up everywhere. Very few of the three million Orange County residents hadn't heard of him or seen the fugitive's image. One person who had somehow missed it was his sister. The massive dragnet for Hilbun continued late into the night. In Newport Beach, every officer in the police department, including 23 detectives, worked overtime in the search. Twenty-three police agencies countywide participated.

That same night, two of Hilbun's victims struggled for their survival in emergency wards. Elizabeth Shea required extensive brain surgery and the repair of her shattered skull. Patricia Salot returned from the threshold of death. Doctors upgraded her condition from critical to guarded and worked diligently to repair the bullet damage. Both patients faced a long painful road to recovery. Shea's boyfriend also survived the gunshot wounds.

About 20 minutes after midnight, in a Huntington Beach

sports bar, two miles from the Wells Fargo ATM shooting, a crowd of more than a hundred customers drank and chattered noisily. They'd been watching basketball and hockey games on large television screens. As the excitement tapered off and the clamorous din of voices diminished, a customer caught sight of a newcomer in the bar who looked familiar. The new arrival, who wore white pants with a blue and maroon Hawaiian-style aloha shirt, didn't have a beard or mustache, but had the same expression as the photo frequently displayed on the news. He stood near a pool table, calmly sipping a 7Up and vodka cocktail.

Trying not to be conspicuous, the customer edged close to the bar manager, tilted his head in the direction of the tropically clad newcomer, and said, "The postal killer is here." He repeated it several times. They called the police.

At 12:30 A.M., Saturday, three Huntington Beach Police Department officers approached Mark Hilbun in the bar and requested that he step outside with them. "Cool as a cucumber," according to witnesses, Hilbun complied. One of the cops asked Hilbun for identification. A police spokesmen later said, "At first, the suspect gave an alias and said his name was Plant. The officer said, 'Well, give us your real name,' and he quickly admitted who he was. After he gave us his name, he just hung his head."

Whisked off to the Orange County Sheriff's headquarters, Hilbun would be interviewed by investigators. Other officers would find the camper shell from his pickup dumped in a Newport Beach vacant lot. On the vehicle, he'd switched license plates, replacing his with ones from Idaho. Hilbun had already shaved off the beard he usually wore and trimmed his hair much shorter. Later, he changed out of the psycho T-shirt into the island-type clothing. Hilbun may have had some emotional disorders, but his methods of evading the massive hunt demonstrated considerable cunning.

At last, Hilbun's sister saw the news about the pandemonium her brother had caused, and his arrest. Worried, she telephoned her mother. There was no response, so she left a message on the anwering machine. "Mom, Mark has committed a serious

crime and is in police custody right now. I'm okay. I'll talk to
you when I talk to you." At the time, she had no way of
knowing that her mother had been murdered.

Before the sun came up on Saturday morning, Sheriff's
Investigator Mike Wallace, along with another officer, faced
Mark Hilbun in an interview room. Before the formal questions
and answers started, the recorder picked up Hilbun asking an
officer, "You got the big chest 'cause you got a bulletproof
vest on? I was wondering why you're so hearty there. It looks
like you have a sunken-in chest."

Ignoring Hilbun's offbeat comment, Wallace offered the suspect some coffee. Hilbun stared into the paper cup after some
powdered cream had been added, and mumbled, "Maybe I just
like that muddy color, muddy, muddy waters."

Wallace made certain Hilbun understood the Miranda warning, then started the questioning. Hilbun gave his birthdate,
May 9, 1954. In about 19 hours, he would turn 39, locked in
a cell, under arrest for murder.

Hilbun had already mentioned being in love with Sue Martin.
The detective asked, "Why don't we just start by you telling
us what's been going on the last few days . . . You were talking
about a girl . . . ?"

"I just felt abandoned and isolated. She wouldn't acknowledge my existence, so . . . I lost my reason for living." His
infatuation had started about one year earlier, Hilbun said.
Wallace asked him to try to explain why the events of the last
two or three days had happened. Hilbun spoke softly. "Uh, I
believe I'm the soul, I'm a sun in the sky, and I'm trapped
here in this body."

Trying not to show his personal reaction to the rambling
rationale, Wallace said, "You kind of got a raw deal from the
post office I guess, haven't you?"

"Yeah. They're just like Sue, they won't acknowledge my
existence." Asked if he'd been looking for Sue Martin on
Thursday morning, Hilbun said, "Probably so. I don't remember exactly. Oh yeah, I went to the post office . . . Thursday
morning. Yeah . . . To get her to come with me. And I had the
idea that the world was gonna end. It's . . . gonna go through

a catastrophe and so Sue and I were chosen as, uh, husband and wife of, uh, the race, the human race.''

Keeping an impassive expression, Wallace said, ''The human race, huh? So you, on Thursday morning, you were going to get her to take off to, basically survive this calamity and get started with a new race?''

''Yes.''

''Why did you have a gun with you when you went into the post office?''

''In case they would try to stop me . . . everyone has told me to stay away.'' About the chance of Martin willingly going with him, Hilbun said, ''I felt like I had to force her to.'' She hadn't expressed her real feelings, he said. ''She really wanted to be with me.''

''Was there anyone in particular trying to . . . keep her from you?''

''Yes, the postmaster.''

''How about Charlie [Barbagallo]?''

''No. Well, I asked him where she was. He wouldn't tell me. He said, 'Go away. Get out of here'.'' That, Hilbun said, made him feel alone and rejected, which led to anger. He'd saved Charlie, he claimed. ''I thought I was helping him. He wouldn't have to live through the catastrophe . . . after I shot him between the eyes.''

''Why did you shoot him?''

''To get some response. I felt like he was pushing me away so I guess I wanted to penetrate him to get my point across.'' Hilbun explained that he meant that he couldn't allow anyone to stop him from being complete. ''I just have it in my mind that Sue and I, we're two halves and together we'd be complete.''

Hilbun admitted that he had held the gun with two hands to shoot Barbagallo at close range.

''What did you do next,'' Wallace inquired.

''I went berserk . . . It was like self-preservation. So I saw Pete [Gates] run back there. I knew he had a gun back there. So I ran back and shot him in the head, too.''

''Why did you choose the head?''

''It was the closest to me. He was on the ground and looking

over at me and he goes, 'Oh shit.' I beat him at the draw.''
Hilbun's answers confirmed that he meant to kill Gates. After
shooting the coworkers, he said, he ran around the post office
looking for Sue. ''. . . and everyone scattered. I went to Don
Lowe's office and he was closing the door. I shot through the
door at him. Again, trying to shoot his brains out.'' Why had
he wanted to do that? ''Cause I was angry at him . . . for
isolating me and not trying to help me in any way.'' Hilbun
felt pretty sure that the bullet he sent through the door had hit
Lowe. It hadn't.

Wallace asked a series of questions designed to make certain
that Hilbun knew what he was doing and that he was deliberately
evading arrest. The answers seemed to confirm that he did.
Hilbun admitted the encounter with the retired probation officer
and told Wallace about trying to shoot the victim more than
once, but the handgun had misfired. At first, he said, he'd tried
to crush the man's skull with the butt of the gun to avoid the
noise of shooting, but it hadn't worked. Hilbun's purpose for
the attack, he told Wallace, was to steal the victim's car.

Hilbun described the ammunition he took with him as ''shot-
shell'' which contains little pellets instead of one slug, and a
supply of ''solid full-metal jackets.''

In Newport Beach, Hilbun said, he tried to steal some magnetic signs from a woman's car to ''camouflage'' his pickup.
The woman followed him, honking her horn and demanding
he stop. ''I got angry and told her to back off or I'd kill her.
And she kept coming and I just got out of the truck and went
back and laid four rounds in her.''

''Where were you aiming them?''

''Maybe the heart.''

After leaving the wounded woman, Hilbun said he hid out
in a vacant lot next to a parked RV camper. ''The helicopters
were buzzing around and I kind of camouflaged my truck. I
ended up taking off the shell and leaving it there.'' To hide
his truck from aerial view, he spread a double-wide sleeping
bag over it. A little later, he hid in a house under construction
for an hour or two.

Detective Wallace directed the conversation to a time before

Hilbun went to the post office. "Do you remember stopping over at your mom's house?"

"Oh, yeah. I went there early. Uh, she was still in bed and I just decided that she was better off dead . . . So I walked in. Her dog, Golden, knew I was coming to take her life and he howled. Then finally, he came up to me and I slit his throat. And then I walked into my mom's bedroom. I said I was going to take off camping so I had a Mother's Day gift for her and then I just jumped up on top of her and showed the knife and she put her hands up and said, 'No, no.' And I said, 'I love you very much and here, you're gonna go see Grandma,' and I plunged the knife in her heart a couple of times and she died—no problem at all."

The stunning litany took the breath away from Wallace. He'd elicited many confessions before, but this one matched anything he'd ever heard. Quickly recovering, he asked, "Did she put her hands up?"

"Yeah. Then at the last it seemed like she kind of welcomed it."

"Did she say anything to you?"

"No. So again I thought I was sparing her suffering from the catastrophe that [would] hit the world on Mother's Day. And my plan was to, uh, I was all provisioned for a South American trip. And when I got Sue, we were gonna go to the southwest . . . and get a couple of kayaks and I wasn't sure if we were gonna drive down to Mexico and take off there or take off out of San Diego harbor or what. I just felt that Mother's Day there'd be a major earthquake and sunomis and apocalypse." Presumably, Hilbun's reference to "sunomis" meant Tsunami, the Japanese word describing a huge sea wave produced by a seaquake or undersea volcanic eruption.

Hilbun told Wallace of leaving his mother's house, loading his pickup with supplies, and stealing his mother's auto license plate to attach to his own vehicle. Why? "I tried to evade the police." Wallace continued to build evidence that Hilbun knew exactly what he was doing. The calm killer even told of using a "Buck filet knife" to kill his mother.

Turning Hilbun's attention to later events that night, Wallace listened as Hilbun admitted trying to rob two men at bank ATMs and shooting a woman. He said that afterwards, he left his gun, a Smith and Wesson .22-caliber magnum, in the pickup truck. He had acquired it while in the Air Force in Guam.

Asked why he'd gone into the bar in Huntington Beach, Hilbun said he wanted to meet a woman. "I just felt all wasted and I couldn't really . . . communicate at all." So he sat and had a drink, which he claimed was beer.

A "Pink Floyd" baseball cap had been found at the retired probation officer's home, and Hilbun candidly admitted losing it there.

During the 39-hour countywide search for Hilbun, investigators had visited a number of people who knew him, including a distant female relative, who mentioned a conversation during Hilbun's recent visit to her home, and some odd comments he'd made. Wallace asked him if he recalled that visit. Sure, he said, he had eaten pizza and watched some videos with her and another woman. They had talked, too. "What did you talk about?"

"Uh, I asked her if she wanted to have sex . . . She said no."

Hilbun also recalled buying some tickets to attend a circus, and watching workmen setting up the tent in San Juan Capistrano. He'd asked one of the men if there were any job openings. There might be big-rig truck driving jobs available, the worker had told Hilbun.

Curious, Wallace asked Hilbun if he was looking for a job. Yeah, Hilbun said. He'd been "waiting it out" for the post office to overturn his dismissal. "They kept saying that we had a deal worked out and it would come through." But it never did. He planned to take his mom to the circus, but changed his mind and decided to ask Sue Martin instead. Later, when he was watching videos with the two women, he asked the visiting guest if she would go with him. She declined. Maybe because he'd made some complimentary comments about her "cute butt."

During his murderous odyssey, Hilbun had switched license plates on his pickup. He admitted stealing the Idaho plate in a

Huntington Beach parking lot, and having five other plates in his vehicle ready to substitute while making his run for the border. "I thought it was all a big game. I thought me and Sue were the main players. We were also responsible for everybody else." He told the officers that he'd stolen some of his mother's jewelry with the intention of giving it to Sue. He'd invaded the post office to "rescue" Sue Martin because he thought "they were holding her."

About the postmaster, Hilbun said, "[As] I remember the past months, I think that he was the cause of all the problems. I fantasized about killing him . . . I just felt he had held Sue. So I thought he might have her in his office after I left there. I was disappointed with myself that I didn't look in there for her like everywhere else." At the post office, Hilbun admitted, he was willing to kill anyone except Sue Martin.

Hilbun had tried to steal money from the ATM customers, and Wallace wanted to know how he planned to use the money. Hilbun thought for a moment, and said, ". . . actually, the plan was to pick up a woman or visit a massage parlor, a prostitute . . . and she would demand fifty dollars and I had to go rob . . ." His voice trailed off.

After taking a break and reviewing some of the subjects already discussed, Hilbun volunteered another tidbit. "One night I broke into Sue's apartment. I thought for sure she'd be there. She wasn't. I looked at all her pictures and stuff. It seemed like she was just like me, not really fitting in. I got her address book to get a street address of her parents. I looked it up in the book and it wasn't there at all."

Before the interview concluded, Hilbun asked, "How's Sue? Is she okay?"

Wallace answered. "Yes, [and] she is a little bit concerned. A little bit frightened actually . . ."

Hilbun interrupted. "I just had a thought. I wondered if she had a demon in her and it's now in me."

Wallace and his team of investigators put Hilbun in an isolation cell, and started the big job of assembling evidence to be used in a future trial.

One of the top prosececutors in Orange County is Deputy

District Attorney Christopher Evans. Tall, slim, articulate, a classy dresser, his studious countenance fools people who don't know that he's a weekend surfer and an excellent sailor. Three other deputy district attorneys (DDA) join him frequently to spend hours in wet suits catching the perfect wave in the cold Pacific waters.

On May 6, 1993, Evans had been through several stressful trials and needed a few days off. He sailed his 32-foot trawler across the channel, to Catalina where he'd planned to stay for two weeks. Unfortunately, he glanced at a newspaper vending machine and spotted headlines that screamed with news about the 39-hour rampage and the capture of Mark Hilbun. A tight, prescient feeling came over Evans. A dozen or more DDAs might inherit the case, but somehow Evans knew, at that moment, that he was going to be caught up in Hilbun's sticky web.

Legal wrangling can consume months or years. In a major case such as the Hilbun murders, it usually takes years. Pretrial motions must be settled, lawyers must assemble reams of documentation to prepare themselves, and a maze of legal issues must be dealt with. One of the major issues with this case related to jurisdiction. Mark Hilbun had killed and wounded postal employees on federal government property, which would usually demand trial in a federal court. But he'd also killed his own mother, attempted to kill several other people, and committed corollary crimes for which the state would try him. In a good example of interjurisdictional cooperation, federal authorities agreed to allow California to try Mark Hilbun on all counts.

More than three years after the crimes, on a warm July day in 1996, Evans stood before Judge Everett Dickey's court to present opening statements. He'd been right on the mark that day in Catalina with his intuition about the case.

The prosecutor knew that Deputy Public Defenders Roger Alexander and Denise Gragg would concede that Mark Hilbun committed the crimes, but would insist that he was mentally ill and incapable of knowing what he was doing. They would ask for a verdict of not guilty of first-degree murder by reason of insanity. Evans argued that even though Hilbun exhibited signs of mental problems, he knew exactly what he was doing. "Even with what mental disorders the evidence shows he may have, he is able to do continuous thinking during this crime spree that turns into a crime party . . . this is a defendant who has a huge anti-authority chip on his shoulder."

Over a span of nearly three weeks, a parade of witnesses took the stand, including Patricia Salot and Elizabeth Shea, both of whom had been so grievously wounded. The confession that Investigator Mike Wallace recorded was introduced. But so were the exceptionally bizarre motivations and movements of Hilbun. A jury of five men and seven women hung on every word. Gallery observers wondered if any defendant accused of stabbing his own mother to death to save her from the coming holocaust could be sane.

When all of the evidence and witnesses had been presented, Evans summed up the state's case. Sure there were some mental defects, Evans conceded, but he has no mental disease that prevents him from forming the intent to kill. He planned and executed a series of brutal murders. Ticking off items he wanted the jury to remember, Evans recalled the four or five license plates Hilbun took with him to avoid being caught, his camouflaging the pickup with a sleeping bag so it couldn't be seen from a helicopter, and a host of other moves to which Hilbun had confessed in his interview with Wallace. And even though the plot to take Sue Martin to Mexico or South America was strange, it clearly demonstrated Hilbun's ability to plan ahead.

To drive home Hilbun's ability to form the intent to kill, Evans cited the defendant's words to Patricia Salot. "If you follow me, I will kill you."

"It's hard to get more clear than that," said Evans.

The cold-bloodedness of the crimes was spotlighted by Evans saying, "Mark Hilbun needed money to party." Referring to the shooting of Elizabeth Shea and the robbery of her boyfriend, Evans said, "When Hilbun gets the money, he goes to a bar . . . to meet a girl." Shea had begged him not to shoot her, but Hilbun didn't hesitate in his attempt to eliminate any witnesses.

Public Defender Roger Alexander, summarizing for the

defense, reminded the jury that Hilbun had undergone years of treatment for mental problems. Alexander's earnest belief that Hilbun was mentally incompetent at the time of the crimes became crystal clear as he spoke. If he could convince the jury of Hilbun's mental illness, the charges of premeditated murder would not stick. Attaching a long list of various witnesses statements to an easel, Alexander laboriously took the jury through each one.

Through the whole trial, Mark Hilbun sat as if in a trance, staring straight ahead, the thousand-yard stare of a man whose mind can no longer deal with reality. He wore a blue pinstriped dress shirt and pleated gray slacks. His curly hair and newly grown beard had turned silvery gray.

The jury started deliberations on the last day of July 1996. Six days later, they found Hilbun guilty in 14 of the 15 counts with which he was charged, dropping only a minor charge of burglary. Court clerk Susan Sedei read the guilty verdicts aloud while Hilbun sat stone still in his trance. The special circumstances that would send the trial into a penalty phase were also true, the jury said.

Now, the jury would be required to sit through more evidence to determine if Hilbun was legally insane, and should be sent to a mental hospital, or if he was sane, and should face imprisonment or the death penalty. The latter decision would require yet a third phase of the trial.

The sanity hearings lasted nearly three weeks. Prosecutor Evans presented evidence to support his theory that Hilbun was within the legal definition of mental competence. Defense attorney Denise Gragg argued that Hilbun suffered from schizophrenia.

When the jury retired again in mid-September to decide on Hilbun's sanity, no one expected them to reach a verdict in just a few hours. They didn't. Two weeks crawled by while the jurors argued. It was 15 days, 16, then 17. Finally, after 18 days of exhaustive turmoil in the jury room, they announced an unbreakable deadlock. Judge Dickey declared a mistrial and asked counsel to meet for the purpose of determining whether or not they wished to repeat sanity hearings with a new jury.

Discussions between prosecutors and defenders went on for two months. At last they reached an agreement. If the prosecution would withdraw pursuit of the death penalty, Hilbun would withdraw his insanity defense, and accept life in prison without the possibility of parole. Evans, saying the agreement served the "overwhelming interests of justice," accepted. "Our goal here has been that Mister Hilbun is unable to ever walk the streets again."

On January 14, 1997, Judge Dickey and a gallery jammed with media reporters heard emotional statements from Patricia Salot, Elizabeth Shea, and Sue Martin. Hilbun, clad in a faded pumpkin-colored jumpsuit labeled "O C Jail," sat impassively as he had during the trial, staring straight ahead.

Salot, recovered from her wounds after years of plastic surgery and therapy, spoke first. Her husband, Monte, and her mother, who ironically had been a postal employee for 20 years, sat in the gallery. Close behind Salot, Carol Waxman of the Victim/Witness Assistance Program, stood holding the trembling woman at the waist to give her physical and emotional support.

"I'm a survivor," Salot said. "Mark Hilbun shot me, inflicting six wounds. The first six months after that were the most traumatic time of my life." She told of having two bullets in the neck and how the left side of her face was virtually destroyed by shrapnel. "My arm was shot and my finger taken off." Her breast had been injured and a bullet remained in her right hip. "I feel raped of my life."

Facing toward Hilbun, who stared toward the front of the court, Salot said she'd experienced a spiritual awakening through three and one-half years of intensive therapy. Out of fear, she had been unable to go near any windows. She'd worn leg braces. "I still have no use of my left arm. My face is half frozen and numb. I must eat small pieces of food because I can't chew." Despite a host of other problems, she said, "God has given me the strength to get through this."

The trauma would not prevent her from being a productive citizen, Salot said. With all the courage she could muster,

Patricia Salot addressed Mark Hilbun. "I forgive you for what you did and I pray that God have mercy on you."

Sue Martin, appearing ready to fly apart at the seams, stepped up to the lectern, also supported by Carol Waxman. For the first time, Hilbun twisted his head to look over his left shoulder at Martin, his eyes bulging. She had no forgiveness for him, she said. "This is unbelievable. This person is capable of so much damage to people's lives. It took a lot for me to come here. I've been waiting four years." Her life, she said, had been torn apart; even though she wasn't wounded with a bullet, she had felt the torment of hell. "I hope he has to suffer what we had to suffer." Martin's voice shook with passion and rage, wavering in volume but not in ferocity. She concluded by thanking the people who had helped her survive.

Hilbun faced forward, immobile again, as Elizabeth Shea spoke. The compassionate Carol Waxman stood with her, too. She said, "I wrote a big speech, but will cut it short."

Judge Dickey advised that she could take all the time she needed. Looking down at her typed notes, Shea said, "On the night of May 7, 1993, a man by the name of Mark Richard Hilbun walked up to me while I was sitting in the car in the parking lot of Wells Fargo Bank. For absolutely no reason at all, he proceeded to raise his handgun and aim it at my head. He pulled the trigger releasing a bullet into my head. The bullet split in two, and shattered my skull on impact."

A piece of the slug and fragments of her skull bone penetrated her brain, Shea said, causing observers to shiver in empathetic horror. "I had debris in my brain for four and one-half hours . . . The doctors say I am very lucky the bullet missed the core of my brain by one-half inch." Now, she had a titanium plate in her skull. She named the surgeons who had saved her life and repaired her. But she still lived with intensely painful headaches, vertigo, confusion, and general discomfort.

Shea expressed special gratitude to Waxman who had guided her from hell back into a world of sanity. In and out of hospitals for years, and still undergoing treatment, Shea hoped to recover a normal life. Sometimes, she said, her "rage makes me want to destroy everything in my pathway and everything around me.'' Sending angry glances toward Hilbun, she said, ''I only ask one thing, that this coward never be allowed out on parole. I don't want to have to worry about this thirty years from now. I would like to put this behind me now, and keep it there.''

No witnesses spoke in Hilbun's behalf, and he declined the opportunity to comment. Both Gragg, for the defense, and Prosecutor Evans presented brief statements.

Judge Dickey, his wavy white hair and mustache giving him a dignified appearance, perfunctorily delivered the sentence.

Mark Hilbun would be prevented from ever leaving prison. The judge imposed nine life terms, plus a $10,000 restitution fine to be paid to a state fund for victims. The judge even tacked on an additional eight-months penalty for cruelty to animals to punish Hilbun for killing his mother's dog.

Chapter 22
The Brighter Side

For every Mark Hilbun or Patrick Sherrill, there are thousands of USPS employees who go above and beyond the call of duty as heroes, humanitarians, and generally nice people who make the day a little brighter. Many of them never receive the recognition they deserve, but one organization goes out of its way to give them their due. The National Association of Letter Carriers (NALC) annually honors selected acts of courage and good citizenship.

Their "National Hero of Year" award went to Joan Barr, a letter carrier from Mechanicsville, Maryland, who delivers mail in Silver Spring. As she drove home on February 16, 1996, through an evening snowstorm, she saw a column of smoke coming from a train wreck. Heavy black smoke and flames poured from the twisted cars. Without considering her own safety, she scrambled down a steep embankment to crawl under the Amtrak train trying to reach screaming passengers. A car of the Maryland Rail Corporation commuter train had been ripped open. Barr worked desperately trying to save passengers from the deadly smoke and fumes. Many died, but Barr helped set up a triage to treat those who did survive. Vincent R. Sombrotto, president of the 318,000-member union, presented the award to Barr in a ceremony at NALC's national head-quarters.

The union also honored three other heroes. Guy A. Young, of Allenstown, New Hampshire, crawled through the broken window of an overturned van in September 1995, ignoring the danger of an explosion from leaking gasoline, to rescue an infant dangling upside down from his car seat. Mark A. Hopkins of Chicago, Illinois, saw a thug attempting to rob a senior citizen in front of a Windy City currency exchange and risked his own life by coming to the victim's aid. Carlos E. Tichenor delivers mail in Topeka, Kansas. In the lobby of his city's main post office, a police officer tried to arrest a resisting lawbreaker and had nearly lost the battle when Tichenor interceded to help bring the combatant under control.

Not only heroic acts are recognized by NALC. Their "National Humanitarian of the Year" award went to Donald F. Coldwell of Upton, Massachusetts, a mail carrier in Natick. He and his wife, Vidia, read a newspaper article that made them heartsick about a young girl who had been abused and abandoned by her family. They opened their home to her as foster parents. The child became one of 22 foster children for whom the Coldwells provided love and care.

Sombrotto said, "There are tens of thousands of courageous brothers and sisters all across America whose daily deeds of selfless bravery and simple compassion make us all proud. They put their own lives and safety at risk. They cast a watchful, protective eye over the neighborhoods they serve. And they give of their own personal time and talents to help the needy. Letter carriers believe that serving the American public means more than delivering the mail. To serve also means to protect, to assist, to help every citizen at any time the opportunity arises."

There are, no doubt, long lists of other admirable deeds performed by postal employees, from both the rank and file of managers, carriers, clerks, mechanics, and all members of the USPS. The media relations folks in Washington, D.C., however, chose to ignore requests to identify and honor them.

In September 1994, the U.S. General Accounting Office

(GAO) issued a two-volume report on their inquiry into U.S. Postal Service operations titled, *Labor-Management Problems Persist on the Workroom Floor*. The report noted that "... academic research has shown that a negative impact on organizations occurs when employees perceive that managerial actions are unfair and the methods available to them to voice their concerns (such as grievance and equal employee opportunity proceedings) are ineffective. In this situation, employees voice their frustration by quitting, withdrawing from the situation (increasing absenteeism), reducing their efforts, or engaging in disruptive behaviors. These unproductive behaviors exist at the postal service, and they impose a heavy cost on all the parties and can limit the postal service's ability to effectively serve customers and meet competitive challenges."

The report also points a harsh finger at postal service management. A "critical problem," it said, was identified by postal service, unions, and management association officials interviewed by the GAO investigators. They concluded there "is a pervasive, autocratic management style in post offices and mail processing plants throughout the country. A union president said that an autocratic culture is prevalent at every level of the postal service, which creates tension on the workroom floor."

Indicating that authoritarian supervision had been the rule in the postal service, the GAO said that a 1989 study by Duke University for the USPS showed a strong culture in the postal service that was "autocratic, task-focused, functionally driven, non-strategic, and moderately risk averse."

Even top management officials acknowledged that an authoritarian management style existed in the postal service. Union leaders agreed, and said it resulted from a tendency to operate "by the numbers."

The GAO issued recommendations for changes, including one that suggested the USPS "select and train managers who can serve as facilitators/counselors and who will have the skills, experience, and interest to treat employees with respect and dignity, positively motivate employees, recognize and reward employees for good work, promote teamwork, and deal effectively with poor performers."

They also suggested that delivery employees be given "greater independence . . . in sorting and delivering mail, incentives for early completion of work, and a system of accountability for meeting delivery schedules."

Requesting a response to the recommendations, the GAO gave the USPS two years to reach a framework agreement with the unions, but to provide Congress a report after one year.

As of January 1997, the office of Congressman John McHugh, chairman of the subcommittee on the postal service, planned to receive a full report from the USPS in April 1997.

Most interested parties hope to see implementation of improvements as soon as possible.

Chapter 23

"Was My Daddy Sad When He Was Dying?"

Montclair, New Jersey
Tuesday, March 21, 1995

A group of girls practicing field hockey in the late afternoon near Watchung Plaza in Montclair, New Jersey, caught sight of a man sprinting by their school at full speed with a gun held in one of his hands. That sort of thing just didn't happen in peaceful suburban Montclair. Panic-stricken, the girls screamed and scattered. Their coach shepherded them back together and soothed their frazzled nerves before calling the police. It appeared to the girls that the runner came from the direction of the tiny substation post office on the corner of Park and Fairfield Streets.

Most Montclair postal customers use the larger main post office on Glen Ridge Avenue, but the one on Watchung Plaza, known as substation A, manned by only two employees, served shoppers, commuters, and folks in the neighborhood. Nearly all of them knew the two men behind the counter by name. Ernest Spruill, 55, was the clerk in charge. The other man, Stanley Scott Walensky, 41, enjoyed a tremendous popularity among customers. Known for his courtesy and good humor,

"Scotty" would even offer customers a ride home on a rainy day. Walensky's retired father, who had been a mail carrier for 40 years, said, "My son replaced me as a postal clerk."

An hour after the girls had been frightened by a sprinting gunman, two calls came into the Montclair Police Department. Something suspicious was going on at the smaller post office. A customer who had been running a little late said she had telephoned one of the two employees there to ask if he would accept a package to be mailed a few minutes past the normal closing time of 4:00 P.M. Of course he would, he said. Just knock on the front door when you get here. But when the customer arrived and knocked, one of the postal employees appeared behind the glass looking worried, and told her to go away, claiming that something was wrong with the plumbing inside. As the puzzled woman left, she heard gunshots coming from the building's interior. After thinking it over for a while, she had decided to call the police.

The second call came from a postal worker who had gone to Branch A to pick up a load of mail, and couldn't raise anyone in the place. That didn't make sense, so he thought the police might want to see what was wrong.

Officers drove over to the small building to check it out. The timing couldn't have been worse. At 5:00 P.M., rush-hour crowds of commuters arrived home from metropolitan New York, 15 miles to the west, on the New Jersey Transit train. The Watchung Plaza station stood within yards of the post office. Confusion reigned as passengers stepped off the train and mixed with gawking groups of curious onlookers who had stopped to see what the police were doing. Crime was a stranger in the upscale town of 37,700, where few people bothered to lock doors, either of their homes or cars.

But the post office was locked up tight. In a medical office next door, which shared a double entrance with the post office, a doctor had just started examining her patient, when the police came in and alerted them to the emergency. A few minutes later, the officer rushed back in. The doctor recalled, "The police came in and said, 'Everyone get out right now'."

At 5:20 P.M., the officers used a battering ram to enter the post office. They found a scene of bloody horror.

In the back room, behind the customer counter, five men lay on the floor, four of them facedown. Each of them had been shot in the head or neck, execution-style. Miraculously, one of the victims showed signs of life, and was instantly transported to an emergency medical center. The other four had expired from the bullet wounds. Both Spruill and Walensky had been killed, along with two customers, Robert Leslie, 38, and George Lomaga, 59. The two customers were longtime Montclair residents. The seriously wounded man, David Grossman, 45, also lived in the town. Medics loaded him aboard a helicopter that had landed in the schoolyard where the girls' hockey team had spotted the fleeing gunman. At University Hospital in Newark, emergency room doctors worked to save his life.

Within hours, detectives visited Grossman, who was able to communicate by giving weak signals with his fingers. He answered their questions in this painful manner, while a doctor stood by to assure that the process didn't harm the patient. Grossman gave the police a reasonably good description of the man who had killed four others and tried to end his life.

The next day, investigators received another extraordinary break. An underworld informant heard the news of the post office slaughter. Needing a bargaining chip to help neutralize problems he had with the law, he told the detectives that he had recently heard an acquaintance talk about plans to rob the little post office substation. The informant's friend had said he knew exactly where the money was kept. "I tried to talk him out of it 'cause I knew he'd be caught," the tipster said. He gave the officers the suspect's name and address: Christopher Green, who lived a short drive to the south, in East Orange.

While preparing to go question Green, detectives ran a computer search on him and found that he possessed a stainless steel 9-millimeter Taurus handgun. The caliber of the weapon matched that of the gun used to kill the four men and wound another. No arrest record turned up, though, which temporarily dampened the prospects of finding a killer. Most murder-robbery suspects have long rap sheets.

The officers drove to a fashionable 24-story apartment building in nearby East Orange. An impressive building, it contained a health club, tennis courts, and a mini-golf course. They found Green, 29, at home in his 16th-story studio apartment. At first he calmly said he had no idea why they would want to talk to him. But within minutes he signed permission to search his apartment, then broke down and confessed to the robbery and murders. He'd taken about $5,000, he said, as he handed over a plastic trash bag filled with bloody clothing and three postal money orders. He led the officers to his refrigerator, under which he had hidden $2,000 in cash, along with the stainless steel handgun. Green told them that he'd given the apartment manager a money order for $2,023 to pay for back rent. That's why he did the robbery, he said, because he had "a mountain of debt" and wanted to pay his overdue rent.

Why did he shoot the five men?

Green said he realized that the two employees could identify him because he had been employed at the post office from July 16, 1992 until April 25, 1993. As a maintenance worker, he had cleaned both the main post office and substation A. Yes, he knew Walensky and Spruill. One of them had called out his name during the robbery, making him realize that he would be identified. So he had to get rid of them.

When he first entered the post office, Green confessed, he aimed the gun at the two employees and the three customers, and told them, "I don't want any trouble. I don't want to hurt anybody. I just want the money." But when he heard his name called out, and realized the danger of being caught, he herded the men into the back room and ordered them to "get down." On their own, Green said, they opted to lie facedown. He demanded car keys, and got them from customer Robert Leslie. When Walensky heard someone at the front door, he realized it was the woman who wanted to mail a late package. Green gave him permission to get rid of her, so Walensky made up a story about faulty plumbing and sent the woman away.

As soon as he returned to the back room and joined the others prostrate on the floor, Green began pumping bullets into his captives. The departing woman outside heard muffled gunshots.

The executions took place quickly as Green fired repeatedly into the back of each man's head and neck. David Grossman realized, too late, what was happening, and tried to get up. As he twisted toward Green, the gunman fired two shots from point-blank range into Grossman's face.

In his rambling confession to the police, Green said, "I felt I was over the line, and there was just no point of return. I was scared and confused."

The investigators reeled at the flimsy rationalization for dealing out death so blatantly. And they scratched their heads in bewilderment when Green revealed his motivation for embarking on the robbery—to pay the back rent on his luxury apartment! As the story of Green's background unfolded, the reasoning made even less sense.

One of seven children, Christopher Green grew up in Montclair in a comfortable middle-class, three-story home with a moral, religious African-American family. He played Little League baseball and graduated from Immaculate Conception High School, followed by vocational school training to become an electrician's helper. At age 18, in 1984, a family-owned small electrical company in East Orange hired him. The proprietors virtually adopted Green, took him on family outings and fishing trips, and said he was an excellent worker.

While still employed there in 1991, Green developed an interest in the Nation of Islam. He became an active member, married another devotee, and resigned from the electrical company. After a brief stay in Maryland, he returned temporarily to the same job in 1992, but his marriage fell apart. In July that year, he joined the USPS in Montclair as a custodian. His job duties included cleaning the main post office and substation A, where he became well-acquainted with two easygoing and friendly workers, Scotty Walensky and Ernest Spruill. His tenure with the postal service lasted until April 1993, when he took a job with Montclair's Department of Public Works. He was headquartered in a garage one-half mile up North Fullerton Street from the Watchung Plaza post office. Driving a truck in

the summer and a snowplow in winter, plus helping a crew
that repaired street potholes, Green earned an annual salary of
more than $26,000. His goal, he said, was to join the police
force. Shortly after changing employment, he visited a gunshop
and picked out a 9-millimeter Taurus handgun, bought it legally,
and took it home.

Solidly built with a broad chest and thickly muscled arms,
well-mannered and soft-spoken, Green looked like a professional athlete, offset only by his eyeglasses which gave him a
scholarly appearance. His acquaintances spoke highly of him,
expressing the opinion that the young man had avoided any
involvement in drugs, gambling, or other illicit activities, and
could never be called flamboyant. The owner of a pizza restaurant where Green often ate said, "He dressed nice, but not
flashy. Nice Dockers and a clean sweatshirt, but no gold or
jewelry." Green replaced his old 1964 Oldsmobile with a 1980
model the same year he took the public works job. The car
caused his only brush with the law. He got four parking tickets
which he casually ignored, causing the court to suspend his
driver's license. Green finally got around to paying the fines,
but there was no record of him ever arranging for reinstatement
of his license. It appeared that Green's only extravagance was
the luxury apartment which rented for over $800 monthly.

Even though Green's squeaky clean reputation suggested
no affiliation with criminals, he apparently knew at least one
underworld figure. Inexplicably, Green confided his plans to rob
the post office to the shady character, who promptly contacted a
police detective he knew, using the information as a bargaining
chip.

The saddest part of a robbery that spirals out of control and
turns into murder, is the deaths of good people, truly innocent
victims. Spruill had worked for the USPS over 30 years, and
had reached the threshold of retirement. He often stopped to
eat and chat with the owner of a deli on Watchung Plaza.
Afterwards, the shocked proprietor said, "Ernie was talking
about taking it easy just the other morning. I said to him, 'Ernie,
you're looking good . . . very fit.' And Ernie said, 'Got to stay
in shape for my retirement'."

Spruill had labored for decades to reach the golden years, and since his two children had graduated from college, he was marking time until his wife would leave her job.

A grieving ex-coworker, who had already retired, said, "[Ernie] was in a station in a nice quiet neighborhood. He loved his job there and he was putting in a little more time, waiting for his wife to retire . . . I was going to call him today, then something came up and I thought, 'No, tomorrow.' Now, there is no tomorrow."

Scotty Walensky would be remembered for his congenial personality. According to a colleague, "Scotty was always joking. He had a real sense of humor."

The deli owner said, "They were both very nice guys. Ernie and Scott. Most days they'd just come in to get their sandwiches for lunch and take them back to the post office."

Walensky left three young children and a wife who worked as a supervisor in a local nursing home. With a heavy heart, his father recalled, "He was given the post office Good Guy award a couple of years ago and just got a fifty-dollar gift certificate to [a seafood restaurant] for not having a single sick day in four years." The elder Walensky, his voice trembling, added, "He had a photographic memory. If you mailed a package at his window, you had a friend for life."

The adult daughter of victim George Lomaga said that she was saddened by the fact that her baby daughter, born just a few months earlier, would never know her grandfather. Lomaga had doted over the infant, and loved babysitting her. "There is no way to describe his love for her. I want the severest penalty under law imposed on this man for the grief he caused innocent people. He has robbed my daughter of a grandfather."

Robert Leslie had lived on Norman Road in Upper Montclair, where he maintained a home office in his sales profession. He spent his off-duty hours with his wife and two young children, often puttering in his garden. A crying neighbor said, "On a nice day, he would take his little girl over to Sunset Park."

The principal of the school where Leslie's four-year-old daughter was a pre-kindergartener said the massacre was, "a

Montclair tragedy, a school tragedy, and a parish tragedy . . . It's just so hard to believe. We all [felt] so safe here.''

David Grossman lay in a Newark hospital gradually improving, having won his battle to stay alive. He'd been shot twice in the head. One bullet entered his left cheek, tore through the flesh and bone, and exited behind his right ear. The second slug ripped through his nose. He'd lain on the floor, pretending to be dead and hoping the shooter would stop pulling the trigger. Grossman was a computer analyst for a New York bank, married, and had a four-year-old son.

Six months after the carnage, Christopher Green stood before U.S. District Judge Joseph Rodriguez, having pled guilty to the murder charges. Before the judge passed sentence, he listened to statements from the principles of the case.

Green said, ''I'm deeply ashamed of my actions and . . . have remorse for the families of the victims. I'm asking to my God that from this day forth there be a healing process for everyone that is involved in this particular case and that from this day forward . . . we can move on with our lives. Whatever days that are ahead for any and everyone involved . . . that they be utilized for a healing process. And I ask the mercy of this court in my behalf.'' Observers thought it sounded hollow and insincere, like a prepared speech.

One of Green's defense attorneys acknowledged that ''Christopher Green must face a sentence of life without parole in the federal prison.'' The other defender, pointing out that ''life within the federal sentencing system means exactly that. . . ,'' asked the judge to consider recommending a prison other than the maximum-security lockup at Marion, Illinois, which has a reputation of being one of the toughest places to serve time.

Prosecutor Faith S. Hochberg countered the request. ''It is the United States' position that the defendant should be incarcerated at Marion because that is the appropriate place to sentence a prisoner who has committed crimes as atrocious as the ones under issue here today.

''A mere six months ago, in less than fifteen minutes Christopher Green shattered the lives of five families and an entire town. Faced with relatively small debt, he chose a cowardly and brutal way out. He robbed the Montclair post office at gunpoint and then turned his gun on five defenseless men. They complied with Green's every demand. They gave him the cash at the post office, they gave him the keys to the getaway car, they obeyed when he told them to lie motionless facedown . . . and yet Green deliberately tried to eliminate all witnesses to his robbery. Green shot his five victims in the back of the head or neck at close range, wasting no time between shots. He murdered four men in execution-style and tried to kill a fifth, leaving him for dead.''

Hochberg explained, for the record, that the wording of federal statue's did not provide for the death penalty in this case, and argued that the defendant should face the sternest possible consequences for cold-blooded, execution-style murders. Serving time at Marion, she said, would be appropriate. She explained why. ''Marion is a maximum-security facility designed to house offenders like Christopher Green who have committed horrific violent federal crimes. More than half the inmates have killed, many . . . more than once. One third of the inmates are serving life sentences. Inmates at Marion remain confined alone in stark cells for up to twenty-three hours a day. And the cells, like the prison itself, are underground. Life in solitary at Marion offers no hope. Each day is starkly like the day before and the day after in a hopeless, endless succession.''

The grim picture Hochberg painted sounded worse than the death penalty. ''Green should be sentenced to Marion to reflect the seriousness of this horrible crime, to promote respect for the law, to provide punishment, and to deter others.''

Postal inspectors, Hochberg said, had interviewed scores of people who knew the defendant and knew him well, and had expressed shock that this defendant carried out such horrifying acts. The consensus collected by the inspectors, she argued, did not accurately portray the defendant. ''The real Christopher Green is capable of cruelty, brutality, and horror . . . Notwithstanding his appearance here today, the real Christopher Green is a violent killer.''

With that, she said, ''We will shortly hear the words of victims of Christopher Green's vicious crime . . . They speak with a collective eloquence and pain that can only come from such an unspeakable tragedy.''

David Grossman walked slowly from his gallery seat, placed some papers on the lectern, and spoke of his experience:

Your Honor, shortly before 4 o'clock in the afternoon of March 21st, I stepped into the Fairfield Street post office in Montclair to send a letter by certified mail. A few minutes later, I lay on the floor in the back room, unconscious, near death from two bullets fired into my head. On the floor beside me, four men lay dead.

Struggling mightily to hold back the tears, Grossman continued:

Christopher Green thought he had killed all the witnesses to the robbery . . . but I survived. He fired bullets that narrowly missed my brain, just missed my vital arteries and nearly severed my spinal cord.

After regaining consciousness, I lay on the floor for an hour, unable to move, struggling for each breath, feeling the blood gurgling in my throat. The room seemed dark and I could not raise my head, but when I called out and there was silence, I knew the others were dead. From where I had fallen, I could see a clock on the wall, an employee time clock. I knew that at five o'clock someone would come into the post office to collect the mail. If I could stay alive until then, if I fought for each breath and each heartbeat, I knew I would be rescued and I would survive.

I was rescued by the Montclair police and the brave men . . . and women of the Montclair Volunteer Ambulance Squad. Thanks to them and to Mountainside Hospital paramedics, the Medivac helicopter crew and the doctors and nurses at the New Jersey Trauma Center, I'm here today . . . to bear witness to the brutal crimes committed by Christopher Green, to bear witness to his cold-blooded execution of four helpless men. Some newspaper accounts of the post office murders give the impression that Christopher Green intended only to rob the post office and not to harm anyone. The stories say the robbery spiraled out of control or that Green suddenly snapped.

Green himself attempted to give this impression. In his confession, he said the shooting began . . . as though he was not the one who made the decision to shoot, as though the gun fired by itself . . . [and] he repeatedly said he blanked out.

When Green pleaded guilty on June 8th, he said he started shooting because he was scared and confused. His family and friends insist that he snapped, that he was someone else for a few seconds in which he took four lives and attempted to take mine.

Christopher Green did not snap. His actions throughout the robbery show that he was in control at all times. I was there, I know. He was cool, deliberate, purposeful. At no time did he appear to be scared or confused. He methodically executed the four men laying beside me and then he shot me. He fired seven times in rapid succession. There was no hesitation.

I believe the facts of this case allow no other conclusion except that Christopher Green premeditated not just the robbery, but the killings . . . for weeks. I believe that he walked into a post office not only willing to kill, but determined to kill . . . If women and young children had been in the post office, he would have killed them too.

Green first planned to rob the post office some three weeks earlier. He discussed the plan with a friend who later told investigators that he thought he had talked Green out of the robbery by pointing out that he would surely be caught. Green was, after all, known to two postal employees who worked for the post office.

Christopher Green had three weeks to think this over. The decision he made was to load his Taurus nine millimeter semi-automatic with fifteen Black Talon bullets and to kill anyone who identified him. The fact that he chose Black Talon bullets argues that he had a desire to kill that became at least as strong a motive for his crime as his need for money.

Judge Rodriguez, when you impose sentence and make a recommendation as to where Christopher Green should be incarcerated, I ask you to try to see him as I last saw him. With the four other men, I was laying face down on the floor. When I heard the first shot, I began to turn. I heard another shot and then another. As I tried to get to my feet, I saw Green standing just in front of me, his gun pointed at my head. I stretched out my arm trying to grab the gun or push it away. Green must have looked into my face then, and aimed. He pulled the trigger. I felt an explosion inside my head. Then he fired again.

The Christopher Green I saw at that moment as he fired the shots he thought would end my life is the true Christopher Green. Nothing about his life prior to March 21st prevented him from pulling the trigger of his gun again and again, seven times. He is a vicious, cold-blooded killer and he should be put to death.

Winding up by asking the judge to recommend Green be imprisoned at Marion, Grossman said, "The intention of his imprisonment must be punishment and the protection of society, not rehabilitation, and he must never be released."

Grossman's wife stepped forward to share her point of view. She said:

On this day, Christopher Green comes before us ... dressed not in bloodstained clothing, but in a suit and tie. He carries no gym bag heavy with death. He holds no gun in his hand loaded with Black Talon bullets, bullets he knew were designed to destroy and kill. Today, we meet Christopher Green in a courtroom of polished wood and marble. But where is the blood that he shed ... when he killed once, twice, three times, four times, and then tried to kill again? Where is the blood that poured onto the floor of the post office he robbed. . . ? Blood two inches thick. That blood has been washed away. Where's the bloody green coat they cut from my husband's body after Christopher shot him twice in the face and left him for dead? That coat has been thrown away.

But surely as he sits here there is blood in this courtroom today because the blood of five men is on Christopher Green's hands, blood that he can never wash away . . .

During the long hours I was sitting in the trauma center in Newark waiting to hear if his bullets had destroyed my husband's brain or severed his spinal cord and paralyzed him for life, where was Christopher Green? [He] was out partying with his friends, drinking beer . . . At the time he was arrested the next morning where was he going? To pick up a girlfriend and take her to lunch with six hundred dollars in his pocket, the money that he stole from the post office the night before.

Mrs. Grossman asked why and how this could happen, and pointed out that nowhere in Green's confession did he take responsibility for his crime. She called Green a man without conscience or pity, and expressed hope that he would be confined in the bleakest prison possible.

The wife of murder victim Robert Leslie spoke next. "I realize that when Christopher Green murdered Bob, he sentenced me to a life without my husband, a life as a single parent with two small children. He sentenced my children . . . to a life without their father . . . he shattered our future. Four families have been sentenced to live forever without their husband or father, grandfather, son or brother. David Grossman lives with emotional pain every day." Nothing would ever be the same again, she said.

When she waited for her husband to come home, "for four tortuous hours," then heard the heartbreaking news, she still hoped that it was all a mistake. She sat up all night, she said, "trying to figure out how I was going to tell our not yet four-year-old daughter that her daddy was killed by a bad man with a gun." Choking back tears, the anguished mother said she could never escape the child's questions. "Was my daddy sad when he was dying? Why didn't Daddy escape from the bad man? How come if God makes everything why can't he make my daddy alive again?'' Mrs. Leslie's voice trembled as she said the child "sleeps with one of Bob's sweaters covering her, it's her only way to keep Bob near.'' The younger daughter, only 10 months old when her father died, would someday ask the same questions.

"He was such a kind and gentle man. He was so much to so many people. He was truly my better half.'' She, too, appealed to the judge to be certain that Christopher Green spends his life in solitary confinement in a maximum security prison.

Ernest Spruill's widow said, ''Each and every day, the picture of my husband lying on that post office floor with his hands under his head, flashes through my mind as though he was praying for deliverance from the evil that was fast approaching. Just to know that I could no longer hold him, protect him, comfort him, to say that everything will be all right makes me feel absolutely miserable . . . Pleasant memories of Ernest will live on.'' Her adult son followed, and told how he regretted that he hadn't said goodbye to his father on that day six months ago, and would never have the opportunity to do so again. He expressed concern about a society in which there is no concrete deterrent to crime, except perhaps to send a strong message by being certain that convicted murderers never have another opportunity to kill.

Scotty Walensky was also well represented by his mourning family. Mrs. Walensky recounted the details of the murders and asked why Green lived in a luxury apartment on his moderate salary. How did he think he was going to pay for it? And if he was concerned about being recognized when he committed the robbery, why didn't he wear a mask? If he needed money, why didn't he get a second job? To her, the crime was clearly premeditated. About the victims, she said, ''Not one of them gave him any cause to be shot and killed; they all marched like soldiers as he barked his commands [while] pointing the gun. He was a big man that day, he had all the power, he had a gun, he could make those people do anything he wanted and he did. He got them to lie facedown on the floor with their heads as close together as possible making it easier to shoot them. He shot them at the precise time the train passed, blocking out the sound of the shooting to any neighbors. This was the plan. He didn't panic . . . he knew he was going to kill them.''

To her, solitary confinement at Marion was too good for Green. "There is no place dark enough for him to spend the rest of his days . . . I hope you, Christopher Green, will burn in hell for the rest of your life.''

When Mrs. Walensky had finished, her eight-year-old son stood and began reading aloud the words he had written. "I think that Christopher Green should get the death penalty. Everybody in this family is very upset that he didn't . . .'' The boy's chin quivered and the lump in his throat made speaking difficult. "Everybody in our family is upset that he didn't get— why didn't he get a job to get money for his apartment instead of killing four people and hurting one very badly? Why did he kill them?'' The lad tried, but the choking sobs wouldn't allow him to go on.

Judge Rodriguez gently asked the mother, "Would you wish to have that statement submitted rather than having him read it?''

"No,'' Mrs. Walensky replied. "No, I will read it.'' She took the paper from the child, who sat with his face buried in his hands, and read on. "He didn't have to do it. All he had to do was take the money and leave.'' She paused to say, "Before I go on, I just want everyone to know that these are my son's words.''

The lad had written about the crying when he, his mother, and sisters had heard of the murder. "I have never seen my mom cry so bad. When my mom told me that [Green] might not go to jail forever . . . I really got upset. I don't think he should play basketball or any sport while he was in jail.'' The plaintive words echoed through a silent courtroom, telling how the fatherless boy would miss playing sports with his dad, and of the bad dreams he and his sisters suffered through. He sympathized with the other families as well, the lad wrote, and suggested that maybe Green should suffer the same bullet-ridden death as his victims. "This morning, I had to wake up at five o'clock to come down here and just look at such a bad man. One day, I would like to see him in jail and to see if he is getting good treatment because I do not want him to get good treatment at all. Thank you."

The eldest daughter of victim George Lomaga addressed the court. Pointing to a whole row of family members, she listed their names and said she spoke for all of them. Also urging that Green be incarcerated at Marion, she described the devastation of her family. "Just this week I had to drive by the post office to do some shopping because we live in the area. I cried every time I go there . . . I think of how my father died, what he must have been thinking as those last minutes passed away and just how terrified he must have been."

She couldn't understand, she said, the callousness of Green's rampage. George Lomaga had believed in the death penalty, and it should apply to his killer. She spoke of the injustice which forced taxpayers to support Green in prison, provide education, food, and entertainment for him, and how he would receive better care than many honest homeless people. For her father's 60th birthday, the family had visited only a cold headstone at the cemetery. Lomaga had given his infant granddaughter, whom he had affectionately nicknamed MiniMac, a teething ring inscribed with the words, "To my dear Mini-Mac—Love, Granddaddy." Now, the sight of it was heartbreaking.

Green, she said, should never again experience any of the simplest pleasures. "He should never feel the sensation of grass between his toes . . . never breathe the first spring air or feel a warm embrace. He should have no reason to rise in the morning other than to ponder his actions. He should be given only the minimal needs to survive, as we believe there is no reason for his further existence.

"There is one last thing, your Honor, and it's been haunting me . . . Green asked for his God's forgiveness. I want him to know that in our minds and our hearts there is no God that will forgive him. He is not worthy of forgiveness for this crime.''

Before imposing the sentence, Judge Rodriguez took the time to explain that he must follow the ''commands of Congress that are contained in the sentencing guidelines.'' He repeated the attorneys' assertions that ''in the federal system, life means life . . . there is no parole.''

In regards to the many recommendations of sending Green to one specific prison, the judge said, ''It appears to be the concern of many of the persons here today that this court designate Marion as the place of confinement . . . I'll simply say this, that one of the things that has been taken away from the court is the authority to designate any specific institution with respect to where the sentence should be served.'' The court can make a recommendation, but nothing more. He explained that some prisons have limited capacity, and that other prisons are expanding maximum custody facilities. The Bureau of Prisons would have the responsibility of determining where Christopher Green would serve his sentence.

With that explanation, the judge returned to the business at hand, and sentenced Christopher Green to five life terms in federal prison. He then turned to Green, advised him of his right to appeal, then added, ''. . . The enormity of the crime, the taking of so many lives and the way you have affected the lives of so many innocent victims make it difficult for me to add to the words I have heard here. I know the words that you have heard will burn in your memory for the rest of your life.''

Chapter 24
"Did I Get Him?"

The City of Industry, California
July 10, 1995

The images of Christopher Green shooting four men to death in the Montclair, New Jersey post office faded in the summer of 1995 as new horrors splashed blood across national headlines. Someone had detonated a bomb in front of the Alfred P. Murrah building in Oklahoma City, destroying the lives of 168 men, women, and children. By early July, federal prosecutors announced they would seek the death penalty if suspect Timothy McVeigh came to trial.

In Los Angeles, an army of media reporters camped around the downtown Criminal Courts building where the trial spectacle of the century unfolded. Football hero, movie-actor Orenthal James Simpson, accused of killing his ex-wife and a young man, watched a parade of experts present a complex, convoluted defense and win an acquittal for him.

If the heat was at least temporarily off the back of the USPS, a veteran employee of 22 years would ignite the torch again before the sun came up on July 10th. He worked as a distribution clerk in the vast, sprawling postal center in The City of Industry

California, 16 miles east of the courthouse where the Simpson trial was held.

Bruce William Clark's personnel file was spotless. It contained no records of disciplinary action, no infractions of rules, and no reports of poor work performance. The 57-year-old employee had simply done his job for more than two decades, day in and day out. Associates knew him as easygoing, soft-spoken, and unexcitable. To call him disgruntled would have made his friends laugh.

It took Clark about 30 minutes each night to commute to The City of Industry facility from his apartment on a quiet cul-de-sac in Azusa, on the southern slope of the San Gabriel Mountains. In his neighborhood, Clark had few close friends, but was recognized in the apartment complex by other residents. They called him the Cat Man out of respect for the compassionate way he fed and took care of several homeless strays. "The cats were his main family," observed one of the tenants. It was quite common to see Clark calling, "Here kitty, kitty, kitty," and searching the area if one of his wandering felines didn't show up for the dinner and water Clark always put in two bowls on his front porch. A young woman who had often noticed Clark said, "He was a little old, fragile man . . . He is very quiet, very clean, very concerned. If people got hurt, he'd be there."

A few of the tenants noticed a recent change in Clark, though. One day, as he helped search for a friend's missing cat, and the tenants stopped to ask Clark if the pet might have wandered into the camper Clark kept parked in a storage area. Clark just gave them a hollow stare. The puzzled searcher said, "It just seemed like he wouldn't recognize you as a person."

The apartment manager also noticed the recent change in the man he'd known for four years. Call it burn out, or depression, or just a case of accumulated weariness—Clark had slid downhill emotionally, and it worried the apartment manager, one of the few people who laid claim to knowing much about Clark. The change perplexed the manager, who said, "Bruce really loved his job. He really loved life. He lived alone and he didn't have many friends. Still, sometimes the guy aggravated me because he loved everybody. I'd tell him how many of my tenants would drive me crazy, and he'd say, 'Aw, they're good people'."

One aspect of the change, the apartment manager said, was that Clark began grumbling about his new supervisor at work. Because Clark's workplace was a busy hive of activity, it wouldn't be surprising to anyone that occasional disputes might erupt. The giant facility on Gale Avenue near Turnbull Canyon Road processed tons of mail each day. Five million letters, parcels, and other pieces of mail passed through the hands of over 1,000 workers in the 24-hour operation, to be delivered by another 1,800 mail carriers. Clark sorted mail in the hours between midnight and dawn, the graveyard shift, during which the force dwindled to around 100. With so many people interacting, friction was inevitable. But Clark had always been so easygoing. The change in his demeanor and personality didn't make sense. The postal complex chief spoke of Clark as a "very quiet and unassuming gentleman who reported to work on time every day . . . and had no history of conflict with other employees. In fact, he was a very soft-spoken man known as a progressive-style employee."

It would later be suggested that there was some racial misunderstandings between Clark and his boss, James Whooper III, age 50, who was African-American. People who knew both men doubted the rumors.

Whooper, like Clark, had a reputation of fine job performance unmarred by disciplinary actions or negative job appraisals from his bosses. He had transferred from a Los Angeles post to nearby Rosemead in 1992, then to The City of Industry in April 1995. Whooper "was a non-confrontational sort of supervisor," said one executive.

"James had no enemies," said a woman who lived on the same street as Whooper in Rancho Cucamonga. "He would honk the horn and wave if he saw me in the driveway. He was a nice guy." She and other neighbors knew him as a generous man who overpaid local kids to water his lawn when he was out of town. Some of the trips he took were to Mount Baldy or Big Bear to ski on the snow-covered slopes.

A woman who had been not only Whooper's coworker, but an intimate part of his life, bearing him a son, said, "He was just a sweet guy . . . a gentle, caring man. I can't think of anything he would do that would make people want to hurt him." Asked about Whooper's reputation as a supervisor, she said, "He was a strict manager . . . He only did his job. He went strictly by the book. But James was not the type of person who would provoke anyone."

A different viewpoint about Whooper came from his subordinates and a postal union. An employee who had worked for Whooper described him as a tough disciplinarian. A union official said Whooper "was mild-mannered, a nice person, but a strict supervisor . . . When he was in Los Angeles, there were problems with him. He was overly stern and heavy-handed." The critic did take the edge off by saying, "He may have changed once he got out of [Los Angeles]."

No one saw the development of any friction or heard any arguments between James Whooper and Bruce Clark. But the apartment manager revealed a conversation in which Clark confided to him that Whooper was targeting him for harsh treatment. At one point, Clark gave his confidante an automobile license plate number. "He wanted me to try and find out something about the guy. The guy had singled him out and he didn't know why."

None of Clark's associates knew about the .38-caliber revolver he kept, or when he took it to his workplace.

Something happened between Bruce Clark and James Whooper in the wee hours of Sunday, July 9, 1995. No one knew exactly what provoked the incident. "There was no argument," a witness would say. "That's why it's a mystery . . ."

With no apparent warning, Clark punched Whooper in the back of the head. Instead of responding, Whooper simply stepped away to report the incident to his boss. Clark, too, spun on his heel and left the room. Within a few minutes he returned, carrying a brown paper bag. When Whooper asked him what was in the bag, Clark didn't reply. Instead, he poked a hand into it, and withdrew the .38-caliber revolver the bag concealed. Instantly, he pulled the trigger. Once, then again. One slug plowed into Whooper's chest, the second one into his face.

Astonished workers reacted with lightning speed, grabbing Clark, pinning him down, and relieving him of the gun. All Clark said was, "Did I get him?"

He did. James Whooper III collapsed to the floor. He died on the spot.

The workers restrained Clark until Los Angeles County Sheriff's deputies arrived to make the arrest. They handcuffed him and transported him to jail where he would be held without bail, charged with first-degree murder.

In the big postal complex, employees who knew both men expressed disbelief. Amidst a cheerless atmosphere, one of them said, "We are just trying to figure out what happened. But I don't know what you do to protect yourself from your own selves." His question would be pondered by top level postal authorities. One worker even suggested the installation of metal detectors at facility entrances. The idea made sense to many people who were beginning to wonder about their own safety in USPS workplaces. For reasons they chose not to reveal, management rejected it.

Postmaster General Marvin Runyon issued a press release from Washington, D.C. saying he was "saddened and shocked by this senseless act of violence. Our thoughts and prayers are with Mr. Whooper's family . . . Violence in our society is too common today and is unacceptable in any form."

A worker among the gloom-shrouded postal force in The City of Industry said, "Hopefully, we'll get over this. But it will take a long time."

When Bruce Clark finally faced trial, he allowed his defense attorney to enter into a plea bargain with Assistant U.S. Prosecutor Patricia Donahue. He would accept the penalty for second-degree murder, but would never speak of his motivation for shooting James Whooper. At a sentencing hearing, Clark sat stone-still, staring at a wall and showing no emotion while Whooper's relatives spoke to the court, appealing to the judge to put Clark away for the rest of his life.

"Give this man the maximum," cried one of the victim's kin, saying that Clark "did it for no other reason than Jimmy was black." Clark's attorney, Richard Satwier, denied the assertion of racial prejudice. No evidence had been produced, he said, to even suggest such motivation.

Another relative, an uncle, said, "This man killed my nephew. He didn't just kill Jimmy, he destroyed a whole family." The grieving man referred to the sad fact that Whooper would never have the opportunity to see his two-month-old grandson.

No one, other than defense attorneys, turned up to speak on Clark's behalf.

Judge Consuelo B. Marshall handed down a sentence of 22 years in federal prison, with no chance of parole. If Clark serves the full sentence, there is a great likelihood he will never experience another day of freedom in his life.

California had experienced more than its share of postal tragedies since 1989, with four incidents involving suicides and murders. Illinois had never had one. Seven weeks later, that record would be shattered.

Chapter 25

"They'd Done a Severe Injustice to Me"

Palatine, Illinois
Tuesday, August 29, 1995

Within two weeks of Bruce Clark murdering James Whooper, USPS officials announced a crackdown on violence in their workplaces. Anyone who carried a gun into a postal facility would be fired, they threatened. Outsiders, and perhaps a few insiders too, wondered if the lip service would have any effect. Would any disgruntled postal worker, whose fevered brain was bent on murder, really be discouraged from carrying the weapon onto USPS property by the fear of being fired? Weren't there better ways of dealing with potential killers, or better programs to head off massacres? Shouldn't postal inspectors be establishing procedures to pinpoint the locations where threats had been made, and concentrate on specific measures against the hot spots? Airports and courthouses across the nation were being equipped with metal detectors. Shouldn't such units be installed at places where threats of violence had been made?

"We'll fire you if you bring a gun to our house!" Several of the killers had already been fired. Certainly, the policy of keeping weapons out of postal facilities should have been invoked anyway, but doubters suggested that it would have little effect on preventing more deaths.

Twenty miles northwest of Chicago, 32,000 citizens dwell in Palatine, Illinois. The Palatine postal distribution center on Northwest Highway employed 1,600 workers from the region, more than a few of whom worried about the growing pattern of bloodshed in USPS facilities nationwide. Union officials voiced concerns about blatant animosity, inadequate security, and the suspicion that some of the workers were violating the new rule about bringing firearms to the job. Some of the employees evidently felt more anxious about self-defense than about the possibility of being fired. Grievances proliferated, many demanding better security measures.

One truck driver expressed his views. "It's a dog-eat-dog kind of place to work. There's lots of stress around here, a lot of tension between the management and the workers."

A mail carrier addressed the issue of bringing weapons to work for the purpose of self-protection. "I think it's ridiculous that we don't have any kind of police on full-time security duty here."

Union officials agreed, pointing out that since the center had opened in 1992, employees had been pressing for an armed force of protective security agents to be on duty 24 hours daily. It would add to overhead expenses for the USPS, but wouldn't it be worth the financial outlay to save lives?

The recent congressional General Accounting Office investigation had branded the postal service as a "dysfunctional organizational culture" in which autocratic managers battle adversarial employees. A former employee who published a newsletter about the USPS wrote, "The violence reflects the frustrating work environment, where you cannot hire the best workers and fire the worst. That's the root of the evil." Expanding on the theme, the article said, "Supervisors engage in harassing tactics to enforce a modicum of discipline, and that only engenders more frustration and anger."

The Palatine distribution center had erupted at least six times during 1995 with fights or rowdy behavior of sufficient magnitude to summon the police. In one case, an employee reported to the officers that his life had been threatened. In two others, supervisors had been accused of physical abuse, shoving a worker out a door and elbowing one in the chest.

The place sounded like a prime candidate for a review by the Postal Inspection Service to determine if extra security measures were needed. Upper management, too, possibly should have stepped in to see what was causing so much friction.

Some individuals raised the interesting point that the mail was given more security treatment than the employees. Registered mail, for example, which often contains checks or money orders, was sorted in a huge, locked room resembling a giant cage. That's where Dorsey S. Thomas, 53, Mike Mielke, 41, and Steve Collura, 45, worked, handling the valuable envelopes and packages.

Thomas had been employed by the USPS for 23½ years, and knew Mielke and Collura enough to socialize off the job with them. On Thanksgiving Day 1993, he'd joined them for a few drinks. The party continued until Thomas blacked out. When he awoke, he reportedly found blood on various parts of his body, and slowly formed some dark conclusions about what had happened while he was unconscious.

Thomas apparently brooded about the incident for nearly two years, until Tuesday morning, August 29, 1995. He left his wife and three children in their Northlake home before the sun rose, and arrived in his workplace at 6:54 A.M. Following his usual routine, he walked upstairs to the second floor where the staccato rattle of mail sorting machines drowned out the morning employee chatter. Mielke stood near the time clock outside the supervisor's office. Thomas walked resolutely to within a few feet of Mielke, and without a word, drew a .380-caliber Beretta semiautomatic, pointed it at Mielke and unleashed five rounds at rapid-fire. Two slugs caught Mielke where he stood; one entering the right jaw, twisting through his head and exiting at the left temple. The second bullet slammed into the right side of his chest and out through his back. Mielke collapsed in a bloody heap.

Pandemonium broke out with workers screaming and scattering in all directions. A witness said, "Everybody was looking around to see what happened, and then . . . started running."

Apparently unexcited, Thomas walked calmly back down the stairs into the lobby of the mail processing plant, the handgun again concealed under his clothing. He spotted Collura, stopped, withdrew the gun again, and aimed from 10 feet away. Only two bullets remained in the pistol and Thomas fired both of them, with remarkable accuracy. The missiles hit Collura in the chest and collarbone. Thomas walked over to the stricken victim who had curled up on the floor, struck him in the head with the gun and then kicked him several times.

A woman who saw the second attack said, "He just pulled out the gun and shot him like that . . . I ran and yelled at my supervisor to call 911 because there had been a shooting. At first, he was very skeptical, and he said, 'Are you sure?' " The entire incident took only seven minutes.

In the confusion, Thomas strolled out into the parking lot, and slid into this Lincoln Continental to take his usual 20-minute drive back home. The police arrested him there shortly after his arrival.

The two badly wounded employees underwent emergency surgery. At Northwest Community Hospital in Arlington Heights, doctors announced that Mielke was in critical condition. Collura fared somewhat better in stable condition at Lutheran General Hospital in Park Ridge. Both men would recover, but would suffer lifelong consequences from the severe wounds.

"I can't understand it," said a coworker who knew all three men. "They talked to each other every day, and you'd never think there was anything wrong between them."

USPS Inspection Service officials promised to review the security at the huge facility. But the media relations people in Washington, D.C. immediately brought out the old defense that violence within the USPS reflects violence in society as a whole. "It's not a postal problem. It's everywhere. With 800,000 peo-

ple, you are going to have a percentage of irrational people.''
The spokesman didn't say what plans the organization had to
identify such employees, or what techniques might be used to
help them with their problems.

When the police arrested Dorsey Thomas, he didn't resist.
They found the empty Beretta in his car.

At a federal court hearing the next morning, authorities
charged Thomas with attempted murder. His defense attorney
said that Thomas had been under a doctor's care for severe
depression and other physical ailments. The defendant refused
to say anything. Eventually it would be revealed that Thomas
had either been psychotic and delusional or suffering from post-
traumatic stress disorder when he pulled the trigger.

In September 1996, Thomas pled guilty to the charges, admitting that he intended to kill the two men, but continued his
mysterious silence regarding the motivation. The judge turned
directly to the defendant, and asked, ''Why did you do this?''

Glancing up as if startled, Thomas replied, ''I felt these two
parties had done a severe injustice to me. It's something I'd
rather not talk about. It had been building for twenty-one
months, and it just boiled over.''

By pleading guilty, Thomas got an agreement from the prosecutor to ask the judge for a sentence of no more than 16 years
and three months in federal prison.

To reporters gathered outside the courtroom, the attorney
representing Thomas, Jeffrey Steinback said, ''This is one
bizarre series of events.'' His co-counsel volunteered information that Thomas had been under medication for severe depression when the shootings occurred.

On Thursday, December 6, 1996, at the sentencing hearing,
Thomas's lawyers at last revealed why he had shot Mielke and
Collura. They said that Thomas believed the two men had raped
him after he'd had drinks with them on Thanksgiving Day
1993. The defendant had passed out, and believed the pair had
trapped him as ''the middleman in a homosexual encounter.''
Beyond that, he became convinced that he'd contracted AIDS
from the sexual assault, and had probably infected his wife
with the lethal disease. None of these accusations were true.

The defense attorneys asked the judge for leniency, saying that Thomas was "living in a nightmare of delusions." Explaining, Steinback said, "There is no evidence of a rape actually having occurred . . . The question is what was going on in this man's head? The reality is this man wasn't thinking rationally at the time." Mental examinations, the defender said, had shown Thomas was psychotic, delusional, depressed and suicidal when he shot his coworkers.

U.S. District Senior Judge William Hart sentenced Dorsey Thomas and commented that, "In a sense, we have three life sentences here . . ." Thomas had wrecked his own life, and his victims would suffer lifetimes of physical pain and disability. Thomas, the judge ordered, must serve 16 years behind bars in the federal prison system.

Could USPS supervisors or postal inspectors have anticipated Thomas's violent outburst and taken action to prevent it? It's difficult to say without knowing details of his behavior leading up to the attack on his coworkers. But if the lawyers' statements about his being delusional, psychotic, depressed, and suicidal were true, there were probably noticeable symptoms in his behavior. If he'd been undergoing treatment, supervisors may have noticed changes in the man's performance or demeanor. Healthy interaction between a worker and his boss can provide a conduit of communication, where a militaristic attitude would tend to block such exchanges. The specifics of this case are confidential, so no conclusion can be drawn on the matter.

Chapter 26

"He's Crying Out For Help"

Paterson, New Jersey
Thursday, August 15, 1996

Halfway between Montclair and Ridgewood, New Jersey, where Joseph Harris and Christopher Green had used guns to end the lives of eight victims, another disgruntled postal worker fumed with anger. In the city of Paterson, at the main post office, diminutive Danny Isku thought his supervisor seemed apathetic to his complaints. At 38, Isku had worked for the USPS motor vehicle maintenance garage for nine years and had taken all the abuse he could tolerate. Standing just a shade over five feet tall, he was fed up with coworkers's sarcastic comments about his height, and their embarrassing imitations of his slight speech impediment. To make it worse, Isku said, his supervisor not only failed to do anything about the frequent complaints he lodged, but actually joined in the harassment. Until recently, Isku had hoped that his position as a union steward would give him the clout to end the tormenting persecution. But that, too, failed when Isku's colleagues voted him out of office.

Gary Weightman, president of Local 190, American Postal

Workers Union, had little sympathy for Isku. Calling the ex-steward eccentric and rambunctious, Weightman said, "He would come in and he would disrupt meetings. He was very strange." Isku's erratic behavior didn't help with what Weightman described as the most contentious labor-management relations of any in North Jersey. "If there was one post office in my local, where I could expect to see violence happening . . . it would be Paterson. It is one of the bigger hellholes I have."

The circumstances surrounding Isku possibly should have set off a warning alarm. Eccentric behavior by an employee, contentious labor-relations problems, complaints of harassment—clues all too familiar in the growing number of violent outbursts by postal employees. And, if management needed another indicator to diagnose the need for corrective action in Paterson, they didn't have to look very far. Danny Isku belonged to a gun club. That wouldn't have been difficult for managers to discover, since it happened to be the Paterson postal workers gun club!

The pressure had been building up for months on Isku. His wife spoke of the alleged mistreatment at work: "He's like a joke to them because of his slurred speech. I think he got high-strung because of all the years of abuse."

The grievances Isku filed seemed to go nowhere, so he lodged complaints with the Equal Employment Opportunity Commission and even advised postal inspectors of his problems.

A sympathetic coworker agreed that management seemed to ignore Isku's plight. The friction between Isku and his supervisor, Jerry Peterson, had grown to a serious level, the colleague said. "They did nothing . . . Jerry Peterson would give Danny jobs, the worst jobs he could find. He didn't like him. Danny was a tire man, and Jerry would say, 'If you refuse to do the job, I'll send you home'." The coworker, who also belonged to the gun club, tried to help. When the tension seemed unbearable, he'd do what he could to soothe Isku, and say, "I don't want you to do anything crazy."

On Wednesday, August 14, 1996, according to Isku, one of his fellow employees started the same old harangue, making fun of the way Isku spoke. "Hey, look," the coworker allegedly said, "The moron's talking." Infuriated, Isku demanded the teasing stop, and waded into the larger man with arms flailing. The two scuffled for a moment, during which Isku's thumb was sprained. A punch in Isku's face brought the brief struggle to an end just as Jerry Peterson stepped in to pry the combatants apart. According to a witness, Peterson "was there to break it up." A postal inspector dropped by the garage to investigate the matter and filled out a routine report.

It is alledged that the same night, a plan is believed to have formed in Isku's mind. He would later say he developed the idea to provide a public service. Perhaps, he thought, he could do some good by making people aware of the reasons for frequent eruptions of violence and murder in post offices across the country.

Danny Isku called in sick Thursday morning. He allegedly changed his mind and showed up at 8:30 A.M. He paused for a minute to watch workmen installing bulletproof glass in service windows of the post office, then is reported to have asked one of his coworkers about Jerry Peterson's location. The colleague pointed to an office. Isku, carrying a brown paper bag, nodded and walked into the office where he allegedly confronted Peterson and Richard Anastasi, a postal service labor representative. The presence of Anastasi appears to have sent up a red flag of warning to Isku.

As Peterson and Anastasi stood up, Isku allegedly reached into the bag and pulled out a .22-caliber Ruger semiautomatic. He is believed to have first pointed it at Anastasi, telling him to get out of the way, then at Peterson, ordering him to step out into the hallway.

Peterson realized the imminent danger and had no intentions of passively allowing himself, or Anastasi to be shot. He apparently lunged toward Isku and reached for the weapon. At the same time, Anastasi allegedly leaped in to help subdue Isku. The gun went off, echoing loud firecracker pops through the building. One slug pierced Peterson's hand. The others bored harmlessly into walls and the ceiling. Anastasi came out of it with a fractured hand as a result of grabbing for Isku's pistol during the fracas.

Isku would later say, "I never had any intention of firing the gun." He explained that because of the sprained thumb from the previous day's fight, he'd lost control of the weapon when the two men jumped him, and it accidentally fired two or three times.

The employee who had witnessed Wednesday's fight said, "I was told Danny had been suspended and he was going to get terminated and lose his job. He came in to find out what was going on."

The whole incident, Isku said, took place for a noble purpose. "I wanted to help prevent tragedies in the post office by showing that the management is being inactive in taking action against employees who are harassing other employees . . . I didn't want this to end the way it did." He had figured the best way to make his point was to take a hostage, which would attract widespread media attention.

The presence of Anastasi, according to a union official, may have further inflamed Isku. Most employees, and certainly union representatives, recognized that Anastasi's position as labor representative for the USPS, put him in the middle of procedures when employees are about to be fired. "If Anastasi was there," said the union official, "they were going to interrogate [Isku] and take action on him." Furthermore, he added, management erred by not having a union representative present if they did plan to question Isku.

At a subsequent hearing, Isku's attorney told the court that his client was simply looking for fair treatment. His method of getting it, the lawyer said, "might have been very poorly executed on his part. He perceived himself to be a victim, being abused and threatened and mistreated, and not getting any redress from the postal service. Maybe his concerns might finally have been addressed." Isku openly acknowledged the anticipation of being arrested.

U.S. Magistrate Dennis Cavanaugh didn't quite see the heroic aspect of Isku's plan or conduct. Announcing that Isku was a threat to the community, he ordered the defendant to be held without bail pending a pretrial hearing. By law Isku is innocent until proven guilty, however if convicted of the charges against him, Isku could face up to 20 years in federal prison. (As this book goes to press, court action against Isku is pending.)

As usual, USPS media relations jumped into the widening breach with comments such as, "Violence is a societal problem. It's not exclusively the post office ... You essentially do a disservice, feeding into a stereotype about postal employees being more violent than other employees. The statistics don't bear it out." Once more, they trotted out the numbers to show that *rates* of homicides put the post office below taxi drivers and employees of liquor stores, gas stations, and grocery stores.

Danny Isku's wife touched the issue more poignantly. "He was crying out for help," she said, choking back tears. "We're living in a world where nobody cares anymore."

Chapter 27

"A Highly Tense and Dangerous Type of Employment"

Controversy over the ability to predict and prevent violence in the workplace spread across the nation, with the USPS bearing the brunt as a topic of discussion.

The rampage by Mark Hilbun in Dana Point caused postal workers and customers to wonder if the USPS could have taken stronger preventive measures and possibly averted the bloodbath. Certainly, Hilbun's bizarre behavior and threats had been no secret. One employee said, "All the signs were there. As far as I'm concerned, this never should have happened."

Murder victim Charles Barbagallo's girlfriend recalled how he had tried to help Hilbun. Barbagallo had tried to see the good side of Hilbun, she said, but she had foreseen the possibility of violence. If an outsider could see it, why couldn't postal management? They should have taken better security precautions, she said. Another employee at Dana Point also criticized USPS supervision, saying that Hilbun had followed in the pattern of murderous postal workers in other locations who were victims of an authoritarian management system.

Even the U.S. chief postal inspector acknowledged that, "It's a classic case of where the system fired him but it didn't solve the problem." He added, "Doors were locked, the back door was locked, but Hilbun knew when the mail drop was and he forced his way in.'' The evidence suggested Hilbun simply *walked* into the building, unchallenged.

One employee pulled no punches in expressing outrage about Hilbun's invasion and killing spree. ''We'd been expecting it . . . because he was that type of person. He had some mental problems.''

To many postal workers and their union representatives, the problems boiled down to two issues: stress on the job and bad management. Others criticized poor or nonexistent security provided by postal inspectors.

After the lethal eruption by Thomas McIlvane in Royal Oak, Michigan, a crisis intervention team counseled employees at that location. The team leader, clinical psychologist James Zander, said, ''People feel they're being treated unfairly, and in some cases, there's an open war between employees and management.'' His observation was borne out by a statistical bulge; more than 5,000 grievances were pending against post office managers in the Detroit area. The ''paramilitary'' management style, Zander said, seemed to focus on petty rules and a tendency by supervisors to harass and berate their subordinates. ''I know of cases where people have been fired for pulling away from the curb without using their turn signals.''

In California, a San Diego psychiatrist suggested that managers, in most cases of violence, fail to respond to advance signals that trouble is coming. ''These kinds of warnings are not subtle. They are statements like, 'Did you hear about the shootings in Royal Oak?' or allusions to recent weapon acquisitions, or actually saying what weapons they might use.''

A two-month investigation by an Escondido, California newspaper staff following the murders by John Merlin Taylor, revealed some shocking management techniques. *The Escondido Times Advocate* article said ''. . . post offices can become vicious, militaristic work environments . . . Postal workers were being disciplined for being bitten by dogs, for being stung by bees, for speaking the word 'junk mail' on television and for driving five miles per hour *under* the speed limit.''

At the same time, Moe Biller, president of the American

Postal Workers Union (APWU), said, "Stress on the job is a big factor these days. I think you'll find that postal work is a highly tense and dangerous type of employment." In the fiscal years 1987 and 1988, over 151,000 worker grievances reached the national arbitration level, according to USPS statistics. That figure may be too conservative, as reflected by the APWU, which counted more than 281,000 arbitrated grievances.

USPS executives hasten to paint a rosier picture. Addressing the problem of grievances, a spokesperson apparently could see no correlation between the rumbling dissatisfaction they represented and the outbreak of violence. Claiming that employee violence, including suicide and murder, is no greater in the postal service than in other workplaces, he said, "We don't have any more or less problems that face society today, whether we're talking about drugs or just plain bad temper." He didn't mention that no other industry had experienced the number of in-house murders that had taken place in post offices. The Postal Inspection Service found encouragement in declining numbers of assaults by postal workers on their coworkers or supervisors. In 1990, there had been 424 such incidents. It fell all the way to 405 in 1991, and plunged down to 398 in 1992.

In an April 1994 USPS bulletin, an article titled, *'Stamping Out Violence'* described current efforts to cope with the problems. "A 24-hour hotline was established in November 1991, following the tragedy at the Royal Oak post office. This allows employees to report threats or other concerns about safety to the U.S. Postal Inspection Service." One result, it said, was the imprisonment of a fired worker who had threatened to kill his boss. "But sometimes," the article acknowledged, "it takes more than a phone call to get results." In its second year of operation, the hotline volume of calls dropped from 1,790 to 593.

More optimism was expressed in the same article about the formation of a national committee of "postal management, union officials, and management associations to devise prevention strategies." The goal would be "extensive retraining of managers and supervisors in 'people skills'." The personnel division "has also been busy. Background checks and preemployment screening have been standardized."

Noting that, "Union publications remain full of complaints concerning what they see as militaristic management style . . . contributing to violent incidents," the article insisted that "management is striving to make things better for its employees . . ."

In a Washington symposium, Postmaster General Marvin Runyon said, "The problem of violence in our society has become a national crisis. The American people want action, and our elected officials recognize we must take steps to stop this outrage."

In another speech, Runyon said, "We are glad that the facts are helping dispel the myth in the media and the public mind of postal violence. But the truth is that violence, itself, is a fact in our society. It is a painful, costly, and debilitating disease that destroys lives [and] alters lifestyles . . ."

In addition to the problem of violence, the USPS, after the 1971 transformation to an independent establishment of the U.S. Government executive branch, faced serious financial problems. They operated for years under huge deficits. The pressure built for the postal service to meet the requirement set by lawmakers to break even over the long haul. As the USPS continued to operate in the red, Postmaster General Anthony Frank cited higher expenses contrasting with lower revenues, and reduced productivity. Meanwhile, managers at all levels pushed for maximum production from employees.

By 1995, snowballing expenses and crumbling revenues caused the USPS to try advertising their way out of red ink. A high-powered former Citibank executive, Loren Smith, headed up a campaign of revamping the eagle logo, merchandising, and widespread advertising. With a whopping outlay of $230 million for ads, only $90 million over budget, they hoped to compete with the competition, including geometrically progressing "E-mail," FedEx, United Parcel Service, and other private postal services. The postal board of governors felt the heat of public and Congressional criticism, so Smith was encouraged to retire. On his way out, he was awarded a $94,000 severance package along with praise from Postmaster General Runyon. The competition continues to soar.

The public wondered why the USPS had lost the highly profitable parcel post and overnight mail business to competitors. Could USPS mismanagement have boosted competitors into dizzying growth? For example, the Federal Express Corporation, known as FedEx, began operations in April 1973. On their first night of operation, a fleet of 14 Falcon jets took off carrying 186 packages. By 1996, 564 aircraft transported more than 2,500,000 packages every day, to be carried to final worldwide destinations in 37,000 vehicles. Ten years after startup, the corporation reached $1 billion in revenues, and by 1996 raked in a one-year take of more than $10 billion. No record could be found of any FedEx employees, numbering in excess of 125,000, murdering each other.

FedEx points to innovative management and the use of advanced technology. It was the first company dedicated to overnight package delivery, the first express company to introduce the "Overnight Letter," the first to offer 10:30 A.M. next-day delivery, the first to offer Saturday delivery and the first express company to offer "time-definite" service for freight. In addition, they offered money-back guarantees of their service.

Why did the USPS, which grew from the old Post Office Department of the federal government, lose such lucrative business? At one time, they were a virtual monopoly. Could they be trying to regain a profitable operation by injudicious cuts in spending and by pushing their employees too hard? Many union officials think so.

Mike Ganino, president of the clerks union, in 1989 said, "People call in sick and it's the immediate hammer. Management is pushing to be more productive and we've noticed a dramatic upswing in the last eight or nine months in verbal, and sometimes physical, altercations on the workroom floor."

At the same time, William Burrus, executive vice-president of the American Postal Workers Union said, "The postal service operates like a quasi-military organization. They have all the trappings of the military . . . they are a monopoly. They are immune from general laws that govern all other workers in the country. Workers can't strike . . . There's stress involved in postal activity, particularly in the style of management they employ—it's autocratic. On occasion, it bubbles over into violence. A lot of it is determined by outside factors, but employers are not helping it by this attitude.'' He gauged the unrest by the volume of grievances filed. ''It indicates you have management not concerned with complying with the contract or interacting with employees.''

A postmaster in one of the major cities didn't give the staggering number of grievances much credence. He said that employees filed petty problems with such complaints as, ''My supervisor doesn't like me.'' Even though acknowledging that the USPS probably processes a higher rate of union grievances than most other industries, he said, ''Under our national agreement, you can aggrieve almost anything.''

Following the massacre in Edmond, Oklahoma, when sympathy cards were posted on a bulletin board, supervisors reportedly warned employees not to read them on company time. In Southern California, a mail carrier was chewed out because she sustained an injury by tripping on the sidewalk. An employee sorting mail was reprimanded for ''excessive motion.'' Friendly mail carriers received warnings for talking to customers too long. A Los Angeles union official complained, ''There is constant harassment. We have sometimes as many as four supervisors for eight employees. We've had a lot of open hostility and a lot of threats because the level of frustration has just gotten to the point that supervisors have no respect for employees. As summer comes it's going to get hot.''

Speaking of hot, a mail carrier in Houston reportedly died of heat exhaustion while frantically trying to complete delivery of the mail in his allotted time.

The picture, of course, is not completely one-sided. The vast majority of USPS managers and workers are fine people. But no reasonable person would think that of 850,000 employees, all of them are shining examples of purity and perfection. The USPS management has a responsibility to supervise them, promote good productivity, and to weed out the bad apples. Excessive absences, poor job performance, and dishonesty by employees can delay mail delivery which is part of America's lifeblood. Millions of businesses depend on prompt delivery, and residential customers can become irate when letters are not delivered promptly. The importance of keeping the system well oiled cannot be overstated. And keeping the postal service operating efficiently is not an easy task.

The question lies in the methods for managing and hearing input from the employees. Among those three-quarters of a million brains, there are an infinite number of valuable ideas and suggestions. Is management listening?

Chapter 28

"We Have An Increasing Number Of 'Captain Queeg' Supervisors"

Ed Dunne, president of NALC Branch 2525 in the San Diego area, says that management-labor relations were full of problems and stress when John Merlin Taylor murdered three coworkers before killing himself in 1989. But when a new postmaster took over the region, conditions improved noticeably. Unfortunately, they began to retrogress in 1995, beginning "a slow drift back to the old ways." The autocratic management style seems to be taking over again in which discipline is overused for petty reasons. Dunne is concerned that if it doesn't improve again, the stage is set for more violence. He testified before a House of Representatives hearing that unions are trying hard to prevent trouble, but facing an uphill battle.

A New Yorker by birth, who still has the eastern sound to his speech, Dunne started with the USPS in 1972 after mustering out of the Army. He carried letters on Long Island, in New York, and became a shop steward after his first year. After relocating to Southern California, he continued his union activities, and became vice-president of Local 2525 in 1989, then president in 1992. He's been reelected three times.

The mail carriers in his local, said Dunne, are being disciplined for petty reasons that could be resolved by simple one-on-one meetings with supervisors. Instead, management seems to be relying more on letters of warning or suspensions. He cites an example in which a shop steward received a warning accusing her of failing to deliver packages at Christmas. When the union investigated, they found that another employee, through a misunderstanding, had failed to place the tubs of packages at the shop steward's vehicle according to practiced procedures. Management chose to handle it with a letter of warning.

Another problem, says Dunne, is dealing with mail deliveries in "rough" areas after dark, when carriers are required to dismount from vehicles and walk. The union advice to the carriers is to use common sense to protect themselves from danger, but, Dunne said, management has chosen to give warnings in some cases where carriers felt threatened by making the deliveries.

The USPS recently announced a profitable year, but some union officials wonder if the ledger is being balanced at the expense of the workers. They chafe also at low wage increases while managers are handed handsome bonuses.

Dunne is especially concerned about the length of time management takes to settle grievances. Some disputes that reach the arbitration stage linger in the pipeline up to 18 months. Recalling that after the tragedy at Royal Oak, Congress recommended shortened grievance arbitration intervals not to exceed six months, Dunne wonders about the good faith being shown by USPS officials.

The problems have spiraled skyward again, says Dunne, pointing to the dramatic upturn in volumes of grievances. "There have been more grievances in the past two years than in the previous twenty-five years," he says, with a frown.

Looking at the national picture, Dunne worries that upper management hopes to persuade a more conservative Congress to pass legislation usurping collective bargaining rights on the pretext of keeping postal rates low. He hopes that publicity about the problems facing the national union constituency can convince upper management to work towards "a kinder and gentler workplace."

* * *

In NALC Branch 458, Oklahoma City, President Don Landis is concerned that management is returning to the militaristic style prevalent when Patrick Henry Sherrill carried out the worst massacre in USPS history.

Landis has been with the USPS for 28 years, over two decades of it as a union officer. He said, "At least two-thirds of the supervisors are pretty good people, but there are some hard-nosed attitudes among the remainder." Regarding the "militaristic" approach used by some of the managers, Landis observed, in a soft drawl, that "in the military, they know when to back off before a subordinate is driven too far. Sometimes, in the postal service, they just can't seem to know when they've reached the point where it's time to back off." Landis tries hard to assure that union officers understand this point. "I tell stewards that we can be in the same position, so always give a person enough room to save face. Don't keep them cornered. Let them have enough room to get out." If you take advantage of someone long enough, Landis said, they get resentful.

One of his frustrations centers on the handling of threats. If an employee threatens a supervisor, he says, they investigate and take prompt disciplinary action. But if a supervisor threatens an employee, management does nothing. And if a customer threatens one of the employees, the inspectors don't follow up on it. Recently, he said, a carrier was shot in the back with a BB gun. Postal inspectors showed no interest in the case. As the incident didn't involve a contract violation Landis felt helpless to pursue any action.

He thinks supervision needs to engender better relations by showing some trust in the employees. Letter carriers are controlled tightly with fixed standards regarding speed of operation and volume, as measured by letters and flats (magazines, etc.) The volume determines how long the carrier will take to complete deliveries. The problem is, they are watched too closely and over supervised. Some of the supervisory demands become petty. For example, Landis recently heard one boss growling to a carrier, "You're putting too many rubber bands on."

The situation in Branch 458, Landis thinks, has deteriorated in recent months, since management arbitrarily and unilaterally pulled out of a local program they'd been using effectively since 1988. It was an informal procedure that used supervisors and stewards to solve problems before it became necessary to file the grievance. It wasn't contractual. From July 1988 to May 1996, with the use of the program, only 40 grievances were filed in eight years. After management pulled out, in a little over six months, 180 grievances were filed.

Prior to the shootings in 1986, Landis recalled, a local USPS executive used a "kick ass and take names" attitude. Landis deeply hopes that management is not headed in that direction again.

Landis holds the opinion that the post offices in Oklahoma City were a trouble spot in 1986. When the tragedy in Edmond occurred, he heard about it from the wife of the previous Branch 458 president when she saw news reports. Landis's first reaction was surprise that it wasn't in Oklahoma City.

Asked if violence in the post office is predictable, Landis gave the question some serious thought, then suggested that certain conditions might give strong hints that an upheaval is about to happen: 1) When employees start complaining about stress, 2) When there are a lot of arguments between employees and managers, and 3) When there is a lot of noticeable tension.

Landis doesn't see any violence on the immediate horizon in his area, but certainly can see the tension rising.

Dean Brewer has been a USPS employee since 1968, and president of the Oklahoma City Local of the American Postal Workers Union since 1991. With his short, graying beard, friendly eyes, big luminous grin and quick wit, he probably should run for state governor. With a twinkle, he refers to USPS headquarters on L'Enfant Plaza, in Washington, D.C., as "Elephant Plaza." When he took office, a mountainous backlog of grievances jammed his in-basket. He brought in help, conducted what he calls a "pre-arbitration blitz" to work out the problems, settled a number of the cases, and within two

years wiped out the "pending" files. Now, he says, because
of management's return to stiff-necked supervision, the backlog
is growing again. Attempts to institute changes are a "long,
slow, agonizing process."

Brewer patiently explains his view of the reasons for management's continuing pattern of recalcitrance: "In a workplace,
there are two classes, the ruling class and the working class.
Those who aspire to be promoted to management will do what
managers do. If, while they are trying to climb the ladder, they
get their butts kicked, they tend to adopt the kick-ass-and-take-
names style when they become supervisors."

His simile resembled one used by a past postmaster general,
who described the same attitude in different words. "I ate dirt
for twenty years, now it's your turn to eat dirt."

Something must change, Brewer says.

Regarding grievances and arbitration, Brewer's goal is to
settle every dispute within 60 days. In the past, he's been
able to meet that objective, but recently has been encountering
obstacles placed by management. The most common disputes
stem from the administration of discipline. The contract, Brewer
says, requires corrective discipline, but too often, management
uses it for punitive purposes instead. And they play some
strange games, too. He cites an example that took over a year
to settle. A supervisor faced disciplinary measures due to his
problems with alcohol. A craft employee, says Brewer, would
be fired. Instead, management evaded their responsibility by
reducing the individual to craft ranks. By law, the union now
had to represent the employee. Thirty days later, management
fired the alcoholic employee saying that he had violated some
"last chance agreements." Puzzled, Brewer investigated, and
found that management had met with the individual, with no
union representation, and coerced him into certain agreements.
The "catch 22" was that he couldn't reveal to anyone what
the agreements were! Outraged, Brewer took the case to arbitration, and won reinstatement for the employee. Management
subsequently fired the arbitrator! Even that didn't end the case.

Reluctant to accept the arbitration, management made the
employee an offer to return as a supervisor. When he asked

Brewer for advice, the union chief said, "Don't do it, they're setting you up." The individual was ordered by management to return to work as a supervisor, and was fired again in two days!

Brewer says there are many such examples of gamesmanship he could cite.

The contract, according to Brewer, is sometimes misused. "It's not a weapon, but a negotiated agreement. Many folks don't seem to understand that concept." He becomes irate when supervisors rationalize actions by saying, "The union won't let us do that." The correct statement, says Brewer, is "The contract doesn't allow that."

Usually, disputes can be settled through simple communication, says Brewer, but all too often, supervisors jump the gun and resort to discipline. In giving an example, Brewer had to suppress his contagious grin. A window clerk, he said, filed a grievance because her boss, without explaining why, wouldn't let her work the public counter. Investigation revealed that the woman perhaps needed to bathe more often to rid herself of an unpleasant aroma. But her supervisor just couldn't bring himself to tell her about it, so he took the easy way out and used his authority to deny her the work she wanted. Brewer says many conflicts could be resolved with more use of common sense instead of dictatorial orders.

Over the years, Brewer has also butted heads with the Postal Inspection Service, causing him to lose a certain amount of respect for some of their personnel and practices.

The last question asked by a journalist, during a rollicking and informative interview, was "Is violence in the workplace predictable?" Brewer immediately reached in a drawer and handed the journalist a 20-page APWU booklet titled, *Facing Workplace Violence*. It's an impressive piece of work with a forward by the union's national president, Moe Biller:

Potential workplace violence can be a recognizable and preventable occupational safety and health hazard. Therefore, it is the Postal Service's responsibility to ensure that workers are protected from it. The APWU, however, could not sit back and wait for the Postal Service to act on this important issue. With that in mind, in May 1993, I created a special APWU Committee on Safety and Violence. The goal of the committee is to help make the Postal Service make the workplace a safe place in which to work, free from violence.

The introduction pages of the booklet list 10 recommendations to the USPS "to help reduce stress and ensure equitable treatment of employees."

Treat each employee with dignity
Take aggressive steps to stop sexual harassment
Take all threats seriously
Solve grievances at the lowest possible level
Consider employees innocent until proven guilty
Apply the same disciplinary actions to supervisors and
    employees
Create a dialogue between union and management on
    problems arising between supervisors and employees
Re-evaluate procedures for hiring and promoting
    supervisors
Staff workplaces with an adequate number of employees
Hold managers and supervisors accountable for their
    actions.

To answer the question, "How big a problem is workplace violence?" the booklet explains that murder is the number two (number one for women) cause of death in the workplace, among industries in general. But most assaults and murders, (all but 4%), are committed by outsiders. It's a different story in the Postal Service. Between 1983 and 1989, a staggering 57% of the workplace murders "involved violence among coworkers and managers." The booklet contains a bar graph that shows a growing trend for in-house violence, including assaults and murders, in the postal service. In 1991, 37% of assaults on postal workers were committed by fellow employees. By 1995, the number had grown to 49%.

The remainder of the booklet is dedicated to methods, procedures, and understanding how to reduce workplace violence.

In Southern California, Art Turner is the president of NALC Branch 1100, the second largest branch in the nation with 6,500 constituents. His executive vice-president is Charlie Miller.

Turner and Miller state that growing stress among employees stems from several major problems. One thorn is that management compensation is tied to measurable performance levels, which "forces them to resort to extreme pressures to improve performances." The second area of friction involves work hours and overtime. Increased workloads and hangups in automated and manual sorting of mail cause carriers to work extra hours, often forcing them to try to complete their deliveries after dark on short winter days. In a recent case, a female carrier was molested by a perpetrator who used darkness to cover the act. Robberies are on the rise, too.

One of the most important issues, they say, is the way employees are treated. And mistreatment is sending the number of grievances skyrocketing. In 1994, Branch 1100 lodged 1,200 grievances, 1,650 in 1995, and in ten months of 1996, they had spiraled up to 1,950.

Ideally, said Turner, most of the issues should be resolved between the supervisor and the worker on the workroom floor, but it seems that very little effort is made to do that. So the majority of problems are escalated through the grievance procedure, which aggravates employees who become frustrated with long delays in reaching settlements. Their perception is that management is just not listening.

As mentioned by the other union officials, petty problems somehow become major conflicts. Charlie Miller cited an example in which a carrier accidentally shut the vehicle door on his finger. He asked a supervisor for a plastic strip bandage. Instead, the boss sent him to a hospital, where a nurse applied a plastic strip bandage. Management then suspended the employee 14 days for intentionally injuring himself.

Turner gritted his teeth and said he's known of employees being disciplined for being in a motor vehicle accident when other cars rear-ended them.

Charlie Miller described a real problem developing throughout the branch. New procedures for letter carriers on foot dictate that they carry up to four bundles of mail, try to pull the letters from the bag, and juggle the sorting process with mail to be delivered in their hands while they walk. In some cases, it can't be done. The carriers struggle in the attempt, and it takes longer to deliver the mail, sometimes well into the night. One 57-year-old carrier, with 20 years of spotless duty, is now being disciplined because she finds the new process impossible. Another carrier became so stressed out, he blacked out and picked up a coworker by the neck. Management, said Miller, could see the problem developing between the two people, but refused to intercede. "We have an increasing number of Captain Queeg-type of supervisors," he said, referring to the insane Captain in *The Caine Mutiny.*

Warming to the topic, Art Turner said that unreasonable harassment of the carriers is becoming commonplace. In a sector of Orange County, he said, "The postmaster and three managers literally followed a carrier until he was so stressed he was ready to explode. All three of the supervisors were harassing him to hurry up. Two of the supervisors would give the man conflicting orders, then discipline him for not carrying out the orders correctly."

Miller said he visited the Union Hall in Royal Oak and by chance met Thomas McIlvane, the Royal Oak employee who killed four employees before committing suicide. "I could clearly see the man was frustrated and upset." Miller wondered why others hadn't seen it.

Both Turner and Miller become frustrated when managers get away with abusing employees. Turner recalled a recent arbitration case in which a decision was made that the postal service would have to remove abusive managers. On the very day of that decision, Miller said, when the USPS knew they had lost the case, the supervisor in question was brought to Washington, D.C. and promoted!

Asked how the USPS had responded to the House of Representatives recommendations to reduce violence, both men growled in unison, "It's a joke." Management has twisted it to their advantage, Miller said. They implement the suggestion to prescreen employees in a reverse way. If, for example, an employee is injured on the job, management goes through a detailed index check looking for accidents that happened before the employee started with the USPS. If they find any, the employee is terminated.

"They are doing some preemployment screening," Turner interjected. "Enough that it takes four months to get a job. But it's still not effective."

The union is trying to help solve some of the misunderstandings on other issues, said Turner. "Our constituents become angry with the union because we can't force management to listen to problems. It's push, push, push, and eventually someone is going to push back. It seems to be all one way. Overdiscipline carriers, and overlook management misbehavior. For example, Charlie can name a dozen supervisors who, when they were craftsmen, were up on charges for assaulting supervisors. And now, they are the most abusive supervisors. One of them got fired as an employee, then fired again as a supervisor, but got his job back anyway. Management now blames employees for all problems instead of trying to come to grips with the core reasons for the problems. I know a supervisor who has slapped carriers twice. If that was reversed, the employee would be fired. The supervisor wasn't even disciplined."

A good example of that, said Miller, happened not long ago. "A carrier who had twenty-eight years on the job, great service, clean record. Was a shop steward. During a discussion, he pointed his index finger at a manager, and was fired for it! The case went to arbitration, but it took nine months to get him back on the job. On the other hand, supervisors can cuss at, yell, scream, and actually strike employees without fear of discipline."

A few big programs were initiated out of Washington after

some of the shootings, said Miller, but some of them are counterproductive. "A bunch of radicals came in as executives." Miller named a few of them, one of whom he regarded as "a dangerous snake."

Some progress was made in violence prevention under Postmaster General Frank, said Turner. But recently, progress has shut down. Miller agreed. "They are practicing a form of industrial terrorism."

"There is a big failure," said Turner, "in any part of the seven points recommended by the House of Representatives. Because the postal service is not addressing real causes of frustration among the work force. And they are not administering equal disciplinary measures to management." He described a manager in the L.A. sector who has repeatedly been involved in acts of sexual harassment, "but he's still there."

Miller knew a similar case. "There's a supervisor who waits for new employees who are single women, with children, to be brought into his office for some disciplinary reason. He has authority to dismiss them for any reason during their first ninety days. He uses that leverage to persuade them to give him sexual favors. Most never say anything because they have a child to support and can't afford to lose the job. But finally, one came forward. And four more followed her brave action. The supervisor was fired. End of story? No. A few months later, the USPS hired him as a carrier, then promoted him again. The woman who came forward found herself under intense scrutiny, and was eventually fired. The same people who conducted the charade of investigating the supervisor also investigated the woman. That really frustrated her fellow employees. Some to such a degree they went out on stress-related medical leave."

With a distressed expression, Turner said he knows of a supervisor who has been transferred to different offices five times because of sexual harassment accusations. But his superiors refuse to fire him. Another supervisor, he said, has also been moved several times because he pats female employees on their butts and fakes masturbation in front of them. "He's still a manager, and he just got a new office full of women."

As in the other union shops, grievances in Art Turner's territory are piling up in a big logjam.

Both Turner and Miller, when asked if the deteriorating conditions suggest the possibility of another violent outburst, said they pray that it doesn't happen, but it certainly wouldn't surprise them.

Obviously, the great majority of management employees of the USPS are not dictatorial brutes. Most of them are conscientious people, dedicated to performing their jobs to the best of their abilities, just as the union officials are. Of course, some human beings abuse authority. And some are driven to malicious behavior by ambition, greed, and personality disorders.

In many cases, supervisors and managers are pressured from above by company policy and executive edicts. It happens in most organizations, especially large bureaucracies. First and second line managers are often blamed for implementing procedures that are not of their own choosing.

If the issues discussed in this book are critical, the criticisms are aimed at the few executives, managers, and employees who are guilty of the misdeeds and behavior described. For those who are doing their level best, and working to avoid violence in the workplace, you have the utmost respect of millions of customers and employees. We salute you, and join in your deep hope that the violence will not be repeated.

Epilogue

As we researched the tragic murders, and interviewed postal employees, union officials, and others, all of them expressed hope that no one else would die as the result of violence in the workplace. Several of the union officials, while praying that it wouldn't happen again, see an increase in frustration and anger among employees, alarmingly similar to conditions that existed in the post offices prior to the murders.

When we gave media relations executives the opportunity to tell the USPS side of the story, they chose instead to accuse us of being unfair for spotlighting violence in post offices. In November 1996, one of the officials said, "Well, there have been no incidents for over a year." We agreed there had been no *murders* since July 1995, but reminded him that employees had been wounded by coworkers in Palatine, Illinois, and Paterson, New Jersey during that time. The executive brushed us off and said he would rather not participate in a mass media book. So we conducted our research without him. We heard from several sources that deteriorating working conditions in some locations are building tensions which could possibly lead to another outbreak of violence.

298 Don Lasseter

Could It Happen Again?

Unfortunately, yes! And it did.

Six days before Christmas 1996, a recently fired employee of the Las Vegas, Nevada main post office allegedly shot and killed a senior labor relations supervisor. Charles Jennings, 41, had started with the USPS in 1978, and transferred to the large Las Vegas facility in 1993 as a mail clerk. He also served as a union steward who, at one time, reportedly had a bright future in the union hierarchy. That all crashed to the ground in May 1996 when the postal service fired Jennings for allegedly fudging on the amount of time he worked, and for which he was paid.

James "Jay" Brown, who spent 23 of his 59 years in the U.S. Air Force, received the Bronze Star for valor while serving in Vietnam. He joined the USPS in 1979 as a letter carrier, and gradually worked his way up through the ranks to become a senior labor relations supervisor. Off-duty, the father of three and the grandfather of two earned community praise as a high school football referee. His on-the-job reputation characterized him as an easygoing, non-confrontational man well liked by everyone. He would be remembered for always having a smile. A colleague chatted with Brown as Christmas approached and recalled the upbeat conversation. "He was talking about how good life was."

When Charles Jennings appealed his job termination, and it went to arbitration, Jay Brown represented the USPS in the final hearing. Jennings lost.

On Thursday morning at 7:00 A.M., as Brown stood in the employee parking lot at 1001 East Sunset Road, across the street from McCarran International Airport, Jennings allegedly arrived. Heated words were allegedly exchanged between the two men. Witnesses reported hearing five or six gunshots, and Brown collapsed within 15 feet of the employees's entrance. At least two bullets had struck him in the head. He died on the spot.

Jennings allegedly drove away. About 30 minutes later, he approached a traffic officer who was issuing a citation to another motorist. Jennings is alleged to have dejectedly told the officer, "I just murdered someone."

In an early January 1997 hearing, Jennings's attorney said, "My client never intended to shoot anyone that day . . . The evidence suggests initially that Mister Brown may have been shot while . . . trying to take the gun away from Mr. Jennings." The district attorney's office said that Jennings will be tried for first-degree murder and a jury will decide if he is innocent or guilty. Jennings defense will be that he and Brown got into an argument and he did not intend to kill Brown.

And so, the problems continue.

One former postal worker commented that management contributes greatly to the stress employees feel. "The real problem is the adversarial relationship between management and the postal employees . . . They get rid of the good and promote the bad into management."

Another retired letter carrier complained, "We were followed on our routes, timed to go to the bathroom, not allowed to talk to other carriers while casing mail. It's the worst job I ever had. Once, when we had a crisis in our family, the supervisor wouldn't even let me accept an emergency call from my daughter."

Ray Madueno, also retired from delivering mail in Southern California, has written a novel titled *'Muther's Day'* in which he chronicles problems besetting the carriers. One of his friends was murdered because he refused to hand over mail to a gangster who knew the schedule for delivery of welfare checks, called "muther's day" on the street. In his book, Madueno chides supervision, in one case for putting a carrier on administrative leave because his mail was stolen, even though it wasn't the employee's fault. The author says he hated the pettiness. He saw a female coworker "go berserk in the post office due to constant harassment from her supervisor." Such militaristic management, says Madueno, can lead to violent acts.

More input came from an expert on workplace violence who said a danger signal should be seen in an organization that has threats, intimidation, and assaults. "In 1992, the post office set up a hotline for complaints and they got a skyrocketing number of calls. The bureaucracy hurts them. If they do a survey of their employees . . . by the time they get that done, guess what? It's time for another survey."

A resident of Las Vegas wrote a letter which was printed in the opinion section of the *Las Vegas Review Journal*. "So there's been another postal worker murder," said the writer, a former California postal employee. He knew, he wrote, why these killings happen. "Workers are treated like criminal fifth graders." The writer described the treatment as condescending and contemptuous. Emphasizing that he didn't condone murder, he said he simply wanted to suggest some preventive measures to be addressed by the postal service. His list included better sensitivity training for supervisors, who, the writer thought, are often former military personnel accustomed to issuing gruff orders to be blindly obeyed. He suggested psychological profiles for applicants, fresher colors on the workplace walls, and plants to soften postal environment. "A better understanding of how people want to be treated is absolutely necessary." He complained that, ". . . we were once told to regulate our bowel movements to avoid doing it on company time." He concluded with, "What a mindset. I hope this may help."

We join you, sir, in hoping that something may help.

Of the 14 tragic incidents involving murder since 1983, four of the killers committed suicide. Two have been committed to mental hospitals. Five are serving either life in prison, or long terms. One is pending trial, and one is awaiting retrial.

The remaining one, Joseph Harris, who hacked his supervisor to death with a Ninja sword, executed her boyfriend with a gunshot to the head, and killed three postal workers, received two death sentences. He appealed the constitutionality of the 1982 New Jersey law which provided for a death penalty, challenging it on the basis of bias against blacks. The New Jersey Supreme Court scheduled a hearing on the matter in

September 1996, but postponed it due to an event on death row in the state prison at Trenton.

On Friday evening, September 23rd, Harris collapsed in his cell and was taken to St. Francis Medical Center in Trenton, where they found severe cranial bleeding. He'd apparently not been taking prescribed medication for his high blood pressure, and slipped into cardiorespiratory failure. He died on the following Monday.

At the beginning of the legal process for Steven Brownlee, the killer of two in Georgia, it appeared that he might be freed after having been hospitalized for psychiatric problems. At one point, a judge ordered him to be released, then reversed the decision following a hearing involving further testimony from experts. But according to Brownlee's attorney, Tony Axam, he is currently still confined in a Georgia institution for psychiatric patients.

The U.S. Congress decided that it no longer needed a full committee to oversee USPS operations, so they relegated the duties to a subcommittee under the chairmanship of Mr. John McHugh of New York. The congressman is optimistic that problems can be solved in the USPS and is working closely with the executive level to achieve those solutions.

In Edmond, Oklahoma, Gene Black still works as a mail carrier at the same post office. While he will never forget the pain of Sherrill's murderous rampage, Black has healed his own emotional wounds. Not long after the tragedy, he met his future wife, Christine. "She's my wife and my best buddy," he says.

AUTHOR'S NOTES AND ACKNOWLEDGMENTS

To the best of our knowledge, all of the events in this book took place as we have reported them. It is a factual account of brutal crimes. We join management and employees of the United States Postal Service, along with the whole nation, in fervent hope that violence in the workplace, including tragic murders of employees and customers, can be eliminated.

In order to protect privacy, the following names of individuals are pseudonyms: David Perez, George Grady, Carlos Siratt, Doris Hazard, Louise Eastman, Herb Cardwell, Vincent Stubbs, June Collins, Harvey Kruger, Tom Gordon, Shantelle Graham, Jerry Peterson, and Sue Martin.

In researching mountains of material for the book, we owe unrepayable debts of gratitude to generous people across the country who gave us vital input.

Gene Black responded unselfishly and eloquently to our request for personal accounts of survivors in Edmond, Oklahoma. Congressman John McHugh and Staff Director Dan Blair answered our needs for government information. Union leaders Tom Fahey, Art Turner, Charlie Miller, Don Landis, Dean Brewer, and Ed Dunne took time out of their busy schedules to share essential stories and important issues with us. Ray Madueno, Gail Carpenter, and other ex-USPS employees contributed their experiences. We are also grateful to active employees who shall remain anonymous. Deputy D.A. Chris Evans in California and Defense Attorney Tony Axam in Georgia helped explain the legal labyrinth. Patricia Salot and Elizabeth Shea helped us understand the horrors of being a gunman's victim. Fred Burger of the *Anniston Star* in Alabama, Esther

Dillingham of the U.S. Bureau of Labor Statistics, along with Dick Laventhal and Ted Formaroli of the U.S. District Court, New Jersey, generously supplied important documents. Rodney Porterfield III, Government Documents Department, Birmingham, Alabama, Linda Wheeler, Rhonda Hollimon, Jeanine Williams in Georgia, along with Maria Dres and Steven Green in the Essex Superior Court, Salem, Massachusetts, congenially cooperated with our requests for assistance. Sue Reeves in Las Vegas, as well as Kim Forsythe and Laurie Reeves in Orange County, California gave us invaluable assistance.

Paul Dinas, Editor-in-Chief of Kensington Publishing Company, recognized the need for this book. Consulting Editor Karen Haas not only sorted out the text, but contributed several items of research. Susan Crawford, Crawford Literary Agency, coordinated the logistics.

READ EXCITING ACCOUNTS OF
TRUE CRIME FROM PINNACLE

A PERFECT GENTLEMAN (0-7860-0263-8, $5.99)
By Jaye Slade Fletcher
On October 13, 1987, the body of 16-year-old Windy Patricia Gallagher was found in her home in Griffith, Indiana, stabbed 21 times and disemboweled. Five months later, 14-year-old Jennifer Colhouer of Land O'Lakes, Florida, was found raped and also slashed to death in her own home. But it was the seemingly unrelated cold-blooded murder of a Beaumont, Texas police officer that sparked a massive, nationwide manhunt across 5 states and 2 continents to apprehend one of the most elusive—and charming—serial killers who ever lived.

BORN BAD (0-7860-0274-3, $5.99)
By Bill G. Cox
On a lonely backroad in Ellis County, TX, the body of 13-year-old Christina Benjamin was discovered. Her head and hands were missing. She had been sexually mutilated and disemboweled. A short distance away was the badly decomposed corpse of 14-year-old James King face down on the creek bank. He had been brutally shot to death. This ghoulish discovery would lead to the apprehension of the most appalling torture killer Texas had ever seen. . . .

CHARMED TO DEATH (0-7860-0257-3, $5.99)
The True Story of Colorado's Cold-Blooded
Black Widow Murderess
By Stephen Singular
Jill Coit spread her lethal web of sex, lies, and violence from one end of the country to the other. Behind the beauty queen smile was a psychopathic femme fatale who took a fiendish delight in preying on innocent men. With fifteen aliases, countless forged birth certificates, and a predatory allure, she married ten men, divorced six, and always stayed one step ahead of the law in a poisonous spree of bigamy, embezzlement, and murder that lasted nearly 35 years.

Available wherever paperbacks are sold, or order direct from the Publisher. Send cover price plus 50¢ per copy for mailing and handling to Penguin USA, P.O. Box 999, c/o Dept. 17109, Bergenfield, NJ 07621. Residents of New York and Tennessee must include sales tax. DO NOT SEND CASH.

GRUESOME REAL LIFE EVENTS FROM PINNACLE TRUE CRIME

BEYOND ALL REASON   (0-7860-0292-1, $5.99)
My Life with Susan Smith
By David Smith with Carol Calef
On a fall evening in 1994, David Smith began every father's worst nightmare when he learned his two young sons had been kidnapped. Nine days later, his wife, Susan Smith, confessed that the kidnapping had been a hoax, a cruel lie. The truth would be even crueler: 3-year-old Michael and 14-month-old Alex Smith were dead, slain by their mother's own hand.

BLOOD CRIMES   (0-7860-0314-6, $5.99)
The Pennsylvania Skinhead Murders
By Fred Rosen
On February 26, 1995, in a quiet suburb of Allentown, Pennsylvania, 17-year-old Bryan Freeman and his 15-year-old brother David slit their father's throat, stabbed their mother numerous times, and smashed the skull of their 12-year-old brother Erik with a baseball bat. Their hideous mass slaughter led to something even more frightening: the Nazi skinhead movement in America.

LOBSTER BOY   (0-7860-0133-X, $4.99)
The Bizarre Life and Brutal Death of Grady Stiles, Jr.
By Fred Rosen
Descended from a notorious carny family, Grady Stiles, Jr. led an unusual life. With a deformity that gave his hands and feet the appearance of lobster claws, he achieved fame and fortune as "Lobster Boy." But beneath Stiles's grotesque sideshow persona lurked a violent man who secretly abused his family for years. Until his wife and stepson decided to do something about it—by entering a conspiracy to kill.

Available wherever paperbacks are sold, or order direct from the Publisher. Send cover price plus 50¢ per copy for mailing and handling to Penguin USA, P.O. Box 999, c/o Dept. 17109, Bergenfield, NJ 07621. Residents of New York and Tennessee must include sales tax. DO NOT SEND CASH.

HORROR FROM HAUTALA

SHADES OF NIGHT   (0-8217-5097-6, $4.99)
Stalked by a madman, Lara DeSalvo is unaware that she is most in danger in the one place she thinks she is safe—home.

TWILIGHT TIME   (0-8217-4713-4, $4.99)
Jeff Wagner comes home for his sister's funeral and uncovers long-buried memories of childhood sexual abuse and murder.

DARK SILENCE   (0-8217-3923-9, $5.99)
Dianne Fraser fights for her family—and her sanity—against the evil forces that haunt an abandoned mill.

COLD WHISPER   (0-8217-3464-4, $5.95)
Tully can make Sarah's wishes come true, but Sarah lives in terror because Tully doesn't understand that some wishes aren't meant to come true.

LITTLE BROTHERS   (0-8217-4020-2, $4.50)
Kip saw the "little brothers" kill his mother five years ago. Now they have returned, and this time there will be no escape.

MOONBOG   (0-8217-3356-7, $4.95)
Someone—or some*thing*—is killing the children in the little town of Holland, Maine.

Available wherever paperbacks are sold, or order direct from the Publisher. Send cover price plus 50¢ per copy for mailing and handling to Penguin USA, P.O. Box 999, c/o Dept. 17109, Bergenfield, NJ 07621. Residents of New York and Tennessee must include sales tax. DO NOT SEND CASH.

AMANDA HAZARD MYSTERIES
BY CONNIE FEDDERSEN

DEAD IN THE CELLAR   (0-8217-5245-6, $4.99)

DEAD IN THE DIRT   (1-57566-046-6, $4.99)

DEAD IN THE MELON PATCH   (0-8217-4872-6, $4.99)

DEAD IN THE WATER   (0-8217-5244-8, $4.99)

Available wherever paperbacks are sold, or order direct from the Publisher. Send cover price plus 50¢ per copy for mailing and handling to Penguin USA, P.O. Box 999, c/o Dept. 17109, Bergenfield, NJ 07621. Residents of New York and Tennessee must include sales tax. DO NOT SEND CASH.